D1175389

THE
African
Iron Age

Edited by

P. L. SHINNIE

CLARENDON PRESS · OXFORD

1971

916.
S 556 a

Oxford University Press, Ely House, London W.1

GLASGOW NEW YORK TORONTO MELBOURNE WELLINGTON
CAPE TOWN SALISBURY IBADAN NAIROBI DAR ES SALAAM LUSAKA ADDIS ABABA
BOMBAY CALCUTTA MADRAS KARACHI LAHORE DACCA
KUALA LUMPUR SINGAPORE HONG KONG TOKYO

© OXFORD UNIVERSITY PRESS 1971

PRINTED IN GREAT BRITAIN
BY WILLIAM CLOWES & SONS LIMITED
LONDON, COLCHESTER AND BECCLES

PREFACE

THE intention of this book is to give a description of present
knowledge of the archaeology of the Iron Age in several
key parts of Africa. The contributors have all been active
in the field and it is hoped that this presentation will be of use to
Africanists, not themselves specialists in archaeology, and to
archaeologists who are unaware of the rapid development of
archaeological field work in Africa. The information is as up-to-
date as it can be made, but the difficulties of contact with contributors widely scattered over the continent makes it inevitable
that some work of recent date will have been omitted. Some
areas are not dealt with, the Mediterranean coast and Egypt
deliberately so, as information is easily available elsewhere,
others because the field work so far undertaken is too limited to
make a reasonable synthesis of knowledge possible.

The study of the African Iron Age is a recent development in
archaeology—twenty years ago a book such as this could not
have been produced. Much of it is still in a very early stage and
field archaeologists are still few—the total number working in
the whole continent is less than that in any one country of
Europe. To have achieved the results shown here in such a short
time is a remarkable feat; if the pace is maintained and if adequate
training programmes are provided for the new generation of
archaeologists the results of the next twenty years should be even
more spectacular.

An important aspect of recent archaeological study in Africa
is the way in which the archaeologist has combined with scholars
in other disciplines so as the better to understand the past. In
many traditional areas of archaeological endeavour, in Europe
and the Near East, the archaeologist is concerned with peoples
and societies of the distant past whose culture has little bearing
on that of the present day. In Africa he is dealing with the past of
still existing societies, a past which may be quite recent. So some

HUNT LIBRARY
CARNEGIE-MELLON UNIVERSITY

knowledge of the languages, oral traditions, and social patterns of the people currently inhabiting the region of his studies is essential, and conversely, the archaeological material can add much to the findings of those researching into many other aspects of African life and history. It has become a truism that the study of African history needs the combined efforts of historians, linguists, anthropologists, art historians and others for a balanced understanding to be reached. This is the aim—it is not always fulfilled. But most archaeologists of Africa are aware of the need to work with others and this book attempts in most of its chapters to combine knowledge gained from a number of sources.

I must thank the colleagues who have made this book possible. They have accepted my harrying in good part.

P.L.S.

CONTENTS

LIST OF PLATES

ACKNOWLEDGEMENTS

I, II, III, IV Margaret Shinnie

V, VI Rhodesia National Tourist Board

VII from Fouché, *Mapungubwe* volume I

VIII Rhodes Livingstone Museum

LIST OF FIGURES

LIST OF MAPS

I

NIGERIA

by
Frank Willett

INTRODUCTION

IT IS inevitable that much that appears in this chapter will already be out of date on publication, and recent discoveries are bound to necessitate substantial reassessments of older views. I have tried to refer to the most important radio-carbon dates: most of them are listed in Shaw's papers.[1] The rapid increase in numbers of radio-carbon dates reflects the great increase in archaeological activity in Nigeria, mostly in the field of final Stone Age and later studies. The reader will be able to keep abreast of further work through the *West African Archaeological Newsletter*, published by the Institute of African Studies of the University of Ibadan, and, when it eventually appears, through the *West African Journal of Archaeology*.

THE ENVIRONMENT

The aspects of human history with which the prehistoric archaeologist chiefly concerns himself are those which reflect the mutual interaction of man and his environment. In Nigeria the varying physical environments are most clearly reflected in the vegetation belts which cross the country from east to west roughly parallel to the sea coast of the Gulf of Guinea. The most

[1] Thurstan Shaw, 'On Radiocarbon Chronology of the Iron Age in Sub-Saharan Africa', *Current Anthropology*, 10 (1969), 226–9; 'Radiocarbon Dating in Nigeria', *Journal Hist. Soc. Nigeria*, 4 (1968), 453–65.

up-to-date map of these is that prepared for the Association pour l'Étude Taxonomique de la Flore d'Afrique Tropicale, with notes by R. W. J. Keay.[1] (See Map I.) This shows a band of mangrove swamp up to 40 miles wide, embracing the coast continuously from west of Lagos to beyond the frontier with Cameroon on the east. This area is not at all well suited to archaeological excavation, though waterlogging or burial beneath the fine silt which replaces the swamps (and ultimately kills off the mangroves) might serve to preserve organic materials better than they are preserved elsewhere in southern Nigeria. No excavation has been conducted in this area, but it seems possible that there was no occupation of the swamps before Iron-Age times, although there were well-established communities here at the time of the first Portuguese contacts at the end of the fifteenth century. They were already fishing from dug-out canoes, which must have been obtained by trade from outside the mangrove area.

Behind the mangroves lies the rain forest (Keay's 'moist forest at low and medium altitudes'), interrupted to the west where the relatively moist savannas sweep down to the sea in Dahomey and Togo. This gap gave easy access to the coast for inland towns situated close to it—e.g. Old Oyo, Abomey, and Kumasi, and may have been a factor in the choice of these sites.[2] Between the forest and the savanna is a belt of forest savanna mosaic, due apparently to the activities of the earlier Iron-Age inhabitants who cleared the forest in order to grow their crops, but lacked a sufficient understanding of the need to leave the land fallow for long periods, and to protect it from fire to allow the forest to recover.[3]

The savannas which stretch inland to the north are divided into four types. First comes the group of very variable habitats marked by a dense growth of tall grass, especially subject to severe burning, with pockets of woodland of relatively moist type, but lacking the genera *Isoberlinia*, *Brachystegia*, and

[1] Keay, *Vegetation Map of Africa, South of the Tropic of Cancer* (Oxford, 1959).
[2] P. A. Allison, 'Historical inferences to be drawn from the effect of human settlement on the vegetation of Africa', *Journal of African History*, 3 (1962), 242.
[3] Ibid., p. 243.

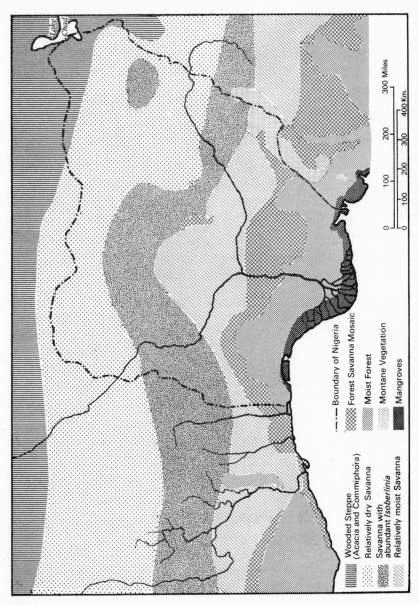

MAP I. Vegetation Zones of West Africa. (After Keay.)

Julbernardia. To the north, interrupted patches of *Isoberlinia*
woodland occur. (These two savanna types together comprise
the area formerly known as the Guinea savanna.) The third type,
formerly known as the Sudan savanna, is again very variable in
its botanical composition, but is characterized by species pre-
ferring a drier habitat. The resultant tree growth is less, the grass
shorter and less dense. Finally comes the belt, formerly known
as the Sahel savanna, of wooded steppe with abundant *Acacia*
and *Commiphora*; the trees may form clumps or be widely
scattered. The short grasses make travelling in this area easy, and
although the modern political boundary of Nigeria encloses only
a small piece of the belt, it is one which stretches across Africa
from the coast of Senegal in the west to only a few miles short
of the coast of the Red Sea and the Indian Ocean. This belt of
open country, together with the only slightly less open country
to the south of it, appears to have played a very important role
in the building up of cultures in Iron-Age Nigeria.

METHODS AND APPROACH

In investigating the archaeology of a country like Nigeria,
where written records are scarce over the last half a millennium
and practically non-existent before that, one has essentially to
adopt the methods of the prehistorian. If one begins at the
beginning, so to speak, one can trace through time the successive
cultures of Nigeria from the Lower Palaeolithic onwards. One
can, however, begin at the other end, and, by utilizing both
written history and oral traditions, work back from the known
to the unknown—from the dated antiquities to those of (as yet)
unknown age. Both these approaches have been used in Nigeria.
In a country where a great deal of historical tradition survives
(difficult to interpret though much of it may be), and where we
know for certain that many of the most important groups of
people have been occupying their present lands for some centuries, it would be foolhardy for the archaeologist to ignore this
additional evidence, even though much of it can only be utilized
at the second stage, when the archaeologist begins to write
history, rather than dig up material remains. So far as the archae-

ologist's primary task is concerned, that of excavation, oral
tradition or customary rituals may point to certain sites as being
possibly worth while to excavate, but for providing reliable dates
for visible monuments, their scope seems to be limited to little
more than the last hundred years. The town wall of Ife, for
example, is said to have been built during the reign of the Oni
Adegunle, nicknamed Abeweila, who reigned for only a few
years before 1849. Paul Ozanne's recent work has shown that
only two short sections of the wall can be assigned to this late
date, and that they were additions to the older system serving to
demarcate Modakeke, the area where the refugees from old Oyo
had been allowed to settle.[1] This is, however, the only antiquity
in Ife which can be positively dated through the traditions. In
Benin much of the palace was destroyed in 1897 after the punitive
expedition. Previously it had occupied about half of the town.
The destruction layer representing this horizon was found in
both Professor Goodwin's excavations in 1954–5 and 1956–7
and Graham Connah's of 1961–4. Such dated recent levels do
provide a *terminus ante quem*, which, however modest in antiquity, is at least a start from which we can work backwards,
pursuing a course comparable to that which Vansina, Mauny,
and Thomas[2] have designated 'regressive history'. In Benin,
however, there are spectacular town walls of immense size,
constructed, according to Chief Egharevba[3], in the reigns of
Obas Oguola and Ewuare. Bradbury[4] has examined the basis
of Egharevba's dating, and concludes that 'Oguola may well
have reigned a hundred years later' than the date suggested by
Egharevba (i.e. in the late fourteenth century rather than in the
late thirteenth); but the dating of Ewuare to the middle of the
fifteenth century may be broadly correct, though it cannot be
taken as entirely accurate. The attribution of the walls to the
reigns of these obas appears to be reliable for the early account

[1] Ozanne, 'A New Archaeological Survey of Ife', *Odu*, N.S. I, (1969), 28–45.
[2] J. Vansina, R. Mauny, and L. V. Thomas, *The Historian in Tropical Africa* (London,
Ibadan, & Accra, 1964), p. 63.
[3] J. U. Egharevba, *A Short History of Benin*, 3rd ed. (Ibadan, 1960).
[4] R. E. Bradbury, 'Chronological Problems in the Study of Benin History', *Journal of
the Historical Society of Nigeria*, 1 (1959), 263–87.

of Benin by the Dutchman known as D.R., published in De Bry's *India Orientalis*, shows that at least one of the walls already existed in the late sixteenth century, whilst charcoal from the forest clearance which immediately preceded the construction of these town walls has recently been dated to A.D. 1310 ± 105 (I-2722).

As a start Graham Connah undertook to plan their course through the thick forest—a formidable task. From the amount he has mapped (nearly 100 miles) we can see that far from consisting of three concentric walls as was once thought, they form a series of enclosed areas abutting on to each other like an irregular honeycomb, without any very clear general arrangement, apart from the nuclear function of the one immediately round the older part of the city of Benin itself, which lies at the eastern edge of the complex, protected to the east by a river. This inner wall is evidently defensive, whereas the others appear to be land boundaries.[1]

THE STONE-AGE SEQUENCE

Although an archaeological excavation begins at the most recent deposit and works backwards through time, it is more convenient to describe the results of archaeological work in a forward direction. Between 1962 and 1964 Robert Soper investigated Stone-Age sites in northern Nigeria, and located some scores of new ones, including one at Beli on the Taraba River which produced a few possible pebble tools.[2] No demonstrably Chellean implements have been found to follow these, but Acheulean implements have been known from the Plateau for a long time[3] and have been described in their succession by Bernard Fagg[4] and Geoffrey Bond[5]. A radio-carbon date of

[1] Connah, 'New Light on the Benin City Walls', *Journal of the Historical Society of Nigeria*, 3, Pt. 4 (1967), 593–609.

[2] Soper, 'The Stone Age in Northern Nigeria', *Journal of the Historical Society of Nigeria*, 3, Pt. 2, (1965), 175–94.

[3] H. J. Braunholtz, 'Stone Implements of Palaeolithic and Neolithic Types from Nigeria', *Geological Survey of Nigeria Occasional Papers*, 4 (1926).

[4] B. E. B. Fagg, 'An Outline of the Stone Age of the Plateau Minefield', *Proceedings of the Third International West African Conference, Ibadan, 1949* (Lagos, 1956), 203–22.

[5] Bond, 'A Preliminary Account of the Pleistocene Geology of the Plateau Tin Fields Region of Northern Nigeria', *Proceedings of the Third International West African Congress, Ibadan, 1949* (Lagos, 1956), 187–202.

'more than 39,000 years B.P.' was obtained from carbonized wood associated with Acheulian implements at Nok[1]. Soper has found that sites with Acheulean types of hand axes appear to be restricted to the Plateau and to the area to the east of it, which probably formed a promontory of savanna projecting from the Sahara into what was forest at the time. There follow a series of industries which have been grouped together under the name Sangoan, but much work remains to be done to separate out the individual cultural traditions which this term hides. The most recent site to produce such implements was discovered by Professor Thurstan Shaw at Asejire, between Ibadan and Ife, and was investigated by Ozanne and Oyenuga[2]. These industries were followed during the Gamblian pluvial period by a Middle Stone Age dominated by flake tools with prepared platforms, utilized as knives and scrapers. It is possible that some were hafted. These industries in their turn were replaced by others which employed very small tools made from quartz, known as microliths.

These have been recorded from three sites: Rop cave on the plateau;[3] Mejiro Cave at Old Oyo[4] and a cave at Iwo Eleru, near Akure.[5] The last-named site is almost certainly the oldest of the three, having produced radio-carbon dates of 7200 B.C. ± 150 (I-1754) and 9250 B.C. ± 200 (I-1753), the latter date being from charcoal found with a skeleton, the earliest man so far found in the West-African forest. At this site microliths are rare, and tools were made from both chert and quartz, with the proportion of chert increasing from 2 per cent at the bottom up to 25–30 per cent at the top. In the upper levels pottery and ground

[1] G. W. Barendsen, E. S. Deevey, and L. J. Gralenski, 'Yale Natural Radio-carbon Measurements III', *Science*, 126 (1957), 916–17. Lab. no. Y–142–8.

[2] Ozanne, and K. Oyenuga, 'Excavations at Asejire', *West African Archaeological Newsletter*, 8 (1968), 32–4.

[3] B. E. B. Fagg, 'Preliminary Report on a Microlithic Industry at Rop Rock Shelter, Northern Nigeria', *Proceedings of the Prehistoric Society*, 10 (1944), 68–9, and Ekpo Eyo, 'Excavation at Rop Rock Shelter', *West African Archaeological Newsletter*, 3 (1965), 5–13.

[4] F. Willett, 'The microlithic Industry from Old Oyo, Western Nigeria', *Actes du IVe Congrès Panafricain de Préhistoire*, Sect. III, Tervuren (1962), 261–72.

[5] C. T. Shaw, 'Excavations at Iwo Eleru, 1965', *West African Archaeological Newsletter*, 3 (1965), 15–17.

2

stone axes occurred, apparently associated with a radio-carbon
date of 1515 ±65 B.C. (Hv 1512). The Rop cave was excavated
originally by Bernard Fagg, who recorded a deposit containing
microliths, pottery, and ground stone axes. A skeleton was
excavated in the lower part of the deposit which was radio-
carbon dated 25 B.C. ± 120 (I-1460). Further work on the site in
1964 by Ekpo Eyo and Robert Soper[1] discovered that there were
two separate layers of microliths with a sterile layer between
them. The upper layer contained pottery and two iron points,
but no ground stone axes occurred in either layer. It looks as if the
burial belonged to Iron-Age occupants of the cave who had dug
the grave into the Stone-Age level, for, as we shall see, iron was
in large-scale production nearby from the fourth century B.C.

In the Mejiro Cave the microliths were not accompanied by
pottery or ground stone axes and so are probably to be equated
with the lower microlithic level at Rop; yet the fact that no
ground axes were found in the second season's excavation there
should warn us that a larger sampling of the Mejiro cave might
have produced some. More sites need to be excavated before the
relationships are clear, but the microlithic industries at Mejiro
and Rop are closely similar, so that we probably have successive
stages of one culture.

In 1966 Donald Hartle excavated a rockshelter in Afikpo
Division called (Ezi-Ukwu) Ukpa. He found stone artefacts
which he described as 'rather amorphous . . . bits and pieces;
although a few definite tool types have been found, such as
knives, balls, scrapers and hoes.[2] Pottery was found throughout
the deposit, that in the upper 12 in. being closely similar to
modern Afikpo pottery and having little stonework with it,
whereas the deeper pottery was thicker, poorly fired, and of a
different colour. Charcoal from a depth of 18 to 24 in. gave a
date of 95 B.C. ±95 years (GX-0932) whilst deeper levels
produced dates back to 2935 ± 140 B.C. (GX-0938).

It is not yet clear at what time the change in the pottery
occurred, or when the stone tools ceased to be used, but this may

[1] Eyo, op. cit.
[2] Hartle, 'Archaeology in Eastern Nigeria', *Nigeria*, 93 (1967), 140.

have been quite late, for there is increasing evidence that Stone-Age cultures persisted till very recently in many parts of Africa[1]. The use of stone tools alongside iron ones in very recent times is well documented from eastern Nigeria and the Cameroons.[2]

The phase of transition from a stone-using to an iron-using economy is one of the most interesting periods in Nigerian prehistory. One of the most important sites which affords evidence of this transition is in north-eastern Nigeria, where, after an exhaustive survey[3] Graham Connah selected the mound at Daima for a major excavation. The site is a veritable tell, an accumulation of occupation material which gradually raised the level of habitation up to 10·63 m. above the surface of the clay of the Lake Chad basin. An apparently continuous occupation was discovered in a trench 6 m. wide, 50 m. long, and up to 11·5 m. deep. Examination of the 11 tons of artefacts is still in progress, but a number of interim reports have already been published.[4]

Connah's tentative conclusion is that the site shows the stages of development of a community as it evolved from a late Stone-Age stage in about the middle of the first millennium B.C., through an early and late Iron Age, ending somewhere in the seventeenth or eighteenth century A.D. The earliest levels had stone axes, grinders, polished bone tools probably for leatherworking, and bone harpoon or spear heads with bilateral barbs, whose affinities seem to lie with sites along the southern edge of the

[1] See Davies: 'excavations at Sekondi have shown that the neolithic stage had hardly been passed in the sixteenth century' in Ghana (O. Davies, *South African Journal of Science*, 52 (1945), 149); and Clark: 'It would not ... be surprising to find that ... small groups of hunter gatherers using stone tools were still in existence in north-eastern Angola in the 16th century A.D. and later.' (J. D. Clark, *Prehistoric Cultures of North-East Angola and Their Significance in Tropical Africa*, Lisboa (1963), 170.)

[2] M. D. W. Jeffreys, 'Stone-age Smiths', *Archiv für Völkerkunde*, III (1948); 'Ibo Warfare', (1956), 77; and 'Notes on the Neolithic of West Africa', *Proceedings of the Third Pan-African Congress on Prehistory, 1955* (1957), 262 ff.

[3] Connah, *First Interim Report*, Northern History Research Scheme, Zaria (1966), 11–21; and 'Summary of Research in Benin City and Bornu', *West African Archaeological Newsletter*, 5 (1966), 22–5.

[4] Ibid., 'Radiocarbon Dates for Daima', *Journal of the Historical Society of Nigeria*, 3, Pt. 4 (1967), 741–2; *Second Interim Report*, Northern History Research Scheme, Zaria (1967), 17–31; and ' "Classic" Excavation in North East Nigeria', *Illustrated London News*, 251, No. 6689, Oct. 14 (Archaeological Section 2276) (1967).

Sahara. Grooved stones of a type commonly called 'bead polishers' were evidently used in making the bone tools, for no beads were found at these levels. Small, solid, fired-clay figurines of animals, mostly cows, represented in a squat legless manner, were also found. Abundant animal bones—cow and sheep or goat—occurred, but no direct evidence of grain cultivation. Pottery was best represented by a fine ware with burnished red surface, often decorated with a toothed comb or roulette. The dead were buried inside the settlement in a crouched position, and one man had a harpoon head in the lower abdomen which had evidently caused his death. At a height of about 1 m. above the base of the occupation material a radio-carbon date of 450 ± 96 B.C. (I-2372) was obtained. The earliest iron object was about 2·60 m. above the base and was isolated. This was thought at first to represent a date around the year 0, since radio-carbon dates of A.D. 480 ± 270 (I-2370) and A.D. 450 ± 670 (I-2371) came from 3·60 to 4·40 m. above the base. However, a date of A.D. 630 ± 190 (I-2943) has since been obtained on bones from the level of this piece of iron so Connah now suggests a fifth or sixth century date for the introduction of iron.[1] Iron occurred next at 5·60 m. and continued to the top of the mound. The bone industry declined sharply at 2·40 to 2·80 m., but stone axes occurred occasionally up to about 8 m., probably as heirlooms, since this area is deficient in stone.

Clay figurines continued after the introduction of iron and the burial traditions remained unchanged. Evidence of circular mud huts was found at different levels in the middle part of the mound, one of which, at 6 m. above base, had been floored with a potsherd pavement in a simple herringbone design. The clay figurines ceased between 5 m. and 6·80 m., but reappeared above this level in a more naturalistic form, often representing cows with long legs and apparently running. Between 7·20 m. and 8 m. radio-carbon dates of A.D. 810 ± 90 (I-2368) and A.D. 980 ± 90 (I-2369) were obtained. At these levels carbonized guinea corn was found. A little earlier than this bronze had appeared

---

[1] Connah 'Radiocarbon dates for Benin City and further dates for Daima, N.E. Nigeria', *Journal Hist. Soc. Nigeria*, 4 (1968), 313–20.

with burials, and grave goods became varied from then on.

The material culture from the later levels has some resemblances to that described by Lebeuf[1] from northern Cameroon and south-western Chad. Increasing trade contacts are indicated. Circular huts and hearths were revealed, and at a very late stage a number of distinctive clay fireplaces with vertical sides. Pottery had changed earlier, and at these levels is very heavy and commonly decorated with geometric rouletting. Clay figurines increase in variety, and include a fish, the head of a gazelle, and a pig-like creature. The burial tradition remained unchanged but the deceased wore bronze discs and bracelets, white stone lip-plugs, and beads of carnelian, rock-crystal, ostrich egg-shell, and glass, as well as pottery. At a very late phase smoking-pipes appeared. Connah suggests a date in the seventeenth or eighteenth century for the abandonment of the site, and that this may coincide with the arrival of Islam.

This excavation reveals the rich rewards Nigeria can offer to the patient and industrious worker. This site has already forced us to look anew at many aspects of Nigerian archaeology.

Previously the classic example of the transition from stone to iron in Nigeria had been considered to be the Nok culture. This is still one of the most important aspects of African prehistory as a whole but recent work suggests that it is exclusively an Iron-Age phenomenon.

THE NOK CULTURE

The Nok Culture first came to light in 1944, when Bernard Fagg recognized the importance of two terracotta sculptures found in 1930 and kept from that time in the small museum of the Mines Department. Soon afterwards a third specimen was reported from Jemaa, some 25 miles away from Nok, and ever since specimens have been turning up, chiefly from the tin-bearing gravels of the Plateau. This has been due entirely to Bernard Fagg's persistent work in educating the minefield labourers (and the Nigerian public at large) in the importance of these relics of the past. As a result sculptures and other remains

[1] J. P. Lebeuf, *La Civilisation du Tchad* (Paris, 1950); and *Archéologie tchadienne* (Paris, 1962).

have been recovered from about twenty sites in northern Nigeria, and a consistent picture of the culture has been built up over the years.

The type-site of the culture is the small mining village of Nok in Zaria Province, where a whole series of cultures occurs, from the Acheulean onwards,[1] incorporated in the alluvial deposits. The antiquities are consequently not *in situ*, but derived, so that doubts have been cast on the association of the separate elements in the deposits. However, the condition of the terracotta sculptures is usually remarkably fresh, which suggests that they have been washed into the river from the banks very close to their find-spots. Moreover, in all the many sites so far known there is a general consistency in the range of material present, so that it seemed not unreasonable to regard the different elements as truly associated, even though a certain amount of caution was required until the association could be proved from a dwelling site. It was expected that proof would come from a site discovered in September 1960 at Taruga, south-east of Abuja. A small excavation was conducted there in December 1960. It confirmed that the two headless terracotta figurines of women, which led to the discovery of the site, really came from there, and that it was an occupation site with remains of iron-working and abundant charcoal,[2] which has been dated by radio-carbon to 280 B.C. ± 120 (I-1457).[3] This is right in the middle of the period claimed for the culture from the evidence of the Nok deposits themselves. Here carbonized wood from grey-black clay containing figurine material gave a date of A.D. 207 ± 50 (Y-474); whilst a sample from abraded logs in the basal gravels and sands gave a date of 918 B.C. ± 70 (Y-142-4), which Fagg interprets as indicating that the culture probably began some time in the middle of the first millennium B.C. and continued at least till the second century A.D., and probably later.[4] This

---

[1] B. E. B. Fagg, 'An Outline of the Stone Age of the Plateau Minefield', op. cit.

[2] 'An Ancient Site in Niger Province', *Bulletin of News*, Historical Society of Nigeria, 5, Pt. 4 (1961), 3.

[3] 'Radiocarbon Dating of the Nok Culture, Northern Nigeria', *Nature*, Jan. 9 (1965), 205, 212.

[4] B. E. B. Fagg, 'The Nok Culture in Prehistory', *Journal of the Historical Society of Nigeria*, 1, Pt. 4 (1959), 292.

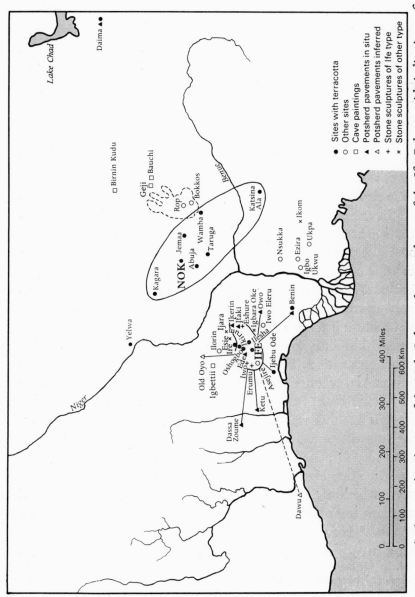

MAP 2. The known distribution of the Nok Culture, the central area of the Ife Culture with indications of its possible influence, and other sites mentioned in the text.

HUNT LIBRARY
CARNEGIE-MELLON UNIVERSITY

conclusion had been reached before 1949, and very cautiously supported by Geoffrey Bond on purely geological grounds.[1]

Further excavations were conducted at Taruga in 1966 and again in 1968. The 1966 season located by proton magnetometer a score of iron-working locations, one of which was excavated and proved to be a furnace. Terracotta sculpture and pottery were also found. The main results of the 1968 season were reported to me in a letter from Bernard Fagg: 'I believe that the use of the site for iron smelting may have lasted for two or three centuries. 440–280 B.C. are reliable dates from the deposits and this was followed . . . [5 April 1968] by another of 300 B.C. for charcoal sealed inside a furnace by a slag layer. It would surprise me if this is not accepted as an absolutely reliable date for the presence of iron smelting in Nigeria. It would of course, not surprise me at all if we discovered other much earlier dates in the course of new investigations.'[2] The cultural contents of the site were entirely Iron Age with no Neolithic elements so Fagg concludes ' that the Nok culture can now be accepted as exclusively an Iron Age phenomenon.'[3]

The site at Taruga is not the only one which is not an alluvial deposit, but only one of the others has proved suitable for further excavation. This is the site of the Benue Middle School at Katsina Ala, where a remarkable head, conceived as a cylinder,[4] and twenty-eight fragments of the body were found beneath a shea-nut tree that was uprooted to make a hockey pitch in 1951. The fragments were stuck together at the Jos Museum and found to comprise a large part of a figure, about 2 ft. 6 in. in sitting height. He sits on a round stool with his hands on his knees, which are apart. The left arm and leg are more or less complete, but only parts of the other limbs and of the trunk have survived.[5] Nevertheless, the figure is a remarkable object to

[1] B. E. B. Fagg, 'An Outline of the Stone Age of the Plateau Minefield', op. cit.; and Bond, 'A Preliminary Account of the Pleistocene Geology of the Plateau Tin-fields Region of Northern Nigeria', op. cit.

[2] The dates are: 440 ± 140 B.C. (I-2960) and 300 ± 100 B.C. (I-3400).

[3] B. Fagg, 'Recent work in West Africa: new light on the Nok culture', World Archaeology, I (1969), 41–50.

[4] Illustrated in Willett, Ife in the History of West African Sculpture (London, 1967), Pl. XI.

[5] Ibid., Fig. 20.

have been sculptured, hollow as it is, from moist clay (presumably by allowing the successive stages to dry), and then to have been successfully fired in an open wood fire, just like a domestic cooking-pot. Indeed, it is not unlikely that it was placed inside a very large pot to protect it whilst it was being fired. A small rescue excavation was conducted on the site after two further heads were found in 1954. Very little cultural material was found, however, which suggests that the site may have been a grove for religious ceremonies rather than a habitation site.

The material found in the same alluvial deposits as the Nok terracotta sculpture includes polished stone axes and adzes, many of which are very small indeed, and may have been intended for use in wood-carving by a pre-Iron-Age population, whilst the large ones were probably hoes used in cultivating the swampy river banks. Stone grindstones give further testimony to the use of vegetable food, whilst the seeds of the oil-bearing *atili* (*Canarium Schweinfurthii* Engl.) have been identified, as well as the shells of palm-nuts (*Elaeis guineensis* Jacq.) and the indented stone anvils and pitted hammer stones with which they were cracked open to extract the kernel. The growing oil-palm needs careful protection from bush fires if it is to survive. This is impossible in the savanna, so the abundance of palm nuts indicates that the area was forested during the period of the Nok Culture, unless, of course, the nuts were obtained by trade from further south.[1]

One of the figurines (from Samban) carried what appears to be a bowl of eggs, whilst another fragmentary one is interpreted by Fagg as possibly representing a domestic cow, but unfortunately no bones of any kind have been recovered from the deposits to confirm this suggestion of mixed farming.

Beads made from tin have frequently been found on sites of the Nok Culture, but never yet for certain from the same horizon. Quartz beads do occur, however, together with ground

[1] D. R. Roseveare, *Checklist and Atlas of Nigerian Mammals* (Lagos, 1953); and Allison, 'Historical Inferences to be Drawn from the Effect of Human Settlement on the Vegetation of Africa', op. cit.

quartz rods probably intended as lip, ear, and nose plugs. One grinding stone for making these ornaments has been recovered. Many of the figurines show a profusion of beads being worn, whilst a recently discovered piece from Kuchamfa seems to be wearing a hemmed cloth.

Domestic pottery, mostly rather heavy and coarse but well-fired, is abundant. The vessels at Taruga were mainly of two types: bowls 14 to 22 cm. in diameter, sometimes deeply scored inside for use as graters, and globular pots 26 to 36 cm. in diameter with everted lips, often with a groove along the edge. There are also potstands. Fragments of burnt clay from wattle-and-daub buildings are found, together with more strongly fired clay from furnaces, and the nozzles (*tuyères*) through which air was conducted into the charcoal fire of the blooming-furnace. Iron slag has been found, though iron objects (as seems to be usual on Iron-Age sites throughout the world!) are rare. Most interesting, however, are two iron axe blades which closely resemble stone axes in their form. One of these is from Nok itself, whilst the other was found at Tree Flats, Makafo, close to a stone axe of very similar size and shape.[1] At least three figurines represent people holding axes, but it is not possible to be sure whether these are of stone or of iron. Other figurines portray features of dress or hair-style which can still be fairly closely matched among the various small pagan groups occupying much of the area of the Nok culture. This suggests that the Nok people may have been their ancestors, and certainly their way of life must have been very similar.

Many of the stylistic features of the Nok terracottas can be paralleled in more recent sculpture in southern Nigeria, especially in Yoruba wood carvings,[2] so it is clear that the basic canon of much West-African sculpture was already firmly established 2,000 years ago. That the Nok sculptures have so much in common with each other suggests in turn that there was a long period of development of the style before these examples were made.

[1] B. E. B. Fagg, 'An Outline of the Stone Age of the Plateau Minefield', op. cit. Fig. 15.

[2] B. E. B. Fagg, 'The Nok Culture in Prehistory' op. cit.; 'The Nok Terracottas in West African Art History', *Actes du IVe Congrès Panafricain de Préhistoire*, Tervuren, Sect. III (1962), 445–50; and Willett, *Ife in the History of West African Sculpture*, op. cit.

There is evidence to suggest that this earlier evolution of the art style occurred in wood, perhaps originating earlier than the manufacture even of domestic pottery.[1]

THE TRANSITION FROM STONE TO IRON

There are two possible routes by which the knowledge of iron-working could have come to Nok. One is from Meroe,[2] which lies at the eastern end of the belt of steppeland which, like the wooded steppe into which it merges to the south, runs right across Africa from east to west. During the second half of the first millennium B.C. the Nakuran wet phase would have caused the vegetation belts shown on the modern map[3] to have lain further north, but the wide belt of steppe and savanna would still have made communication between the Kushitic Kingdom of the time and West Africa quite easy. The alternative route (which Mauny prefers)[4] is by diffusion from the Phoenician settlements in the Maghreb to the Berbers, and then via the long-established caravan routes across the Sahara, which was at that time much less formidable to cross than it is now. Either of these routes is feasible, and more evidence is needed to resolve the issue. It is not impossible that the knowledge came by both routes, but the early dates of iron-working at Taruga together with the late date for Daima which lies on the route to Meroe appear to make the trans-Saharan route the more probable.

Hamo Sassoon[5] has studied the general problem of the spread of iron in Africa, and suggests that a study of the distribution of furnace types of the last hundred years would be likely to reflect the routes by which the knowledge of iron-working spread. This is a task of great urgency, as in most parts of Africa traditional methods of preparing iron are being abandoned in favour of ready-made iron scrap provided by old motor-cars and

[1] Ibid., Fig. 19.

[2] P. L. Shinnie, *Meroe*, (London 1967).

[3] Keay, op. cit.

[4] R. Mauny, 'Essai sur l'Histoire des Métaux en Afrique Occidentale', *Bulletin de l'Institut Français d'Afrique Noire*, 14 (1952), 574–83; and *Tableau Géographique de l'Ouest Africain au Moyen Age* (Dakar, 1961).

[5] H. Sassoon, 'Early Sources of Iron in Africa', *South African Archaeological Bulletin*, 18 (1963), 176–80.

lorries. The use of European metal saves labour, but the resulting tools, although of purer metal, are apparently less effective in cutting. In the traditional method of preparing iron by bloom-ing, a considerable quantity of finely divided slag is left scattered through the metal. The wrought iron itself takes a very sharp edge, but is rather soft. The hard inclusions resist wear, and make the edge more durable. Forest clearance with these tools was probably easier than it is now with European matchets.

The Nok culture belongs to prehistory, but the later Iron-Age cultures are ethnohistoric, that is to say, we know the names of the people who handed on the culture, so that we can use evidence of traditional history, and, for the latest period, even written documents, to throw light on the archaeological remains. Indeed the study of the corresponding modern societies is an essential adjunct to archaeological investigation among them, for it can be of great help in interpreting the finds made by excavation, even when, as at Ife, there seems to have been extensive corruption of historical tradition. At present we appear to have a gap between the early Iron-Age Nok Culture and its later Iron-Age successor, but already this gap is being filled. Priddy has excavated terracotta sculptures near Yelwa with dates ranging between A.D. 100 $\pm$ 115 (N-361) and A.D. 700 $\pm$ 105 (N-363).[1] We do not know when the Nok culture ended when so many of its culture traits are still found in West Africa. Nor do we know the date of commencement of the Ife culture, which appears to have drawn extensively on the Nok tradition, or perhaps on a wider one of which the Nok culture happens to be the chief manifestation known to us, because it has lain in deposits which have merited commercial exploi-tation. (It is important to remember also that any chart or map of the archaeology of Nigeria is also a distribution map of the efforts of a very few archaeologists in a country of over 350,000 square miles. Now that archaeologists have been working from the universities of Ibadan, Ife, Lagos, Nsukka, and Zaria, as well as in the Department of Antiquities, this accidental bias is being eliminated.)

[1] See Thurstan Shaw, 'Archaeology in Nigeria,' *Antiquity*, 43 (1969), 196 and frontispiece.

It is especially important for us to know about the dates of the first penetration into the forests of the south, where polished stone axes have played an important role in the traditional religion of the Iron-Age peoples of the area. They have been found in later Iron-Age contexts at Ife, Ilesha, and Benin. (Graham Connah[1] has published an account of such axes brought to him in Benin, and of others, including some of very unusual length, from the altars to the deceased Kings of Benin in the palace.) This appears to indicate a substantial pre-Iron-Age penetration into the forest, as does the discovery in alluvial deposits near the Green Springs Hotel, Ibadan, of quite fresh-looking stone axes with polished edges.[2]

The radio-carbon dates from Iwo Eleru show that at least one group penetrated deeply into the forest at a very early period, but we remain ignorant of the later occupants of the forest. It would be interesting to know the relationship between the late Stone-Age forest dwellers, or their iron-using successors, and the Nok people. It is not impossible that the Nok culture, or something related to it, was widespread in the forest area already in the early Iron Age, and that it formed the basis for the cultures of the later Iron Age, with their great development of sculpture and metal-working, and, in the case of the Yoruba and Benin, towns of considerable size. The population of the forest in early times may well have been much greater than we have imagined, for it appears that little, if any, of the rain forest in Nigeria is genuinely virgin; it has all probably been cleared by man at some time and allowed to grow again.[3] It should be remembered that the principal tool for forest clearance today is fire, so that even a Stone-Age people would have had no difficulty in clearing the forest very efficiently.

THE LATER IRON AGE

The Iron-Age cultures of the Yoruba are known to us so far from excavations at three principal sites: Ife, Old Oyo, and

[1] Connah, *Polished Stone Axes in Benin*, Department of Antiquities (Lagos, 1965).

[2] E. L. Kostick, and C. N. and S. A. Williams, 'Stone Implements from Western Nigeria', *Nature*, 184 (1959), 124.

[3] Allison, 'Historical Inferences to be Drawn from the Effect of Human Settlement on the Vegetation of Africa', op. cit.

Ilesha, though finds related to the cultures revealed on these sites have been made elsewhere, and their distribution is indicated on Map 2. The Yoruba today number something approaching 10,000,000, and are clearly divided into separate groups, of which the largest are the Oyo, Ilorin, Ibadan, and Ekiti, who inhabit chiefly savanna-woodland country, and the Ife, Ijesha, Ijebu, Ondo, Owo, and Egba, who are principally in the forest. There was a considerable amount of population movement during the wars of the nineteenth century, which led to the abandonment of many towns, and the establishment of new ones, usually further south; there was in consequence a certain amount of mixture of population, though often a family will still remember the precise quarter it used to occupy in its former town. Despite these movements which have blurred the distinction, the northern Yoruba of the savanna-woodlands have a rather different culture from the southern Yoruba of the forest and its fringe. The forest of the Guinea Coastlands seems to have operated in rather the same way as did the Highland Zone in Britain,[1] i.e. when new cultures reached the forest their free spread was limited and only certain elements were absorbed into the pre-existing culture of the forest dwellers, so that a new synthesis was slowly evolved. It looks as if the southern Yoruba have retained a more truly indigenous culture than have the northern Yoruba, whose way of life is of a more noticeably savanna type.

There are two patterns of traditions of Yoruba origin—one that the world was created at Ife and that all mankind spread from there; the other that the Yoruba came from the east across the Sudan. What seems to have happened is that a relatively small group came into the area across the savanna from the east or north-east, possibly bringing knowledge of brass-casting and town-dwelling; these people settled among the indigenous population, probably on the fringes of the forest in the Ife area, intermarrying with them, and becoming completely absorbed into the population. A new culture was born of the blend,

[1] Sir Cyril Fox, *The Personality of Britain, Its Influence on Inhabitant and Invader in Prehistoric and Early Historic Times* (Cardiff, 1943).

exemplified by the continuing manufacture of terracotta sculpture ultimately derived from the Nok tradition, but supplemented by its translation into brass castings, a technique perhaps introduced by the newcomers.[1] The new way of life established at Ife spread outwards, as we can see from the material remains, a spread which is commemorated in the traditions under the names of individual founder-heroes who established their individual city states throughout Yorubaland. Even Benin claims to have renewed its dynasty from Ife when its own became powerless to rule the country.[2]

THE IFE CULTURE

Because of its central position in these traditions of origin, Ife became, if it had not been earlier, an important centre of religious cults; there are shrines there still for the founders of many of these new kingdoms. Its religious importance sets it apart from other Yoruba towns, yet its way of life was probably similar to that of other Yoruba kingdoms. Iron agricultural tools became increasingly important, and Yoruba blacksmiths became skilled at wrought-iron sculpture required for various cults; yet stone continued, and indeed still continues, in use for grinding vegetable foods, and for cracking shells of palm nuts. Certain stones were prized for beads, especially carnelian, agate, and jasper, examples of which have been found also at Old Oyo, Ilesha, and Benin. The raw material is still imported from Niger into Ilorin, where the industry is still carried on. In Ife glass beads were manufactured, and fragments of the crucibles in which they were made are commonly found in excavations. The crucibles show a great variety of colours, but the most common beads are tubular, of blue glass, and known as *segi*; they were traded widely in West Africa.

The domestic pottery used in Ife was very varied in its decoration, which included incision (straight lines, zigzags, stabs, and curvilinear designs), burnishing, painting, rouletting (with a great variety of carved wooden rollers, commonly giving a

[1] See Willett, *Ife in the History of West African Sculpture*, op. cit., pp. 119-28.
[2] Egharevba, *A Short History of Benin*, op. cit., pp. 6 ff.

basketwork effect, though twisted-string rouletting was also common, together with the use of a cob or ear of maize), and decoration with applied strips of clay.[1] This last technique was especially important in ritual pottery, where relief sculpture, sometimes of a very elaborate type, was usual. No pottery of Ife type has been found at Old Oyo over 100 miles away to the north, but a certain amount has been found at Ilesha about 20 miles to the north-east. Pottery of Old Oyo type has, however, been found in considerable quantities in what are probably nineteenth-century deposits at both Ife and Ilesha. This could be the result of movements of population as a result of the Fulani wars in the early nineteenth century, but it could be due to trade, as the descendants of the Old-Oyo potters now carry on a thriving long-distance trade in much poorer wares which they make in Ilorin. Scientific analyses of sherds from these sites are awaited.

A striking characteristic of the Ife culture was the habit of using sherds of broken pottery (including occasionally even ritual pottery) set on edge to form pavements inside their houses. They lived, as they still do in the older parts of Ife, in very extensive rambling compounds, consisting of many inter-connected houses, separated by narrow passages, with rooms of varying size, and frequent courtyards with open verandahs where the women would sit at their domestic chores—cooking, spinning, weaving, and perhaps potting. The larger rooms frequently had *impluvia*; the roof was open to the sky in the centre, with either a tank or a group of large waterpots to collect the rainwater for use, usually supplemented by drains of pottery or of worn-out grindstones with a hole right through, to lead away the excess water. These *impluvia* were often floored with potsherd pavements, clearly more effective than rammed earth in the days before cement, whilst similar pavements were used under verandahs round courtyards, and in passageways. Sometimes very neat cobblestone pavements were inserted in doorways, and often very decorative use was made of a mixture of

[1] Willett, 'Pottery Classification in African Archaeology', *West African Archaeological Newsletter*, 7 (1967), 44–55.

quartz pebbles and potsherds to produce striped or chequered pavements.[1] This particular culture trait has been found to be widely distributed, as far as Benin in the south-east, through northern and southern Ekiti, across to Ketu in Dahomey. There is indirect evidence of similar pavements at Old Oyo, Ilesha, and at Dawu in Ghana.[2] This distribution could be interpreted as a reflection of the influence of Ife, but Connah's discovery of similar pavements at Daima in a context earlier than the ninth century A.D. throws doubt on the idea that such pavements originated in Ife. They may have been introduced to Ife by the small ruling group who seem to have effected a number of other changes in the culture of the Yoruba area, or they may prove to be a widespread and ancient feature of West-African architecture.

An even more striking use of pottery than to make pavements is very important in Ife, namely naturalistic sculpture of terra-cotta figures, usually elaborately dressed, with bead necklaces, bracelets, and anklets, wearing beaded crowns on their heads, and having cloth wrappers tucked in round the waist if they are male figures, but usually just below the armpits if they are female. These sculptures are mostly about two-thirds life-size, though often larger or smaller than this, and seem to derive from the Nok tradition of sculpture, where naturalism had already made its appearance in the animal sculptures, and where some of the human heads show some naturalistic feeling. However, the limbs and trunks of Ife sculptures are often very simplified and resemble the corresponding parts of the Nok sculptures very closely. Elaborate beadwork is also characteristic of the Nok sculptures. But the most important resemblance of all lies in the fact that they are the only two ancient styles of terracotta sculpture we know, in the whole of Africa, ever to attempt to represent human beings at anything approaching life-size. This is such a remarkable achievement that it is hardly conceivable

[1] Examples are illustrated in Willett, 'Bronze and Terracotta Sculptures from Ita Yemoo, Ife', *The South African Archaeological Bulletin*, 14 (1959), Pl. VIIIa; 'Ife and Its Archaeology', *Journal of African History*, 1 (1960), Pl. VIII; and *Ife in the History of West African Sculpture*, op. cit., Figs. 16, 17.

[2] Shaw, *Excavation at Dawu* (Legon & Edinburgh, 1961), p. 54.

3

there should be no connection between them, especially when they are geographically so close together. Moreover, a small part of a face, apparently in a style intermediate between Nok and Ife, has been found at Ire, 35 miles north of Ife[1]; whilst a complete head of unusual but undoubtedly Ife style has more recently been found only 5 miles from Ire, at Ikirun.[2] Alongside these naturalistic sculptures, however, there are heads which are so stylized that they are scarcely more than symbols, whilst one or two show a curious mixture of stylization and naturalism.[3] There is a very large amount of terracotta sculpture now known from Ife, though we have yet to find a site where the sculptures were clearly new in the archaeological context from which they were excavated. Two shrines in which the sculptures were evidently in current use at the time the site was abandoned have been excavated at Ita Yemoo, Ife, a site which represents a vast compound covering several acres, but in both these cases one had the impression that the sculptures were already antique. Radio-carbon dates have been obtained from this site: A.D. 1060 ± 130 (BM-262) and A.D. 1150 ± 200 (M-2119) indicate the date of abandonment of the site, whilst an occupation level beneath a potsherd pavement, itself beneath the city wall, gave a date of A.D. 1160 ± 130 (BM-259). Charcoal from the bottom of a pit below another pavement gave a date of A.D. 960 ± 130 (BM-261). These dates show that the conventional dates, based on con-servative interpretations of Benin traditions, for the flourishing of Ife art in the twelfth to fourteenth centuries, which William Fagg and I have called the Classical Period, may well be too recent. More recently Ekpo Eyo has excavated a shrine at Lafogido in the centre of the town where he found a number of terracotta animal heads placed on the necks of globular pots set round the edge of a rectangular potsherd pavement. These appear to be *in situ*.[4]

[1] Illustrated in B. E. B. Fagg, 'The Nok Culture in Prehistory', op. cit., Fig. 8; and Willett, *Ife in the History of West African Sculpture*, op. cit., Fig. 27.

[2] Allison, 'A Terracotta Head in the Ife Style from Ikirun, Western Nigeria', *Man*, 63 (1963), 194; and Willett, *Ife in the History of West African Sculpture*, op. cit., Pl. 16.

[3] Ibid., Pl. 61.

[4] Eyo, '1969 Excavations at Ile-Ife', *African Arts*, 3, no. 2 (1970), 44–7.

An excavation conducted in 1963–4 by Oliver Myers at Igbo Obameri, near Ita Yemoo, revealed fragments of large size, including some in previously unknown styles, but these were, as so often in Ife, fragments evidently recovered from the ground in farming or building, and not understood but placed in an existing grove. The radio-carbon date is A.D. 1730 ± 100 (M-1686).[1] Sometimes, as at Olokun Walode, a grove was specially prepared for them. So many terracotta sculptures have been recovered that they deserve independent study, for several distinct styles can be recognized, some of which appear to be late.[2]

The terracottas are the most varied and probably the most rewarding aspect of the Ife culture, yet it is the bronzes (actually made of brass or nearly pure copper) that have become better known. All the bronzes are naturalistic in style and are either heads, usually of life size (in one case actually a mask complete with eye slits), or else figures up to 18 inches in height, or ritual equipment decorated with human heads or a human figure. These are all closely related in style, and since they number only twenty-seven items all told, they may have been cast in a very short period of time. It has even been suggested by Kenneth Murray[3] that they were all the work of one man, though William Fagg has detected two hands at least.

The bronzes and terracotta sculptures mostly represent royal figures in ceremonial dress. It is tempting to believe that they are to be associated with the cult of the divine king, but their precise significance is obscure. The life-size heads can hardly all represent individual kings unless our impression that they were made in a short period of time is entirely false. They seem almost certain to be heads from figures, probably of wood (the necks have holes for nails), used for elaborate second burial ceremonies for important persons who may or may not have been kings.

---

[1] O. H. Myers, 'Excavations at Ife', *West African Archaeological Newsletter*, 6 (1967), 6–11; and Willett, 'The Date of Igbo Obameri', *West African Archaeological Newsletter*, 7 (1967), 5–6.

[2] See Willett, *Ife in the History of West African Sculpture*, op. cit., pp. 68–9; Pls. 55–6, 59–60, and 62.

[3] [Murray], *An Introduction to the Art of Ife* (Lagos, 1955).

The effigies probably bore the emblems of royal or chiefly rank to symbolize the continuity of the office despite the death of the individual office-holder.[1] The terracotta sculptures might, of course, represent kings, or they might, like the mud sculptures of Benin,[2] represent gods conceived as kings, a concept perhaps encouraged by the belief that the king was divine and would become a god after his death.

An outstanding characteristic of the Yoruba is their great urbanism, which Bascom[3] has shown to be of considerable antiquity. It seems very strange that the Yoruba should live in such large towns, when their neighbours, the Ibo, do not. It seems likely that the small group of immigrants we have postulated as being absorbed into an indigenous stock (which in Ife is still called the Igbo, the same name as they use for the Ibo of the East Central State of Nigeria) brought with them some knowledge of town-dwelling, apparently in advance of the foundation of the towns in the Sudanic North of the country. These Yoruba towns are usually walled, but in most cases the walls now visible may be of the nineteenth century, though not enough have been excavated to find out whether any of them are simply refurbishings of older walls, as seems likely. It is equally possible that older walls have now become obliterated by later rebuilding of houses in these towns.

OLD OYO AND ILESHA

Old Oyo has been much less studied than Ife,[4] and much of the evidence recovered there has been mentioned already. The pottery from the site is especially interesting, as the fine grey-

[1] See Willett, 'On the Funeral Effigies of Owo and Benin and the Interpretation of the Life-size Bronze Heads from Ife, Nigeria', *Man*, N.S. 1, Pt. 1 (1966), 34–45, and 138.

[2] Anon., 'Mud Shrines of Olokun', *Nigeria*, 50 (1956), 280–95.

[3] W. R. Bascom, 'Urbanism as a Traditional African Pattern', *Sociological Review*, N.S. 7 (1959), 20 ff; 'Les Premiers Fondements Historiques de l'Urbanisme Yorouba', *Présence Africaine*, N.S. 23 (1959), 22–40; 'Lander's Routes Through Yoruba Country', *Nigerian Field*, 25 (1960), 12–22; and 'The Urban African and His World, *Cahiers d'Études Africaines*, 4 (1963), 163–85.

[4] Willett, 'Investigations at Old Oyo, 1956–7; An Interim Report', *Journal of the Historical Society of Nigeria*, 2, Pt. 1 (1961), 59–77.

black wares are of superb quality—the fabric is only slightly inferior in fineness of texture and hardness of firing to Samian ware—and examples of it have been found widely distributed. There is, however, a distinctive series of elegant pots which is restricted to one part of the city, and may have been made by a stranger element in the population. The paste, like the form, appears to be distinct from the other Old Oyo wares. Among the coarse wares there are remains of a great number of perforated pots similar to types still used in smoking meat. These may indicate that hunting persisted as a more important element in the economy of the savanna that it was in the forest. There are also pots intended to hold fire, with three lugs on the inside of the rim to support a cooking pot; this type occurs rarely at Ife, though a sheet-metal copy is in common use throughout the country nowadays. Stone bracelets occur at Old Oyo, but have not yet been discovered elsewhere. Grindstones of the usual type are rare, for there are many natural outcrops of rock which can be used for grinding basins. Sassoon[1] has demonstrated that some of these might have been used for metal-working.

A single terracotta sculpture of no great distinction was found here,[2] but at Ilesha, in ground which was formerly part of the palace, a large series of sculptures, best described as baked clay figures, was excavated. These are to be dated to near the middle of the nineteenth century, and have much in common with certain rare pieces from Ife, but even more in common with modern Yoruba wood and ivory sculpture. In the same excavation a royal burial was discovered. The king wore red stone and blue glass *segi* beads round his neck, though his head had been carefully removed after death and placed on his chest. He wore bronze bracelets on his arms, and two iron daggers lay beside him, both with brass fittings on the handles, one of which survived in such complete condition that the knotwork decoration could be clearly seen carved in the wood. He was accompanied by nine other people: two men, two women, and the

[1] H. Sassoon, 'Grinding Grooves and Pits in Northern Nigeria', *Man*, 62 (1962), 232.
[2] Willett, 'A Terracotta head from Old Oyo, Nigeria', *Man*, 59 (1959) 286.

rest ranging in age from six to seventeen. Many of these too were wearing bracelets and beads. The grave also held an undecorated ivory trumpet. The burial perhaps dates from the third quarter of the nineteenth century. Its excavation caused local misgivings, so the bodies and grave goods had to be reburied. The clay sculptures did not need to be reburied, which was fortunate, as they are an important link in demonstrating the continuity of the Yoruba style of sculpture from Ife through to the present day.[1]

THE BENIN CULTURE AND ITS RELATIONS WITH IFE

The present dynasty of Benin traces its descent from Oronmiyon, a great Ife warrior, and in recognition of this, the head of the deceased King of Benin was sent to Ife for burial on the site (Orun Oba Ado) from which Oronmiyon set out. This was last done in 1888. In return a bronze head used to be sent from Ife to Benin, until Oba Oguola somewhere about the end of the fourteenth century persuaded the Oni of Ife to allow the heads to be made in Benin.[2] The Benin heads can be placed in typological sequence, with relatively rare thin castings in a fairly naturalistic style at one end, and the thick, heavy, highly stylized heads, which we know to be late, at the other.[3] Six of the burial pits at Orun Oba Ado have been excavated in the hope of finding antiquities from Benin to provide cross-references between the two sequences, but unfortunately no Benin pottery was found, nor any human skulls. It seems possible that the 'heads' consisted of hair and nail-parings from the corpse, buried in a bark box, which would all disappear. However, radio-carbon dates have been obtained from four pits, A.D. 990 ± 130 (B.M.-264), A.D. 940 ± 150 (M-2116) (Pit VI), A.D. 800 ± 120 (M-2115) (Pit V), A.D. 800 ± 120 (M-2114) (Pit III) and A.D. 560 ± 130 (B.M.-265) (Pit XI), which are surprisingly early and suggest that the

[1] 'Recent Archaeological Discoveries at Ilesha', *Odu, a Journal of Yoruba, Edo, and Related Studies*, 8 (1961), 4–20; and *Ife in the History of West African Sculpture*, op. cit., Pl. 107, pp. 179–80. A report on this escavation is almost ready for the press.

[2] Egharevba, *A Short History of Benin*, op cit.; and Bradbury, 'Chronological Problems in the Study of Benin History', op. cit.

[3] W. B. Fagg, *Nigerian Images* (London, 1963), p. 32.

site of Ife has indeed a long history, despite the doubts expressed by Ryder.[1]

In Benin itself, however, a small excavation on the site of the Baptist Church discovered, among vast quantities of Benin pottery, a few sherds of European stoneware, probably of the eighteenth or possibly of the nineteenth century. The excavations which Connah conducted in 1961–2 on the site proposed for the new Benin Museum revealed wide deep pits into which the ruined buildings of the palace had been thrown in 1897 after the fire. These included a dozen blocks of potsherd pavement, somewhat less regular than the Ife ones, but made from thinner pottery. They had apparently formed part of the floor of the palace. The following year he excavated a different area of the former palace, where Goodwin had dug in 1954–5 and 1955–6. Goodwin's first season had revealed four successive rebuildings of that part of the palace, each consequent upon a fire. His second season cleared a courtyard in which he found the cast head of a snake formerly decorating the tower of the palace. This probably got into its place of finding some time before the destruction of 1897.[2] Nearby Connah was able to isolate the Palace wall with its characteristic horizontal fluting, and a succession of occupations (one radio-carbon dated A.D.1490 ± 90 (I-2723)) culminating in a pit more than 50 ft deep containing thirty human skeletons. Accompanying charcoal produced dates of A.D. 1180 ± 105 (N-377) and 1310 ± 90 (I-2722), whilst *iroko* timbers above the burial gave dates of A.D. 1230 ± 105 (N-376) and 1385 ± 100 (I-3622). A quantity of sheet brass decorated with repoussé ornament was found at a late level; it was crushed but still had tacks in it, which suggested that it had been stripped off a wooden support, perhaps a box. Another site nearby provided more substantial brass objects in the form of elaborate wide

[1] A. Ryder, 'A reconsideration of the Ife–Benin relationship', *Journal of African History*, 6 (1965), 25–37; Willett, 'New Light on the Ife–Benin Relationship', *African Forum*, 3 no. 4 and 4 no. 1, 1968 (1970), 28–34.

[2] A. J. H. Goodwin, 'Benin Palace Excavations', paper contributed to the Second Conference on African History and Archaeology, London (1957) (mimeographed); 'Archaeology and Benin Architecture', *Journal of the Historical Society of Nigeria*, 1, Pt. 2 (1957), 65–85; and 'A Bronze Snake Head and Other Recent Finds in the Old Palace at Benin', *Man*, 63 (1963), 174.

bracelets cast in sections. These sites all produced large quantities
of pottery of good quality, much of it richly decorated in relief.[1]

EASTERN NIGERIA

The former Eastern Region was until recently sadly neglected
in comparison with the West, the Midwest, and the North,
although pottery sculpture and metal castings have long been
known from this region. In 1959–60 Thurstan Shaw investigated
the site at Igbo Ukwu, near Awka, where a hoard of elaborate
bronzes of types not known from anywhere else had been found
in 1939, when a cistern was being dug. The original find-spot
still contained enough material to indicate that the site had
originally been a treasure-house where these elaborate bronzes
were stored: great bowls copying calabashes, smaller ones
pinched together at the top and perhaps used as cups, several
types of bronze pendants, many with red stone and blue and
yellow glass beads, potstands of differing types, large mace-
heads, smaller finials probably from the other end of the same
maces, massive bracelets, a belt constructed of bronze plates,
vessels modelled on a large land-snail, and an iron sword in a
bronze scabbard. But the most remarkable find of all, and the
first to be unearthed, was a vase cast in one piece, on a stand, with
an interlaced rope enveloping the whole but attached only at the
top and bottom. All the bronzes have a richly ornamental surface
which often employs crickets, beetles, and mantids as decoration.
Their style is quite unrelated to the Ife/Benin tradition and
bears no resemblance to any other style we know as yet.

Nearby a further excavation revealed a burial chamber,
apparently originally lined with wood; this had rotted, allowing
the sides and top of the chamber to collapse onto the body,
scattering the rich grave goods. Careful recording and patient
work in the laboratory afterwards have revealed that the figure
was seated on a round stool, probably of wood, decorated with
bronze bosses. (This gave a radio-carbon date of A.D. 850 ± 120

---

[1] Connah, 'Archaeological Research in Benin City', *Journal of the Historical Society of
Nigeria*, 2, Pt. 4 (1963), 465–77; 'Summary of Research in Benin City and Bornu', op. cit.;
also private communication with author.

(I-2008)). His arms were supported on bronze brackets sur-
mounting rods stuck in the ground beside him. He held a staff
in one hand and a fly-whisk, with a bronze handle topped by a
fine casting of a horseman, in the other. In his lap, perhaps leaning
against his shoulder, was a bronze 'sceptre', terminating in a
semicircular plate, pierced round the edge, probably to receive
feathers to turn it into a fan. (The length of the handle suggests
that it was intended to be used by an attendant.) The skull lay
inside a mass of red and blue beads, evidently the remains of a
headdress, outside which there was a simple crown constructed
from sheet bronze. On his wrists were bracelets of blue glass
beads set in a bronze framework. Tens of thousands of beads were
scattered round the grave, which suggests that he wore beaded
anklets and probably necklaces, and that his other clothing may
have been elaborately adorned with beads. He wore also a bronze
pectoral plate, in the centre of which were the remains of a woodcarving. Beside him was set a staff surmounted by a leopard's
skull cast in bronze, and there were three elephant tusks on the
floor. The bronze work in the grave was noticeably different
from that found in the treasure-house. All except two items
were made by smithing and chasing, not by casting, and were in
consequence much less elaborate. Later analysis showed that
the smithed and chased objects were of nearly pure copper,
whereas the castings were of leaded tin-bronze, presumably
obtained from a source different from that which supplied Ife
with its brass.[1] The early dating of this complex is confirmed by
radio-carbon dates from pits in different parts of the site: A.D.
840 ± 145 (I-1784); A.D. 840 ± 110 (Hv-1515) and A.D. 875 ± 130
(Hv-1514).

The grave is evidently that of an important ruler, whom Shaw,
before he obtained the radio-carbon dates, took to be an Eze Nri,
the priest-king of the Umueri clan in whose domain the sites,
now in Igbo Ukwu, formerly lay. This clan is reputed to have

---

[1] Shaw, 'Spectrographic Analyses of the Igbo and Other Nigerian Bronzes', *Archaeometry*, 8 (1965), 86–95; 'The Igbo Bronzes', *Actes du Ve Congrès Panafricain de Préhistoire et
de l'Étude du Quaternaire*, Tenerife (1966), 249–59; and Willett, 'Spectrographic Analysis
of Nigerian Bronzes', *Archaeometry*, 7 (1964), 81–3.

brought an intrusive culture to Iboland from Idah,[1] but whether it did so as early as the ninth century is not sure. Idah does seem to have been a place of great importance formerly as a centre of bronze-casting, and Shaw excavated the Ateogu mound at Idah, which provided radio-carbon dates of A.D. 1495 ± 95 (I-2262) and A.D. 1540 ± 95 (I-2263). Unfortunately it has not been possible to follow up this exploratory season, but it is interesting that these dates are of the time when Idah and Benin were competing with each other. Whether large-scale bronze-casting was going on there earlier has yet to be demonstrated.[2]

Most interestingly the Igbo Ukwu and the Daima dates indicate that bronze was known at opposite ends of the eastern side of the country by the ninth century. William Fagg has pointed out[3] that there are two traditions of bronze-casting in West Africa, probably introduced at different times; the Igbo Ukwu castings belong to one, and the Ife-Benin pieces to the other. It will be interesting to know to which tradition the Daima pieces belong, since at the moment we have no direct radio-carbon dates for Ife bronzes, though those from Ita Yemoo came from the same layer as the terracotta sculptures and appear to antedate the twelfth century.

When this paper was originally written, Igbo Ukwu was the only excavated site in eastern Nigeria, though Donald Hartle had begun his survey of the area, which has since located some 400 sites, on fourteen of which he has conducted excavations. A site on the University Farm at Nsukka produced pottery with radio-carbon dates of 2555 ± 130 B.C. (GX-0529) and 1460 ± 115 (GX-0591). The most interesting excavation, to judge from the

---

[1] Shaw, 'Excavations at Igbo-Ukwu, Eastern Nigeria', an interim report, *Man*, 60 (1960), 210.

[2] Ibid.; also 'Royal Tomb at Igbo, Eastern Nigeria'; 'The Regalia and Ritual Instruments of a Nigerian Priest King: the Treasure-house of Igbo', *Illustrated London News*, 241 (1962), 358-9, 404-7 (Archaeological Sections 2101 and 2102); and 'Radiocarbon Dates from Nigeria', *Journal of the Historical Society of Nigeria*, 3, Pt. 4 (1967), 743-51. The definitive report is, *Igbo Ikwu: an account of archaeological excavations in eastern Nigeria* (London and Evanston, 1970).

[3] E. Elisofon, and W. B. Fagg, *The Sculpture of Africa* (London, 1958), pp. 60-1.

brief accounts so far available,[1] is the Ifeka Garden Site, Ezira, where a burial of an important man was excavated, revealing bronze anklets, bracelets, bells, and other ceremonial objects. There were iron gongs round the body and an iron sword beside him. A radio-carbon date of A.D. 1495±95 (GX-0942) was obtained. Other bronzes have been found in the eastern states and in the Niger delta,[2] and much work remains to be done in establishing their relationships.

OTHER SITES

Conjecture has been unavoidable in this chapter; it has been kept to a minimum by avoiding references to antiquities of uncertain date, even though many of them are of great intrinsic interest. There are, for example, rock-paintings from several sites in northern Nigeria,[3] petroglyphs from Igbara-Oke,[4] stone-carvings from Esie,[5] Ijara,[6] Igbajo,[7] Ofaro[8] and the Cross River area.[9] Bernard Fagg has defined a whole complex of rock gongs and rock slides which have since been found in Europe; this may be a Stone-Age culture trait, but it persists throughout the Iron

[1] D. Hartle, 'Bronze Objects from Ezira, Eastern Nigeria', *West African Archaeological Newsletter*, 4 (1966), 25–8; 'Archaeology in Eastern Nigeria', ibid. 5, 13–17; and 'Archaeology in Eastern Nigeria', *Nigeria*, 93 (1967), 134–43.

[2] R. Horton, 'A Note on Recent Finds of Brasswork in the Niger Delta', *Odu*, N.S. 2, Pt. 1 (1965), 76–91.

[3] B. E. B. Fagg, 'The Cave Paintings and Rock Gongs of Birnin Kudu', *Proceedings of the Third Pan-African Congress on Prehistory, 1955* (1957), 306–12; Sassoon, 'Cave Paintings Recently Discovered Near Bauchi, Northern Nigeria', *Man*, 60 (1960), 70; and P. Morton-Williams, 'A Cave Painting, Rock Gong, and Rock Slide in Yoruba Land', *Man*, 57 (1957), 213.

[4] Unpublished.

[5] J. D. Clarke, 'The Stone Figures of Esie', *Nigeria*, 14 (1938), 106–8; W. B. Fagg, 'On a Stone Head of Variant Style at Esie, Nigeria', *Man*, 59 (1959), 60; E. L. R. Meyerowitz, 'The Stone Figures of Esie in Nigeria', *Burlington Magazine*, 82 (1943), 31–6; K. C. Murray, 'The Stone Images of Esie and Their Yearly Festival', *Nigeria*, 37 (1951); and P. Stevens, 'The Festival of the Images at Esie', *Nigeria*, 87 (1965), 236–43.

[6] Allison, 'Newly Discovered Stone figures from the Yoruba Village of Ijara, Northern Nigeria', *Man* (1963), 115.

[7] 'A Carved Stone Figure of Eshu from Igbajo, Western Nigeria', *Man* (1964), 131.

[8] F. de F. Daniel, 'Stone Figures at Ofaro', *Nigeria*, 18 (1939), 107–8.

[9] R. L. Harris, 'A Note on Sculptured Stones in the Mid Cross River Area of South-east Nigeria', *Man* (1959), 177; and Allison, 'Carved Stone Figures in the Ekoi Country of the Middle Cross River, Eastern Nigeria', *Man* (1962), 15; *Cross River Monoliths* (Lagos, 1968); *African Stone Sculpture* (London, 1968).

Age right up to the present.[1] The stone bridges at Bokkos in the Ron country to the south of the Plateau are remarkable engineering achievements, which may well be of the Iron Age.[2] All of these require further evidence for their date before we can interpret them adequately.

DATING METHODS

Establishing the age of an antiquity is, of course, the archaeologist's greatest difficulty, but the invention of new techniques of dating and the improvement of old ones should help to clarify the picture of Nigeria's Iron Age. Trade goods from Europe are one thing we must seek, whether they came in from the coast in recent centuries or across the Sahara at any time during the last two or three millennia. Asiatic beads are beginning to turn up, but these are still ambiguous as evidence for date. Imported plants are of great economic importance in West Africa today, and it seems unlikely that those from America were imported at the same time as those from Asia (unless, perhaps, they came by way of Asia); pollen analysis may serve to sort this out, and then to give us relative dates for our archaeological deposits. If on historical grounds we can give a positive date to such importations, then we have a datable horizon. I have attempted to do this for maize, which is of American origin and is now extensively used as a tool for decorating pottery.[3] My conclusions have been attacked[4] but a recent re-examination of pottery from levels in Ife now dated earlier than Columbus has failed to find any with maize impressions. Thus it appears that maize impressions may be taken to indicate a date later than the beginning of the sixteenth century. Robert Stanton has even suggested a technique

[1] B. E. B. Fagg, 'The Discovery of Multiple Rock Gongs in Nigeria', *Man* (1965), 23; 'The Rock Gong Complex Today and in Prehistoric Times', *Journal of the Historical Society of Nigeria*, 1, Pt. 1 (1956), 27–42; 'Rock Gongs and Rock Slides', *Man* (1957), 32; and J. H. Vaughan, 'Rock Paintings and Rock Gongs among the Marghi of Nigeria', *Man* (1962), 83.

[2] B. E. B. Fagg, 'Archaeological Notes from Northern Nigeria', *Man* (1946), 48.

[3] Willett, 'The Introduction of Maize into West Africa: An Assessment of Recent Evidence', *Africa*, 32 (1962), 1–13.

[4] Jeffreys, 'How Ancient is West African maize?', *Africa*, 33 (1963), 115–31; and G. F. Carter, 'Archaeological Maize in West Africa: A Discussion of Stanton and Willett', *Man*, 64 (1964), 95.

of relative dating by means of the maize impressions themselves, but very large samples are needed, such as could only
be provided by excavations on a much larger scale than has
usually been attempted in West Africa.[1] Thurstan Shaw has
pointed out the importance of the tobacco-pipe as indicating
a level which can be easily identified,[2] and this is now being
successfully used in Ghana. Cowrie-shell currency probably
also affords a similar horizon, since shells seem to be more
resistant to decay than bone, whilst glass beads seem not to
have been made before the Iron Age—a crude measure of dating,
but useful where stray finds are concerned. Trade in local
products is a normal archaeological method of correlation,
and trade in Old Oyo pottery and red stone and blue glass beads
has already been mentioned. Less commonly, fragments of Ife
glass-making crucibles have been found elsewhere, whilst one
was sold to Lander at Old Oyo on 15 May 1830.[3]

The balance of this picture of Nigerian archaeology is less
uneven than it was five years ago. This is largely because of
a deliberate policy intended to fill in the more obvious gaps
as rapidly as possible. From the work so far carried out it is
clear that many peoples of the present day have been in their
present habitats for 1,000 years or more, and that the country as
a whole has been an important centre of sculpture for at least
2,000 years. Already we can see that the old view of pre-colonial
Africa as wholly dark and savage is even less true of some parts
than Caesar's picture of the Iron-Age British as woad-painted
savages.

[1] W. R. Stanton, and Willett, 'Archaeological Evidence for Changes in Maize Type in
West Africa: An Experiment in Technique', *Man*, 63 (1963), 150.

[2] Shaw, 'Early Smoking Pipes: in Africa, Europe, and America', *Journal of the Royal
Anthropological Institute*, 90 (1960), 272–305.

[3] R. & J. Lander, *Journal of an Expedition to Explore the Course and Termination of the
Niger* (London, 1832), I, 180.

2

GHANA

by

P. C. Ozanne

SECOND to Ethiopia, Ghana may be regarded as the oldest of the existing states of sub-Saharan Africa. Many of its distinctive features were defined in the eighteenth century:[1] its borders, to within a few miles; its bureaucracy and centralization of government; its acceptance of strangers as members and even officials of the state, no matter what their origin; industrial concentration, and the combination of private enterprise and state control; and most of its cultural accoutrements. By the middle of the eighteenth century, Asante was the richest country in Africa, and from that time onwards its material culture is of little meaning to the archaeologist unless he relates it to the intricate details of political and economic history yielded by the documents of various nations. This chapter will be concerned with the long series of processes which may be regarded as having culminated in the creation of the commonwealth of Asante two centuries ago. The account can only be given through the kindness and generosity of colleagues, especially Mr. R. B. Nunoo, Mr. R. York, and Mr. D. Mathewson, who have allowed the writer to refer to their unpublished work.[2]

[1] For a detailed account see I. G. Wilks, 'The Ashanti Government in the Nineteenth Century', in *West African Kingdoms* (London, 1966).

[2] I wish to thank these scholars, and Dr. Alexander, Mr. S. Owusu, and Mr. D. A. Penfold, for permitting me to use such material; in many cases the suggested interpretations are mine, and are likely to be superseded in the excavators' reports. Mr. York, Professor Wilks, and Mr. Anquandah have kindly criticized the text, and Mr. D. Coursey the agricultural points.

We must start by looking for the first settlement of the country by the ancestors of the present population, which the archaeologist might expect to be represented by a definite break in the sequence of cultural development. The last such hiatus was between the end of the Old Stone Age, and the beginning of what we may call the Mesolithic Age, the latter characterized by hunting and fishing communities making their tools from minute quartz microliths.[1] A radio-carbon date from Takoradi suggests—though not very reliably—that the hiatus occurred after 3700 B.C., and it is thought to have taken place in the third or second millenium.[2] Subsequently, although there were several changes of the greatest importance, there was no great break in development which might lead us to believe that the stock of the mesolithic people had been replaced; the people of present-day Ghana would seem to be mainly derived from those of mesolithic times. This, be it noted, utterly contradicts the suppositions of historians of 10 or 20 years ago, such as Ward, who remarked that 'there is no nation now dwelling in the Gold Coast which has been in the country much longer than the European'.[3] But it finds strong support in the attitudes of the experts in the young science of West African linguistics; for example, Armstrong has said of the population of the sub-continent that 'the linguistic situation suggests great age and little movement.'[4] The archaeologist can say little about the early ethnic history of the country other than that his material indicates a beginning at least 3,000 years ago; and questions of 'which tribe came first' are better left to those who have more exact evidence.

The mesolithic settlers of Ghana exploited a wide range of environment. They were by no means restricted to the open woodlands of the northern part of the country; indeed, several areas in the heart of the rain-forest were occupied, as for example

---

[1] A detailed description of the stone age cultures is given by O. Davies, *The Quaternary of the Coastlands of Guinea* (Glasgow, 1965).

[2] O. Davies, 'The Stone Age in West Africa', *Ghana Journal of Science*, 3 (1963), 3.

[3] W. E. F. Ward, *A History of Ghana* (London, 1958), 58.

[4] R. G. Armstrong, 'The Use of Linguistic and Ethnographic Data in the Study of Idoma and Yoruba History', in *The Historian in Tropical Africa* (London, 1964), 129.

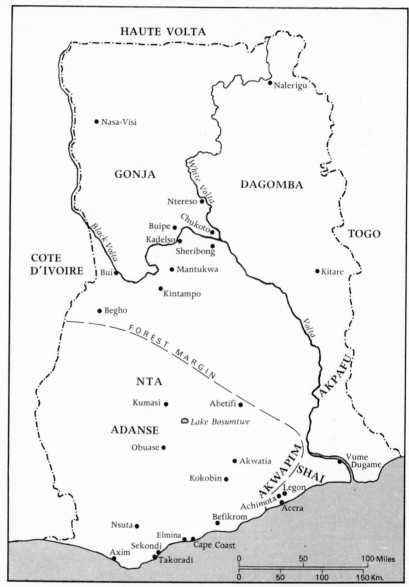

MAP 3. The Early and Medieval Periods in Ghana.

between Kumasi and Lake Bosumtwe, and one can only assume
that the scrub vegetation under the high tree cover was removed
by fire. These people took little care in the manufacture of their
stone tools, and the vast majority of their surviving artefacts are

irregular in shape, undefinable in purpose, and unrelatable to those
of cultures outside the country. The only standardized type of
microlith which is found frequently is the crescent, used perhaps
in a wooden shaft as a square-tipped arrow-head; but this type is
common to so many parts of the world that it tells us little of the
cultural affinities of the early societies. Rectangular and trapezoid
arrow-heads are more rare, and similarly uninstructive. Occasionally in the north, however, tanged points, worked on only
one face, suggest a lingering influence of the cultures of Aterian
type of the Western Sudan and Sahara.

The writer's impression is that at some period between about
500 B.C. and A.D. 500—the dates cannot be defined in the present
stage of knowledge—a series of cultural changes occurred in
rapid succession, with the introductions of cultivation and
stock-raising, of pottery-making and iron-working. Little
evidence of early practice in these activities has been recovered.[1]
With few exceptions, the soils of Ghana rapidly dissolve bones,
iron objects, and even potsherds; they may preserve ancient
pollen, which could inform us of the introduction of domestic
plants, were it not for our present ignorance of West African
palynology, both of the past and of today. The sequence of these
innovations is therefore most obscure. Consideration of the
recurrent legend of Ghana folklore, that in early times iron was
known but was more expensive than gold—first recorded over
two hundred years ago—may help us to understand the early
development of the country more clearly than would be
possible from the surviving archaeological evidence.

The first important technical innovation of which evidence
has survived was a large stone tool, in the form of a pick or hoe,
which was usually made too crudely to serve any purpose other
than as a digging implement. Such are very common in the
Accra area and southern Togo, where evidence of mesolithic
communities is comparatively rare; it is a reasonable hypothesis
that the increased exploitation of this area, by people specially

[1] This view has recently been shown to be too shortsighted. Carbon dates from Kintampo have shown that pottery was certainly being produced by the middle of the second
millenium B.C., though there is as yet no direct evidence of stockraising or agriculture.

equipped for digging, was due to the introduction of agriculture. Ghana lies near the centre of the African 'yam-belt', which extends from the Cameroon mountain range to the Bandama river in the Ivory Coast, through the forest and southern savanna. Here, the yam (*Dioscorea sp.*) is the staple food, and the one which figures in the important annual festivals. The two most common species, *D. cayenensis* and *D. rotundata*, are indigenous, and there is every reason to suppose that they have been culti- vated since the beginnings of agriculture in the zone.[1] Three other important cultivated plants, the taro (*Colocasia esculentum*), the oil-palm (*Elaeis guineensis*) and the cayenne pepper, are also likely to have been cultivated in antiquity, especially palm oil which is used for cooking yam, fish and meat. Fish and yam, cooked in palm oil and pepper, provide most of man's dietetic needs. Furthermore, a distinct stock of cattle is to be found in the south of Togo and Dahomey, and spreading thinly westwards all along the coast; this must have taken some centuries to diverge in type from its northern relatives, and it is possible, although the earliest archaeological evidence is of sixteenth century date, that this breed of cattle was introduced by the first cultivators. Cattle, however, could not be kept by the forest communities, largely because of the sparsity of grazing grass; the only livestock in these parts would have been the ubiquitous sheep, goat, and chicken, and perhaps the pig.

The stone-hoe users of the Accra area appear to have been intrusive, probably spreading thither from east of the Volta. A site at Legon, excavated by Davies, exhibits the strangeness of this new culture.[2] The hoes and some other tools, such as borers, were made of quartzite, as was usual in south-east Ghana and Togo, but there were also quartz microliths. The latter include two new types, a diminutive tanged arrow-head and a leaf- shaped one. Here also appear for the first time the two most common types of stone tool of the Ghana Iron Age—the ground stone axe, in this case a fat rectangular one of gneiss, and the

---

[1] D. G. Coursey, 'The Role of Yams in West African Food Economies', *World Crops*, 17 (1965), 74–82.

[2] O. Davies, 'Galets Perforés du Ghana et des Pays Voisins', *Notes Africaines*, 86 (1960), 37.

quartz pebble, conically bored from each side to make a minute perforation. The latter type may have had various uses, as a measurement of weight, as a unit of currency, as a large bead or pendant, and so on.[1]

Whereas in south-eastern Ghana agriculture may have been brought by intrusive people, in the rest of the country the neolithic arts were probably introduced to the mesolithic population by culture-contact.[2] In the forest especially, assemblages of quartz microliths indistinguishable from mesolithic ones are found with flakes of greenstone (hornblende-schist), and in many cases these seem to have resulted from the manufacture of crude hoes and picks, such as for example those found by Nunoo in the grounds of the University at Kumasi,[3] and not from the making of ground axes. It is unlikely that the people yet knew the use of iron, but they were able to make substantial clearings in the forest, leaving, no doubt, the large trees.

The Kintampo Culture,[4] concentrated in central Ghana, has the strongest claims for the introduction of pottery and iron-working to the country. The two industries are closely related in several parts of West Africa; for instance, in Mande communities from the Gambia to northern Ghana the potter is traditionally the wife of the blacksmith. This relationship may have been much more common in the past, when both activities were conducted on a small, unorganized scale. Industrial development in medieval Ghana can be seen to have separated the industries, the areas where the best ore is found becoming iron-working centres, and exposures of first-class clays supporting expert potting communities. A strong indication that the two industries were introduced together is to be noted in the Accra area, where the earliest pottery, belonging to the Kintampo Culture, is found with stone hoes and picks, but not with microlithic tools; one may infer that from this time onwards such

[1] C. T. Shaw, 'Report on the Excavation of the Cave known as Bosumpra, Abetifi', *Proc. Prehist. Soc. X*, (1944), 47–51.

[2] O. Davies, loc. cit., note 4.

[3] R. B. Nunoo, 'An Archaeological Survey at the College of Technology', *Journal of the Kumasi College of Technology*, 1 (1959), 17–19.

[4] This terminology, as used by Davies, op. cit., note 17 is the most acceptable.

small tools as arrow-heads, borers and knives were made of iron.

The Kintampo Culture may be divided into several groups, of which the central one may be called the Chukoto Variant. Chukoto, excavated by Mathewson, yielded all of the classic types of this Variant. The pottery is simply shaped; perhaps the surfaces were originally polished—they have been worn so much in the soil that one cannot tell. Many vessels are attractively decorated, by horizontal grooves dividing the body into zones, of which alternate ones are filled by oblique impressions, made with a twisted cord or notched blade. Similar pottery is found in the western Sudan, and even on the shores of the West Mediterranean, but no undue significance should be attached to this. Above all, the pottery in all these places looks like copies of pre-existing basketry, as if its makers had learnt the art of potting, but used it in making vessels like those already familiar to them. Form and ornament are very limited in scope in basketry, compared with the plastic medium of pottery, and therefore it is no surprise that ceramic 'skeuomorphs' of baskets should look alike in many parts of the world. This point is strengthened by the identity between the Asante verbs to mould a pot and to weave a basket. We need not therefore postulate an invasion to account for the introduction of pottery; the new medium may have been acquired by aborigines from their neighbours.

A puzzling characteristic type of the Kintampo Culture is a scored tablet, looking like a flattened ear of maize. Most commonly they were made of pottery,[1] but at some sites stone ones occur, and at Chukoto there were also stone rough-outs for them discarded before they were finished. The only function which has been suggested for them is to mould and smooth pottery vessels before firing, in the way maize-cobs and palm-nuts are used today.[2] Other diagnostic types are miniature triangular ground axes of greenstone, polished stone arm-rings, D-shaped in section, of great beauty, and sandstone bead-polishers—pebbles which bear deep rounded grooves, resulting from the manufacture of small disc beads of stone and of shell. Such beads were

[1] Mr. C. Flight questions this assessment and proposes to examine it.
[2] J. Anquandah, 'Ghana's Terracotta Cigars', Ghana Notes and Queries, 7 (1965), 26.

flaked into shape, and perforated by a conical bore-hole on either face, before being ground smooth in this way. Microliths are found on sites of Chukoto type, but apart from crescents and trapezes, they are of little interest.

Chukoto type sites are spread across central Ghana nearly from border to border, and towards the east they are linked, through the Volta Gap which breaks the forest belt, with the settlements of the Christians' Village Variant, which is represented by four sites on the edge of the Accra Plain. At Christians' Village, half-way between Achimota and Legon, Davies found pottery quite like that of Chukoto, with scored tablets and bead-polishers.[1] Typical stone arm-ring fragments come from Peduase, 10 miles north of the type-site. The miniature triangular axes are not represented; the only fragment of a ground axe of this group is of sub-cylindrical form, from a minor site near Achimota.[2] These sites differ from those of the Chukoto Variant in two ways; first, as has been mentioned above, they do not yield microliths, and one may guess that iron was being used for delicate equipment; and second, quartzite hoes and picks, identical to those of the preceding period, were commonly used. Here we seem to find an amalgamation of the intrusive farming culture with new technologies in pottery, stone, and perhaps iron, introduced from the north. An analogous mixed culture is represented by the Kumasi Variant, best known from Nunoo's excavations in the grounds of the University referred to above. Here, in the heart of the forest, Nunoo found similar scored tablets—although only stone ones—with typical stone arm-rings, and also crudely worked hoes of greenstone. The pottery from this site was so crudely made, and had been worn so badly, that none can tell its affinities. Elsewhere in the forest, however—for example, at the cave Shaw excavated at Abetifi[3]—one can see very clearly the influence of the Kintampo Culture upon the earliest known pottery. Altogether, it seems that the Chukoto Variant of the Kintampo Culture played a part of the utmost

[1] O. Davies, 'Neolithic Cultures of Ghana,' *Acyes du IVe Congrès Panafricain de Préhistoire et des Études Quarternaires* (1962), 300–1.

[2] P. Ozanne, 'An Early Settlement near Achimota', *Ghana Notes and Queries*, 8 (1966).

[3] C. T. Shaw, op. cit., note 9.

importance in the development of Ghana in early times, a part rivalled only by that of the Mande peoples in the fourteenth to seventeenth centuries.

Davies has published[1] his first comments upon the most exciting aspect of the Kintampo Culture, which might be called the Ntereso Variant. His excavations at Ntereso revealed not only a Chukoto-type assemblage, but also differing styles of pottery, 'perhaps a new type of thick stone bracelet; probably cattle and horses; a decline in the workmanship of small quartz tools, as if the incomers were unskilled at making them; a little iron; and beautiful arrow-heads with long tapering barbs'. There are other features which made this Ntereso Variant one of the most fascinating subjects of West African prehistory, the publication of which is most eagerly awaited. It is possible that a group related to the Ntereso Variant developed on the Black Volta near the Ivory Coast border; at Bui, York has found long quartz arrow-heads of expert workmanship, round-based and straight-sided associated with bead-polishers and a small perforated pebble.

After these radical innovations, the societies of Ghana seem to have developed very gradually, until, we may guess, about A.D. 1200. The clearest picture of life in the intervening period is obtained in the Legon-Achimota area near Accra.[2] Here were two clusters of compounds, with 200 m. or so between the units, comprising open villages very like some which are still built by peoples of northern Ghana, such as the Talensi. A compound excavated at East Legon was rectangular, with clay-built rooms enclosing a stone-paved patio 6 or 7 m. across. Differences in pottery fabrics and styles between the compounds of each cluster suggest that potting was not a specialized industry, but was perhaps a feature of life of every household. Iron was smelted from the low-grade ore of the laterite in circular clay kilns, each of which had several clay pipes for the air to flow in and the iron out. It is quite likely that the farmers were still making their own

[1] O. Davies, 'The Invaders of Northern Ghana', *Universitas*, IV (1961), 134–6.

[2] A detailed survey of the Accra area in this and in the medieval period is given in P. Ozanne, 'Notes on the Later Prehistory of Accra', *Journal Hist. Soc. Nigeria*, III (1965), 3–23.

picks and hoes of stone, and using iron only for more delicate equipment. The coast, eight miles away, was not greatly exploited, and it is unlikely that any fish or shell-fish were obtained except by sporadic strand-loopers. In all, the general picture is one of simple, self-sufficient peasant life. Some connections with communities 40 miles or more to the west are indicated by the increased use of ground axes of Birimian hornblende-schist, but the areas were by no means interdependent. Pottery styles were simple, conservative and not very imaginative. This picture may be representative of the whole country before the thirteenth century or thereabouts, but this period is very poorly known away from Accra. In the northern part of the forest, where sandstone scarps extend half-way across the country and into the Ivory Coast, caves were commonly occupied, and these provide the only evidence of artistic work of the period, in the form of simple geometric engravings on walls and ceilings.

In medieval times—roughly between 1200 and 1600—many areas became specialized in their economy, and interdependent for their foodstuffs and equipment. Three phases of development may be distinguished in the area east of Accra by changes in pottery styles. The main characteristics of the period here were the steadily increasing size of settlements—culminating in such towns as Ladoku, over a mile long—and the desertion of the quartzite downlands of the Accra Plain in favour of the lagoons on the coast, the hilltops of the Akwapim ridge on the edge of the forest, and the rugged eminences of the Shai Hills, which project sharply in a small area from the flat Accra Plain. The people of Shai were undoubtedly living primarily from the industry for which they have been famous ever since—the manufacture of pottery. Their wares were of very much better quality than those of earlier times, and, in all three phases, imaginatively ornamented, and often finely polished. One of the most excellent forms was the handled jug, the handle being thin but strong, and in some cases surmounted by a model head and neck of a goat or chicken. Such pottery was sold inland, in forested Akwapim and beyond, and to communities on the lower Volta, represented by sites like Vume Dugame.[1] The only structures which can be attributed to the medieval period in this area are in Shai, consisting of small agricultural terraces at Cherekecherete—probably enclosing no more than kitchen-gardens—and small rectangular hut foundations at Adwuku, only 4 m. long, built of double-lines of stone slabs with rubble between. Beside the lagoons, large villages—half a mile long or more—were built on the sand-dunes, and these depended very largely upon the fish and shell-fish of the lagoons and rocky beaches. There is as yet no archaeological evidence to contradict the traditional claim that the people of the Accra area did not fish in the sea before the eighteenth century. They were, however exporting considerable amounts of shell-fish to inland peoples; and considering the persistently high demand for salt in the dry heat of the lands north of the forest, it is likely that they were producing this essential commodity for trade. Similarly, the people of the lower Volta had originated the famous 'Volta Oyster' industry, and may have been trading their produce, and salt, inland. The forest area of Akwapim, one must presume, was producing vegetable foods in exchange for such commodities; the salt soils of the coast, and the dry stony soil of Shai, could hardly yield enough food to support the large communities living upon them.

Iron-smelting became very infrequent during this period, and slag is rarely found on these sites in the Accra area. Most of the iron tools used were probably purchased from blacksmiths in the hills of southern Togo across the Volta; this area remained a centre of the industry until the present century, and its work was recorded at Akpafu by Rattray.[2] During the medieval period, iron-working tended to become concentrated in three parts of the country, namely the Akpafu area, parts of Dagomba and southern Gonja (York has examined an iron-working site on the Sheribong stream), and the far north-west corner. In the forest area, presumably because of the difficulties of communication, the village blacksmith seems to have been more common than

---

[1] O. Davies, *Archaeology in Ghana* (Edinburgh, 1961), pp. 35–45.
[2] R. S. Rattray, 'The Iron Workers of Akpafu', *Journal Royal Anth. Inst.*, XLVI (1916), 431–5.

elsewhere, but even so it is likely that much metal was imported from the north and east. Two forest export industries are represented in the archaeological record, the manufacture of greenstone axes,[1] and of red bauxite beads. The former were made in many parts, wherever Birimian hornblende schist out-crops, but by far the most specialized in this industry was the area inland from Axim and Takoradi. The axes continued to be made until about 1500, and old ones have been used ever since, for scraping and polishing pottery and for medicine. In Shai, they are traditionally used for digging clay for pottery, their smooth-ness presumably making the clay stick less than to a rusty iron blade. Originally, this may have been their function throughout the country. The makers were very highly skilled, and through appreciation of the cleavages of the harder, fine-grained rocks they were able to make such technological masterpieces as finely facetted axes of polygonal section, and ones up to 70 cm. long. This excellence of axe-manufacture, in the western forest especially, may have resulted from the anomaly that heavy iron tools could not be made economically from the poor ores of the forest, whereas it was in exploiting the rich gold resources of these parts that heavy tools, such as these axes, were most needed.

For, above all, the medieval period in Ghana was distinguished by the rise of gold-working to overriding importance. Trade in gold may have started as a secondary component in the inter-community trades which, it has been suggested above, resulted from medieval industrial specialization. Certainly by A.D. 1400 the gold-fields of southern Ghana were known to the traders of the Mali Empire, who took the metal for export across the Sahara. Traditions recorded in Arabic texts refer to the great gold market of Begho, founded by Mande people just north of the forest;[2] before the end of the fifteenth century, this town was known to the people of the Gambia, who described it to Duarte Pacheco Pereira as "Beetuu'.[3] It remained the pivot of the coun-try's economy until the seventeenth century, and did not finally

---

[1] Discussed at length by C. T. Shaw, op. cit., 28–46.
[2] I. G. Wilks, 'Begho and the Mande', *Journal of African History*, II (1961), 25–34.
[3] G. H. T. Kimble (trans.), *Esmeraldo de Situ Orbis* (London, 1937), p. 89.

decline until early in the next. In close relation to it—even derivative from it—other towns originated: Nasa-Visi, the old Muslim town of Wa beside the Lawra gold-field; Buipe, a key town for any trade to the north-east; Yagbum, capital of Gonja; Denkyera, the first town of dazzling wealth of the forest gold-field, founded, according to tradition, by people from 'Kramo-fokrom', 'the town of the Muslims'—presumably Begho. We know little about these towns, however, before the seventeenth century.

Southern Gonja, and the parts to the south of the Black Volta, were densely occupied in medieval times; to such an extent, in fact, that large areas became dessicated by over-cultivation, and have not been suitable for a large population in recent times.[1] The most remarkable feature in this area is a widespread series of painted pottery,[2] best known from a site at Kadelso and mainly concentrated in the triangular peninsula above the Volta con-fluence; the work of the Volta Basin Research Project is revealing more sites lower down the Volta. The pottery is burnt to a yellowish or brownish colour, and subsequently painted with red or purple colours. The forms are varied: wide-rimmed jars, hemispherical bowls, and pedestalled dishes are the most frequent. The designs of the painting are also diverse, but are mostly formed of narrow straight or curved lines, often forming cross-hatched motifs; these are found on several parts of vessels, including the inside of dishes. Similar—but probably earlier—pottery styles have been found at Koumbi Saleh in south-east Mauretania, but it is unlikely that these were directly connected with the Ghana wares.

In the forested area, the population seems to have increased considerably during the medieval period. Interest here is centred upon a group of earthworks, which are restricted to a small area around Akwatia.[3] Each is an enclosure up to a mile across, defined by a deep ditch with a bank on either side—the outer one usually

[1] O. Davies, 'Soil and Water', *Universitas*, IV (1960), 80–1.

[2] O. Davies, 'Gonja Painted Pottery', *Trans. Hist. Soc. Ghana*, VIII (1964), 4–11.

[3] Some of these are described in the Annual Reports of the Gold Coast Geological Survey for 1931–2 and 1934–5; H. J. Braunholz describes excavations in the Report for 1935–36 and *Antiquity*, X (1936), 469–74.

being the higher. The enclosure is irregular, the ditch roughly following a contour. The only close analogies are in the south-east corner of the Ivory Coast. Some of these enclosures, such as Akwatia, were densely occupied, and contain many mounds full of broken pottery; but others, such as the one excavated by Davies at Kokobin, show little sign of settlement. It has been suggested that these enclosures were fortified strongholds, built by the Akwamu in the seventeenth century to defend their north-western border from Akyem, but this interpretation is improbable. The absence of tobacco pipes and the typology of the pottery, indicate an earlier date; and the structure is unusual for a fortification. Defensive works usually have the highest rampart inside the ditch, so that the garrison has a clear view, from the top of the bank, of the approaches. Sites like Akwatia look as if they were intended more to keep people inside, than to prevent access, and it is most likely that they were labour camps for the working of the rich alluvial gold deposits of the River Birim and its tributaries, designed to prevent slaves —and the precious gold dust—from leaving except under supervision. A fine modern parallel is the C.A.S.T. diamond field enclosure which incorporates the Akwatia earthwork.

Another exciting earthwork was recently excavated by Mathewson near Kitare, beside the Oti River, and soon to be inundated in part by Lake Volta. Its general character is strange in Ghana. A roughly rectangular area nearly a mile long is enclosed by rampart and ditch, and two similar earthworks demarcate concentric ovals around the centre, which contains large irregular mounds. Outside the outer oval, the enclosure is subdivided into eight or nine fields of varying shape and size. Mathewson found much pottery, but no tobacco pipes or trade goods, and the site is probably medieval in date. It is the kind of earthwork which one associates with Nigerian town sites, although it is on a smaller scale; and perhaps it was a trading station on the route from North Asante to Northern Nigeria— a route for the export of kola which, according to the Kano Chronicle, was in use in the fifteenth century, if not before. In this case, the various fields may have served to separate stocks and package animals, and the property of various merchants. Elsewhere in Ghana, the only remotely similar structure known surrounds Nalerigu, the capital of Mamprusi in the far north-east, at a radius of about a mile, but this may be as late as the eighteenth century.

Two medieval sites near the coast on either side of Elmina have been excavated. At Sekondi[1] Davies examined a cemetery which he ascribed to the fifteenth century on account of the presence of fragments of plaster, believed to have come from a Portuguese fort. The argument is not wholly satisfactory, since similar plaster has been found in the Accra area in circumstances suggesting local manufacture, but the typology of the many pots found with the burials supports a dating of this order. Several beads were found, but only of stone, biconically perforated as in former times. Also, there were fragments of waste from the manufacture of groundstone axes, showing conclusively that such 'primitive' tools were still being made during a highly developed stage of the iron age. Smelting sites which are most likely to be of fifteenth or sixteenth century date have been excavated nearby in the grounds of the University College of Cape Coast by Penfold, and show a remarkable proficiency, the iron having become fully molten in the smelting. At Befikrom, Nunoo excavated a similar iron-working settlement which showed no signs of European contact, and found pottery which is typologically antecedent to that of seventeenth-century Asebu,[2] and quite like that from the University College. The prime interest of Befikrom is in the presence of distinctively Akan cultural types, namely, human portraits of earthenware, such as are traditionally used to commemorate dead chiefs or priests. These are the earliest known specimens, and it is notable that they should be found in a suburb of Mankessim, which, from the seventeenth century, was the capital of the Borbor Fanti, who succeeded in bringing the whole coastal zone from Elmina to Agona under their suzerainty.

[1] O. Davies, 'Native Cultures of the Gold Coast at the Time of the Portuguese Discoveries', *Congresso Internacional de Historia dos Discobrimentos*, III (Lisbon, 1961).

[2] R. B. Nunoo, 'Excavations at Asebu', *Journal West African Science Association*, 3 (1957), 12–44.

Otherwise, apart from material excavated by Shaw at Abetifi of which little can be said, our knowledge of medieval sites is restricted to the implications of collections from the surface and from gravel-pit sections. There are many such sites in the south which have yielded large assemblages of pottery, and the latter shows close similarities from site to site, and to the better-known wares of the Accra area. A site beside Elmina Lagoon exhibits the early importance of this part; similarly, many years ago the collections of Wild[1] and Rattray demonstrated the ancient importance of such hill-top villages as Nsuta[2] and Obuase, in the heart of the forest gold-fields. Although no accurate dates can be given there is every indication that, by the time Azambuja built the first castle at Elmina, the forest area inland was already populated quite densely, by communities of gold washers and miners, and the workers in other industries and in farming who supported them. Societies of which hazy memories survive in traditions, such as Nta and Adanse, must surely have been in existence at this time.

With the coming of European traders to the coast, a great series of changes came over the societies of the country. Furthermore, through the European documents, through the spread of Islamic literacy in the north, and through the oral traditions which have preserved quite accurately[3] the early history of political entities created since the sixteenth century, the archaeologist has a very great range of material outside his own field which is of the utmost value in interpreting his finds. The terminal dates of some ruined towns can be fixed within very few years, and even in cases like the capital of Agona to within a few days.[4] Apart from documentary references to the destruction of

---

[1] R. P. Wild, 'Stone Age Pottery from the Gold Coast and Ashanti', *Journal Royal Anth. Inst.*, LXIV (1934), 203–15.

[2] For an account of this site see R. B. Nunoo, 'A Report on Excavations at Nsuta Hill', *Man*, XLVIII (1948), 73–6.

[3] Many anachronisms, up to a century or more in extent, are to be found in traditional accounts of the period from 1650 onwards, but most of these can be explained sociologically. On the other hand, many sequences of events described in traditions can be largely supported from documentary sources, and in such cases the traditional details may be accepted with some confidence.

[4] P. Ozanne, *Tobacco Pipes of Accra and Shai*. Forthcoming.

towns, the most accurate dating evidence is provided by European imports and by locally made tobacco-pipes. Late sixteenth-century German pottery was found by Nunoo at Asebu, and in the seventeenth century European wares were imported in sufficient quantity to make the dating of towns in coastal areas fairly simple. Even before 1650 such imports were taken far inland; a good example is from a burial group recovered by Ameyaw at Bokuruwa, far inland near the forest border. Here a grave—probably that of a priestess—contained local pottery, beads, brass dishes and a gold-dust spoon, and also a fine Cologne stoneware jug. The jug has been dated by the Victoria and Albert Museum, and the grave by traditions related to dated events, to the early or mid-seventeenth century. Fifty years later, such imported pottery was commonly used one or two hundred miles from the coast, as has been demonstrated by York's excavation at Bui.[1]

Locally made tobacco-pipes changed in design very rapidly in the seventeenth and early eighteenth centuries, but subsequently became conservative in design. In the limited period, not only can accurate dates be applied to various styles, but also regional peculiarities can be distinguished, which, by their spread outside their areas of origin, can be used to trace trade connections.[2] The primary evidence for dating pipes comes from two sites near Accra, Ayaso, the 'Great Accra' referred to in early documents, and Ladoku, a Labadi settlement built on the ruins of the Adangme town mentioned above. We know that Ayaso was destroyed in 1677, and stratified fragments of German pottery excavated by Owusu and the writer have dated levels of the earlier seventeenth century. At Ladoku, a site for which a terminal date of 1702 is indicated by circumstantial documentary evidence, many European objects of the preceding quarter-century were found in association with locally made tobacco-pipes.[3] In other parts of the country, at Agona, at Begho, at

---

[1] R. York, 'Excavations at Bui: a Preliminary Report', *Research Review*, Institute of African Studies, University of Ghana, 1 (1965), 36–39.

[2] P. Ozanne, op. cit.

[3] P. Ozanne, 'Ladoku: an Early Town near Prampram', *Ghana Notes and Queries*, 7 1965), 6–7.

MAP 4. Ghana from 1550–1750.

Yendi Dabari in Dagomba, and at several other sites, the dates
suggested by tobacco-pipe typology are in agreement with the
documentary and traditional evidence available. The pipes

are thus of the utmost importance to the study of the seventeenth
and eighteenth centuries, and a brief description of their stylistic
development is a necessary introduction to the culture of the
period.

All native pipes of Ghana are built in two pieces, a bowl and
stem-socket of clay (more rarely, of iron or brass) and a long
vegetable stem. The habit of smoking was introduced to the
country from two directions. First, in the early seventeenth
century, it spread in from the north, having been diffused across
the western Sudan from Senegambia. By the time tobacco
reached Dagomba, distinct types of pipe had evolved; the earliest
found at Yendi Dabari have a waisted bowl standing on a high
conical foot, and a plain cylindrical stem. A little later, in about
1640, tobacco was independently introduced to the Accra area.
Here the earliest forms were very like European ones indeed,
apart from their short stem-socket; shortly later, a solid flat base
was added to the bowl to protect it from wear, and a hook built
between the bowl and the stem-socket so that the vegetable stem
could be firmly secured. After about 1690, this hook was
discarded in favour of a quatrefoil terminal to the stem, which
feature, with a quatrefoil base to the bowl, is common to all
areas of the country in the early eighteenth century, including
Begho and Yendi Dabari. The hook is very characteristic of
Accra pipes of the second half of the seventeenth century, and its
sporadic occurrence elsewhere shows how great a part Accra
played in the diffusion of smoking in the country. A few hooked
specimens, of about 1660-80, of Accra style, were found by
Nunoo amongst the earliest pipes at Asebu, with ones of a purely
local design—with long facetted spurs, looking more of wood-
work than of earthenware.[1] To the north-east, hooked pipes—of
styles more like those of Shai than of Great Accra—are found
sporadically on seventeenth century sites up the Volta as far as
Ahinkro, a small town excavated by York. The earliest pipes in
Asante present a variety of designs, some northerly in style,
others clearly derived from Asebu types, and others from those
of Shai, via the Volta variants. Detailed study of these pipes is

[1] R. B. Nunoo, op. cit., Pl. III.

slowly revealing the seventeenth-century trade routes of the southern half of the century.

Seventeenth-century towns have various layouts and structures. Except on rocky hill-tops, such as in Shai, most houses were built of clay, although often the walls were set upon stone foundations. In the south of the country, towns were laid out in very orderly fashion, and the dwelling areas, the rubbish dumps, and the quarries for building material were clearly separated. This is fortunate for the archaeologist, because the stratigraphy of deposits is well preserved. In the north, however, the soil of rubbish dumps was often used in the building of new houses, and consequently the material of several centuries may be mixed together. The difficulties of the archaeologist are well shown in present-day Bonduku, just within the Ivory Coast, the house walls of which are full of ancient pottery and beads! Begho was such a town—or rather, a complex of townships, for it was unusual in having several distinct quarters, sited over an area 5 miles in diameter. (Nasa-Visi seems to have been scattered in a like manner.) Villagers point out its market place, the Mande-speaking blacksmiths' quarter, the Muslim quarter (the latter perhaps surrounded by a wall, such as is ascribed to the town in a document of 1629), and the quarters of three social groups, the Akan-speaking Brons, the Guan-speaking Dumpos, and the Senufo-speaking Nafanas. At each quarter, however, little can be seen but undulating mounds of rubbish, of unknown depth. More typical of a large northern town is Yendi Dabari,[1] which was probably ravaged by Gonja in 1713/14; here an area 3 miles across is covered by irregular mounds of laterite and rubbish. Unique to this site, however, is a form of building-complex which was excavated by Shinnie. An area 160 m. long was divided into rectangular enclosures of varying size, by high walls and by rows of rooms, some of which were two or three storied. Since buildings other than of circular plan are foreign to Dagomba, and houses of more than one storey rare, it is likely that this was a strangers' complex of warehouses and paddocks

[1] P. L. Shinnie and P. Ozanne, 'Excavations at Yendi Dabari', *Trans. Hist. Soc. Ghana*, VI (1962), 87–118.

for package animals. However, of the many mounds which can be found in southern Dagomba and Gonja, several have been seen to be the remains of rectangular multi-storied buildings, and such may have been quite common three centuries ago. Goody has remarked that in some parts 'are to be found complete circles of such mounds, and remains of defences of the kind used until the beginning of the present century at the interesting town of Bute in Central Gonja with its remains of three-storied houses'.[1] One large mound, perhaps the ruins of such a fortification, has been excavated by York, at Buipe.

Another form of town lay-out is well represented at Ahwene Koko[2] on the edge of the forest near Begho; this was the ancient town of Wenchi, and was probably destroyed by the first Asantehene, Osei Tutu, in about 1690. It extended in patches along a line of 9 miles, the alleged 'assembly-place' being a treeless glade at one end, the 'market-place' being at the other; the 'palace area' and other parts between show much signs of occupation. Near Accra, the capital of Agona (destroyed in 1724) and that of Akwamu at Nyanaoase (abandoned partially in about 1660, and completely in 1730) were strung out in a similar way, but only over 5 miles or so.[3] The Accra capital at Ayaso, however, and the smaller town of Wodoku examined by Alexander, are more typical of southern Ghana, with little sign of regularity in their plans.

Of particular interest is a small village on the top of the hill of Adwuku[4] in Shai, although its features are as yet without close parallels. One very rocky part is fortified, full use being made of the enormous natural boulders, but the spaces between them being closed by dry-stone walling 3 ft. thick, except for a few narrow and precipitous entrances. Gun-ports are built into the walls, each covered by a broken or worn-out grinding stone

[1] J. Goody, 'The Mande and the Akan Hinterland', *The Historian in Tropical Africa* (1964), 201.

[2] P. Ozanne, 'Ahwene Koko: Seventeenth Century Wenchi', *Ghana Notes and Queries*, 8 (1965), 18.

[3] A general survey of the Accra area in the seventeenth century is given by P. Ozanne, 'Notes on the Early Historic Archaeology of Accra', *Trans. Hist. Soc. Ghana*, VI (1962), 51–70.

[4] P. Ozanne, 'Adwuku: a Fortified Hill-top Village in Shai', *Ghana Notes and Queries*, 7 (1965), 4–5.

forming a one-piece lintel. Outside this defended part, various forms of enclosure are marked out with stone slabs. Circles about 4 m. across have floors of burnt clay, and others only half that diameter are paved with pebbles; it has been suggested that the former are pottery-working floors, and the latter the foundations for fires in which to bake vessels. Surrounding the circles are various small irregular enclosures which usually contain one or more grinding-stones of 'saucer' shape, a type used by Shai people not only for pounding food but also for grinding the grit they use to temper their pottery. The sides of the hill have massive terraces, partly intended perhaps to support small kitchen gardens such as are represented in one part by very small terraced plots, but possibly also, topped by thorn-bush, to add to the defences. The hill was probably abandoned in 1702.

Few burials have been excavated in the country. Shinnie and Wilks found skeletons under a mound at Vitin[1] in Dagomba, which contained much pottery; two male skeletons each had a disc, made from a broken pot, in its mouth. Burial under the floors of houses is quite frequent outside the forest area, and near Accra, can be traced back to medieval times. At Bui, York has found shafts dug through house-floors, and containing extended burials.[2] In the forest, bodies are usually placed in wooded cemeteries, different areas often being reserved for the various ranks. The burials at Bokuruwa, mentioned above, was laid out in the manner typical of a priestess, on the back and with the arms spread out, each hand lying on a brass dish—the other grave-goods were at the feet. At Ahinkro, York found extended inhumations in the morning shade of baobab trees, and at Krenkuase an empty shaft, possibly an unused grave, in a similar position. Burials are never found in rubbish-dumps, although odd fragments of human bone may be present—perhaps through the over-zealous sweeping of house-floors under which ancestors had been inhumed.[3]

The potter's wheel has been introduced only very recently

[1] P. L. Shinnie and I. G. Wilks, 'A Burial Mound near Tamale,' *Journal West African Science Association*, 6 (1960), 47-8.

[2] R. York, op. cit.

[3] Mathewson has pointed out exceptions to this, as for instance babies dying before they had been named, and victims of certain diseases.

into the country, and only for purposes of art and industrial production. Ghana may be divided roughly into two nearly equal provinces, the North and the South, for the purpose of describing the potteries of the last 400 years. In the north, the wares are comparatively poorly made, and both limited and conservative in design. Jars of simple profile usually have thick walls, and are either plain or ornamented by simple grooved motifs, bands of red slip, or grass-impressions similar to those of very much earlier pottery. Spouted water jugs and small hemispherical bowls often have an overall red slip, which is brightly polished. Differences can be seen between the styles of various areas, but these are not great. In the south, however, the wares show far greater expertise, and, especially between 1600 and 1750, a very wide range of form and ornament, and local variation. At this time, in many parts there were groups of villages specializing in the manufacture of pottery for sale in adjacent towns and villages; the area served by a particular group bore little relation to the geography of political units, languages, sociological systems, and so on, but was determined by the trade pattern of the area. Perhaps as a result of the enormous wealth yielded by the gold industry, the potters could afford to spend much labour and skill in their work, and their customers seem not to have been concerned by the breakage of vast quantities. One great difficulty before the archaeologist, when publishing his material, is created by the great quantity of pottery found, and its extreme variety of form and ornamentation. After 1750, the variety decreases; a deliberate policy of Asante was the localization of specialists in each industry in centres which would serve most of the nation's needs, and Tafo, just north of Kumasi, became the main producer of pottery, which was still exported in the present century to places as distant as Sekondi and Accra.[1] Furthermore, the wide range of social restrictions by which Asante was bound together included limitations upon the variation in design of vessels used for particular purposes.

The great skill of seventeenth-century potters is shown in

[1] R. S. Rattray, *Religion and Art in Ashanti* (London, 1927), p. 203.

several ways. Many of the shapes are extremely complex, combining smooth curves, sharp angles, and various forms of pedestal, and yet these were formed with an accuracy closely approximating to that of wheel-made forms elsewhere. Even large vessels often have walls less than a quarter of an inch thick, and of regular thickness around the pot. Ordinary cooking-pots, palm-wine collecting vessels, and other simple receptacles would often be left with a plain matt surface—York, in particular, has noted exceptions—but 'table-ware' and other particular forms were treated in various ways to give a more attractive finish. Most commonly, they were placed after firing in a smouldering fire, which produced a very shiny black surface, often rivalling a guardsman's boot.[1] Sesquioxide clays were used as slips on other vessels, to give a glossy red surface. Ornamentation varied; evenly executed scratches and grooves were often filled with white-clay; various designs of stamp were used to apply particular motifs; and on special pots clay might be added to the surface to form representations of proverbs and other ideas. It is possible that, as with gold-dust weights, the meaning of some of these representations was known only to the owner. These points will make it clear that a proper description of the pottery of the seventeenth century would take several volumes.

The tobacco-pipe has been mentioned as a particular earthenware form; the other most distinctive one is the human portrait. Such models have several purposes. Some are simply for play; others are used to cure a woman of barrenness, or to ensure the beauty of an expected child; others represent dead chiefs or priests in the cemeteries, stool-rooms or shrines; and so forth. At Ahinsan, Davies excavated part of a late seventeenth and eighteenth-century site which yielded many such models. He has suggested[2] that this site was used for funerary rituals before corpses were taken to the cemetery, but such a custom would be unique in Asante. Wilks suggests more plausibly that this was a

---

[1] Ibid., p. 304.
[2] O. Davies, 'The Archaeological Evidence for the Iron Age in Ashanti', *An Ashanti Research Project: First Conference* (Legon, 1964), pp. 44–9.

typical Asante factory, in this case specializing in the manufacture of these portrait models. Several designs of model head were represented here. Some were three-dimensional and hollow, and in style somewhat reminiscent of those of Ife and Nok in Nigeria; others were flat in form, although the backs of some were adorned with coils representing hair. Several flat ones end in a knob at the base of the back, and may have been fixed into stands of clay or wood. Many of the portraits would originally have been built onto pottery vessels, especially on the shoulder or on the lid of large containers used in funerary customs. Cylindrical supports, for 'lids' surmounted by such effigies, were also found here.

Similar portraits were excavated by Owusu at Twenedurase, and some of these can be seen to be of distinct Kwahu style. Indeed, sites on the Volta at Nkami and Akroso (the latter excavated by Davies, was a mound containing all sorts of local pottery made over a long period, and destroyed on German orders 60 years ago in order to open an export-market for the German colonists!), are claimed to have been founded by Kwahus, and they yielded effigies very similar in style to those of Twenedurase. Complete statues, in the form of seated figures, of the nineteenth century have been collected by Ameyaw[1] in Kwahu and Agona, but the archaeological sites of earlier times have not yet produced effigies of this form.

Earthenware portraits in the Accra area show most interestingly the spread of Akan influence in the middle of the seventeenth century. They are very rare; Shaw found fragments of fourteen at Dawu,[2] nearby Abiriw and Larteh Amnafro have each yielded one, Wodoku three and Adwuku, in Shai, one. At Dawu the earliest specimen was in a level dating to about 1640,[3] at the time when Akwamu was beginning to expand into the area, and the only one excavated at Wodoku, by Alexander, was found in a layer of like date. All of these settlements were probably destroyed by Akwamu in 1677–81, except Adwuku which

[1] Such effigies are discussed by K. Ameyaw, 'Funerary Effigies from Kwahu', *Ghana Notes and Queries*, 8 (1965), 12.

[2] C. T. Shaw, *Excavations at Dawu* (Edinburgh, 1961), pp. 55–6.

[3] For the revised date see P. Ozanne, *Trans. Hist. Soc. Ghana*, VI (1962), 119–23.

probably survived until 1702. Subsequently, earthenware figures do not re-appear in the material culture of Accra.

Most of the beads surviving from the seventeenth century in southern Ghana are glass ones, which present such a great variety in shape and colour that few can be used as evidence of date. Most of them were imported from Europe, but some tubular blue ones are so like those of Ife that they may have been brought from Nigeria. The local manufacture of glass beads, however, began within the century, although nearly all were made by melting down imported ones. Bui has yielded fragments of locally made glass bracelets. The nature of the beads described as 'accory' in early documents is still unknown, but it seems most likely that they were of blue glass, made in some part or parts of West Africa. In central parts of the country, York has found beads of earthenware to be predominant. Stone beads were still used commonly, and others were made out of bone and shell. The teeth of various animals and fish were perforated to form pendants on strings of beads. In the Accra area, much care was expended on the manufacture of bracelets and combs of bone or ivory—the combs, which usually have only two, three or four teeth, would have been used both to comb the hair and as large hair-pins to hold it in place. The handles of the combs are often cut into open-work forms; and both they and the bracelets are engraved with various designs, most of which depend mainly upon the circle enclosing a dot. Similar ornament is found on other bone objects, such as toggles and whistles, but these are rare.

The history of brass-working in the country is confusing. There is no evidence that it began before the seventeenth century, and yet the earliest known local manufactures are very distinctive in design and decoration, as if the industry had already been developed over some centuries. Brass vessels had certainly been imported from across the Sahara. Arabic-inscribed pans of Moroccan or Muslim Spanish manufacture, one of which has been ascribed to the thirteenth century, are preserved in at least four towns—including Nsawkaw, a quarter of Begho which survived the others—and medieval Arabic writers tell us that the

emperors of Mali derived a large part of their income from the
sale of copper to the producers of gold. Only one archaeological
site has yielded brasswork of North African manufacture; this
is Ahwene Koko, where a fragment of a fluted basin has been
found on a seventeenth-century midden. One can assume, then,
that brass vessels imported from the north were, when broken,
melted and re-cast even in medieval times. Two gongs or bells,
dug up by a farmer at Ahwene Koko, may have been made out
of such metal; they are typically south-Ghanaian both in form
and in their simple ribbed decoration. But there can be no doubt
that it was the sale by Europeans of vast quantities of brass
vessels and 'manillas' that gave rise to the copper-working
industry as one of archaeological significance. Indeed, the
student of the archaeology of Ghana, a country so rich in gold
and therefore, one would expect, relatively rich in imported
copper in medieval times, cannot avoid the suspicion that the
abundant copper and brass objects of Ife and Benin, in comparatively impoverished Nigeria, are also made of metal bought
from European traders, and that the weakly founded claims that
many of them were products of the medieval industry are
extravagant.

The midden at Dawu excavated by Shaw has provided the
only detailed evidence of the seventeenth century brass industry;
here not only finished objects, but also crucibles, casting moulds,
and waste metal were found. The whole showed great skill in the
art of *cire perdue* casting. Among the brass objects found here
and at nearby sites of the same date are finger and arm-rings,
cones(perhaps for pouring powder into muskets), rivets for bone
knife-handles, a superb armband from Ladoku, dress-pins,
finger-bells for use in dancing, and fragments of basins. *Forowas*
(for containing the grease of the shea nut, used as soap and as a
food oil) and the lid, decorated with various emblems, of a *kuduo*
(a container of valuable personal effects) have been dug up by
villages at Nyanaoase, and may be of pre-1730 date.

Europe also re-invigorated local iron industries, by the sale of
bars of raw metal, and most seventeenth-century sites produce
some evidence of iron-working. The metal was used mainly for

making knives, hoe-shoes, nails and rivets, arrow-heads, and other tools, but rings and bangles were also produced, especially in the north. Dennis Williams has reached an interesting conclusion on early iron wire: 'Of the two types of iron chain used (by Yoruba blacksmiths), one rectangular-sectioned . . . and the other circular-sectioned . . . the first can be regarded as of entirely local manufacture, while the second would be of local manufacture from imported material'.[1] Most seventeenth-century rings and bangles of northern Ghana are of rectangular-sectioned wire, but a few are circular.

Amongst the miscellaneous other objects found on sites of the seventeenth and eighteenth centuries, European imports figure largely. German pottery has been mentioned above; on coastal sites, some English wares are found. Near the coast, Dutch and English clay tobacco-pipes are abundant, and several specimens of the early eighteenth century were found far inland at Mamponten by Davies, and even as far north as Bui, by York. By the mid-eighteenth century, the Accra area had virtually ceased to produce its own pipes, importing all that it needed from Europe. Guns, we know, were being bought in substantial quantities; and Adwuku and Bui have produced several flints—mostly, it seems, made in Holland, but one or two look like products of Brandon in Norfolk—and at the former site, lead shot. Fragments of liquor bottles are abundant on some sites of the Accra Plain. Locally made miscellanea include very small engraved earthenware lids, presumably used as bottle-stoppers, and stone plugs which may have been used to re-cork gun-powder barrels—cannon of pre-1730 date still lie at Nyanaoase, and cannon balls amongst the ruins of Great Accra at Ayaso. The African game known here as *Owari* is represented on many seventeenth-century sites by small disc counters, made from potsherds; and in some parts, *Owari* boards have been found, in the form of groups of twelve holes ground into natural rock platforms.

Examples have already been indicated of close relationship

[1] D. Williams, 'The Iconology of the Yoruba Edan Ogboni', *Africa*, XXXIV (1964), 160.

between archaeological, documentary, and traditional evidence.
A classic one is the dating of the site excavated by the writer
within the Akwamu capital of Nyanaoase. This was part of the
alleged Queen-Mother's quarter, and the excavation caused
some concern because, on the evidence of tobacco-pipes, this
part seemed to have been deserted at about 1660, 70 years earlier
than the rest of the town. Traditions collected recently by
Ansah, however, claim that the Queen-Mother and her followers
left Nyanaoase during the reign of an *Omanhene* (a paramount
chief) which can be dated, by documentary evidence, to this very
time. In such cases, archaeology serves to confirm other
evidence; but equally important is its use in complementing the
results of other fields of enquiry. The process of Akwamu
expansion in the seventeenth century has been very much
elucidated by the dating of the destruction of towns near Accra,
in the hills of Akwapim, and in and below the Shai Hills; and
the fabric and typology of contemporaneous pottery and pipes
is of assistance in showing the trade patterns, which were the
prime cause of warfare and imperial expansion. The foundation
of Asante is abundantly illustrated by a mass of town sites in the
area of the original *amanto*,[1] some of which—like Juaben—can be
seen to go back to early in the seventeenth century, but most of
which seem to have been created towards the end of the century.
The degree of concentration of population in the *amanto* at the
time of its foundation could not be assessed from other evidence.
Similarly, the process of Asante expansion in the eighteenth
century is being dated, gradually, by archaeological means;
fortunately, certain parts of the story are accurately fixed by
Arabic or European documents, and these serve as checks upon
the archaeological dating. The principal archaeological features
of use in this enquiry are the apparent dates of the desertion of
sites which are said to have been destroyed by Asante, and the
appearance as at York's Ahinkro site (this town was headquarters
for Asante officials in the nineteenth century) of tobacco-pipes

[1] P. Ozanne, 'The Archaeological Contribution to the Ashanti Research Project', *An
Ashanti Research Project: First Conference* (Legon, 1964), pp. 50–9. *Amanto* refers to the
original Ashanti towns established in the late seventeenth century around Kumasi.

of typical metropolitan Asante design in areas which hitherto had followed other stylistic schools in the making of their pipes.

In all, the iron age of Ghana can be said to be well known, in comparison with that of other African countries. A picture of most of the skeleton has been constructed, which is unlikely to need very much modification. This picture, however, exposes the enormity of the tasks before us; the amounts of labour which will be required in adding the flesh, and of luck and skill necessary for the application of absolute dates to the earlier periods, which would give the blood, to the corpus of knowledge.

3

THE WESTERN SUDAN

by

R. Mauny

THE aim of this chapter is to describe the period between the end of Neolithic times and the beginning of history. This is no easy matter, for texts are few before the arrival of the Portuguese on the coast during the fifteenth century A.D. and excavations on early sites are rare, the focus having been on medieval south Saharan Negro-Arab towns, and little is known from the region south of the great Empires of Ghana, Mali, and Songhai. The region studied here is the southern edge of the Sahara and the savanna from the Atlantic to Lake Chad, north of the forest.

THE END OF THE NEOLITHIC AGE AND THE COMING OF METAL

When did the Neolithic period come to an end in this area? It is perhaps worth recalling what happened in the north in Mediterranean Africa. Copper was known in Egypt as early as the fifth millennium B.C., and such things as beads, nails, needles, chisels, arrow heads, and rings have been found, and in later protodynastic times, cups, daggers, axes, harpoons and so on. In the third millennium B.C. true bronze, an alloy of copper and tin, was discovered in the Middle East and diffused along the Mediterranean shores and into Europe.

Bronze was known in Egypt from this early period as it was along the Libyan shore west of the Nile Delta, as we know from the lists of booty plundered from there by the Pharaohs during the thirteenth century B.C.[1] The Carthaginians, further to the west, also had bronze, so we can speak of a Bronze Age in Mediterranean Africa at the end of the second and the beginning of the first millennium B.C. Camps, who has studied the problem in North Africa, points out that the Maghreb had poor natural resources of copper and tin, bronze was scarce and its inhabitants had to import it from outside, but the use of bronze weapons is certain and Bronze Age pottery is known from several sites in Algeria and Morocco.[2] Iron appeared late in Africa. It was being exported to Egypt by about 1300 B.C. as we know from a letter written by a Hittite king to Ramses II, but Egypt, always traditionalist, seems to have been reluctant to use the new metal and it remained rare until the Assyrian invasion of the seventh century B.C. and was not extracted from ore in Egypt before the 25th Dynasty (712–663 B.C.).[3] Known on the Syrian coast since the end of the second millennium B.C., it was therefore known to the Carthaginians too. It may be remarked however that it is only from the sixth century B.C. that iron appears in their tombs. From the third century on it definitely replaces bronze as a material of ordinary use.[4]

Along the valley of the Nile iron seems to have moved slowly south. In Egypt, even in the seventh and sixth centuries B.C., iron was rare enough for chariot wheels to have been tired with copper or bronze[5] and in Nubia, only a few iron implements dating from before 400 B.C. have been found.[6] In Xerxes's army (c. 480 B.C.) the Ethiopians are the only ones to use stone arrow heads (as Herodotus tells us), and the first royal burial to contain model tools of iron in place of bronze is that of Harsiyotef (c. 400–370 B.C.), so that we can place the real beginning of iron

[1] Oric Bates, *The Eastern Libyans* (London, 1914), pp. 142 ff.

[2] G. Camps, 'Les Traces d'un Age du Bronze en Afrique du Nord', *Rev. Afr.*, 462–3 (1960), 31–5.

[3] A. Lucas, *Ancient Egyptian Materials and Industries* (London, 1954). An exhaustive work has been written on the problem: J. Leclant, 'Le fer dans l'Egypte ancienne le Soudan et l'Afrique', *Annales de l'Est*, 16 (1956), 83–91.

[4] S. Gsell, *Histoire Ancienne de l'Afrique du Nord*, IV (Paris, 1913–30), 74–5.

[5] T. A. Rickard, *Man and Metals* (London, 1939).

[6] G. A. Wainwright, *Sudan Notes and Records*, XXVI (1945), 5–36.

working in Nubia in the first decades of the fourth century B.C.[1]

We have been obliged to digress from our chosen area in order to explain how iron spread to other parts of tropical Africa including West Africa. What we know of the industrial stage reached by Negro Africa during the first millennium B.C. points to an external origin of metal working almost certainly in the Mediterranean area.

The Carbon-14 dates that we have for the Nok culture of Nigeria (918 ± 70 B.C.; A.D. 207 ± 50 for Nok and 280 ± 120 B.C. for Taruga), except for the first, which is too early for knowledge of iron, give an indication of the date of its introduction. Most probably it arrived there about the second or third centuries B.C., coming either from the north by the intermediary of Libyan peoples like the Garamantes who were in contact with the Carthaginians and later with the Romans, or from the east from Meroe by pastoral savanna peoples. Nowhere else in West Africa do we have dates for Iron-Age sites of so early a period; the other radio-carbon dates that we have are mainly from Neolithic sites.

Imported copper weapons, dating probably from the first millennium B.C. have been found in various parts of the southern Sahara, and almost all of them in Mauretania. They consist of axes, tanged arrows, and spears.[2] They may be of local manufacture, for important copper mines exist in western Mauretania. Their shape recalls those of the Spanish Bronze Age, and rock engravings in Morocco show that these bronze implements, if rare, were not unknown there.

How metals and other techniques crossed the Sahara we may infer from the study of rock engravings. Among the hundreds of sites now known from the Atlantic to the Red Sea, some fifty have representations of chariots, vehicles which are already mentioned by Herodotus as used in Libya by the Garamantes to fight the Troglodyte Ethiopians in about 450 B.C. Thus we may assume that the Neolithic continued in the western Sudan till the

[1] A. J. Arkell, *A History of the Sudan* (London, 1955), pp. 144–55.

[2] R. Mauny, *Bulletin I.F.A.N.*, XIV, (1952), 545–95. N. Lambert excavated a gallery of the copper mine of Akjouit in 1968. Radio-carbon dates are all from 5th century B.C.

third and second centuries B.C., to be replaced directly (except for a transitional copper age in Mauretania) by iron.

TRANS-SAHARAN CHARIOT ROUTES AND LAND EXPEDITIONS IN CLASSICAL TIMES

The distribution of sites showing chariots is quite remarkable; they are grouped in two series, one in the centre of the Sahara, connecting the gulf of Syrtis with the bend of the Niger at Gao, with an offshoot to Tibesti, and the second between south Morocco and the region west of Timbuctoo, through Zemmour, the Adrar of Mauretania, and the Tichit-Walata cliff. There are no rock drawings representing chariots in the eastern Sahara, for instance, along the Darb el Arbain track joining Asiut in Egypt to Darfur.

The texts dealing with Saharan Expeditions during classical antiquity are scarce, giving the impression that it was only occasionally that Carthaginians and Romans and even North African Libyo-Berbers, like the Garamantes, attempted to cross the great desert. Herodotus tells the story of five young Nasamonians, a people living in the Syrtis region, who planned all sorts of extravagant adventures, one of which was to explore the Libyan desert. They departed (probably on chariots) with a good supply of food and water, passed through the inhabited parts of the northern Sahara, then entered the desert, proceeding in a generally westerly direction. After travelling for many days they saw some trees and picked their fruit, and while doing so were attacked by little black men, and carried off through marshy country, to a town by a great river with crocodiles, flowing from west to east. Most probably the route they followed was the central Saharan chariot track already mentioned, and it is possible that they reached the bend of the Niger somewhere between Bourem and Timbuctoo, in the region where the Niger flows west to east.

The Romans, later on, made several expeditions to protect and to explore the land south of their fortified frontier, the Limes, and probably also to prospect the commercial possibilities of the Sahara, and to find a supply of wild beasts for their circuses.

Cornelius Balbus in 19 B.C. went to Gadames and Garama, the
capital of the Garamantes; Suetonius Paulinus, who was later on
to fight in Britain, crossed the Atlas and arrived at the river Guir
in A.D. 42; and from Tripolitania, two Roman expeditions
probably under Septimus Flaccus (A.D. 70) and Julius Maternus
(A.D. 86) reached the northern limit of the Sudanese Sahel, then
more northerly than today. The country of Agisymba which
they reached, where rhinoceros were found, has not yet been
satisfactorily identified.

We can thus be sure that the savanna was linked—but not
closely—with the Mediterranean in the last centuries B.C. and in
the first century A.D. It is therefore most probable that the
Libyo-Berbers, crossing the Sahara for trade or war brought
iron metallurgy to the savanna belt, where it had every reason to
flourish, since iron ore is plentiful everywhere in the form of
laterite and wood is available as fuel. To defend themselves
against the attacks of Saharan nomads, the negro agriculturalists
needed to have the same weapons as their aggressors and not only
their ancestral stone arrow-heads.

We have proof of this in the change in armament shown on
rock drawings, the large iron spear replacing the formerly
predominant bow and arrow, and by the defensive grouping of
later neolithic agricultural villages of southern Mauretania,
sometimes half a square mile in area, with stone walls, on rocky
promontories near water points. The Tichit-Walata cliff has
many such neolithic villages which still await excavation. Indeed
we have there perhaps the most remarkable group of neolithic
settlements in the world, wonderfully preserved for they
are situated in a country practically empty, even today, of
nomads.[1]

EARLY VOYAGES ALONG THE SAHARAN COASTS

Paradoxically indeed, it was the Sahara that was the link
between North Africa and the western Sudan during the Iron
Age, and not the Atlantic Ocean, whereas on the East African

[1] Important work has been carried out in the Tichit area by P. Munson, and many
radio-carbon dates are now available, ranging from 1255 to 220 B.C.

coast, the Arabs, Greeks, and Romans sailed south of the Equator to the Azanian ports and even reached China.

The Canary Islands and Cape Juby were, till 1434, the limit of navigation to the southward in the Atlantic Ocean. The reason for this difference between the east and the west is easily explained. All year round the winds blow on the Saharan coast from north-east to south-west, whereas on the Somali and Zanzibar coasts they change round. In winter they blow from north to south, allowing ships to go from Arabia and India to Zanzibar and even to Sofala south of the Zambezi, and in summer, from south to north, so that the same ships, after having traded on the coast, can easily return to their Near Eastern harbours in the same year.

In the case of the Atlantic, no return voyage was possible, for the ships of antiquity, square rigged and rudderless, could not tack and thus sail against the wind and return to the Mediterranean or Moroccan harbours. It was only after the progress of navigation made during the Middle Ages, with the use of lateen sails, of the stern-post rudder, of marine charts, of the compass, and of other improvements, that the navigators could work against the trade winds for the home-bound voyage. Gil Eanes, a Portuguese, was the first to succeed, in 1434, in returning from beyond Cape Bojador with his ship. The problem of the return to the north when a ship was south of the limits of variable winds was the insuperable difficulty that prevented the navigators of antiquity from visiting the West African coast.

Several attempts were made to circumnavigate Africa or to reach the country south of the Sahara,[1] but only one may have succeeded, that of Necho's Phoenicians. This Egyptian Pharoah ordered sailors to round Libya, departing from the Red Sea and coming back by the Mediterranean. It is impossible to be sure if this circumnavigation really took place, but an objection by Herodotus, who relates the voyage, suggests that it did. He says that during a part of this navigation the voyagers had the sun at their right. He could not believe this to be possible but

---

[1] On these voyages see M. Cary and E. H. Warmington, *The Ancient Explorers* (London, 1963), pp. 110 ff.

of course we know today that when one rounds the Cape of
Good Hope coming from the east, one has the sun on the right.
So that on the basis of this argument many authors believe the
voyage did in fact take place.

What then of their navigation along the Saharan coast which
we just said above was impossible for ships in antiquity? The
answer may be that when the Phoenicians reached Senegal, they
met Libyans coming from the north. The Senegal river is today
the frontier between Arabo-Berbers and Negroes and was
already so in the Middle Ages. Possibly it was so during classical
antiquity. Although Negroes peopled southern Mauretania,
Libyans with their herds had already reached the grassy country
at the mouth of the Senegal river. Some of these nomads were
crossing the Sahara for trade and were thus in contact with the
Carthaginians of the southern Moroccan coast, even speaking
their language. We may be sure too that some members of the
Phoenician crew had been chosen for their knowledge of
Moroccan Berber dialects. So that it is not impossible that the
survivors of Necho's expedition crossed the Sahara with their
Libyo-Berber friends on chariots, following the western trans-
Saharan track we have already spoken of, running here some
100 to 150 miles to the interior, parallel to the coast; there was no
difficulty in making this journey during the winter.

Herodotus gives us also another interesting account of an
Atlantic voyage, that of the Persian Sataspes, condemned by
king Xerxes (485–465 B.C.) to circumnavigate Libya from the
west. He sailed from Cape Spartel to the south, but after crossing
'over much seas in many months', he came back to Egypt, having
seen at the farthest point of his voyage 'dwarf men, wearing
clothes made of palms who, whenever the voyagers put their
ship to land, fled towards the mountains.' Xerxes suspected
Sataspes of having not told the truth and it was certainly so. The
sailors, and above all their Carthaginian pilots, knew better than
anyone, that they could not navigate the Saharan coasts beyond
the zone of variable winds. They must have persuaded Sataspes
that the best thing to do was to remain quietly in some remote
south Moroccan port and then to come back and say that they

had not been able to go further. Xerxes, who certainly had had information about Sataspes's real behaviour, caused him to be impaled.

We know, again from Herodotus, that the Carthaginians landed at some place on the south Moroccan coast to carry out silent barter for gold. The navigators, when they arrived at the chosen spot made a fire to warn the natives, and placed their goods on the shore. They then retired and the Africans came, putting in front of every heap of goods a heap of gold. Then they retired in their turn, and the Carthaginians came back. If the gold was considered to be of sufficient quantity, they took it away, leaving the goods. If not, they left their goods, retired, and the Africans had to put more gold on their heap. The silent barter went on until everybody agreed. It is impossible to say where this traffic took place; certainly not in northern Morocco where the Carthaginians had permanent settlements and not beyond Cape Juby for the reasons already given—the impossibility of returning to the north.

Another voyage is well known—though it probably never took place—Hanno's Periplus. None has been more discussed, commented on, or refuted than this famous text, said to have been written on the return of the expedition and put up in the temple of Moloch in Carthage, where according to the version we have of it today, it was copied and translated into Greek.

It is by far the longest ancient text we have dealing with voyages on West African coasts. It is therefore of great importance for all those who have to write on the history of navigation and on African exploration. At last, instead of the laconic texts we have been used to, we have pages of 'information', with sailing distances in days, names of towns, peoples, capes and gulfs, mountains, flora and fauna, and other details. According to this text, Hanno, a Carthaginian admiral, appears to have had two objectives. The first was to establish or to reinforce colonies along the Moroccan coast beyond the Strait of Gibraltar, already known to the Carthaginians, and the second was to explore the coast beyond the Lixus river. The 30,000 people he brought in his sixty vessels of fifty oars each were left in the various settlements he mentions. With a few boats only—he does not give us their number—he put out for the south, reaching a big river, the Lixus, where he took on interpreters.

After a few days of sailing, he found at the head of a gulf a small island called Cerne. He left colonists there. Thence he sailed to a river Chretes and to a lake containing three islands larger than Cerne, dominated by a high range of mountains, peopled by wild men in animal skins, who drove off the navigators with stones and would not let them land. Sailing from that point they came to another big river infested with crocodiles and hippopotami and thence turned back to Cerne. He put out from that island a second time and after 12 days of navigation, skirting a land peopled with Ethiopians, whose tongue was unintelligible to the Lixite interpreters, he reached a high wooded mountain and having doubled it, found himself after 5 days in an immense gulf which the interpreters called *Hesperus Cera* (the West Horn). He landed on a large island lying in it, but left for fear of its inhabitants. After 4 days of navigation along the coast, unapproachable because of the heat, he reached a high mountain covered with flames, the *Theon Ochema* (Chariot of the Gods).

Three more days led him to a gulf called *Notu Ceras* (the South Horn). Having landed there on an island full of wild people, chiefly composed of hairy bodied women the interpreters called gorillas, the crew secured three females who bit and scratched their captors, so that they had to kill them. They brought their hides back to Carthage. That was the end of the voyage, owing to lack of provisions.

What should we think of this famous cruise? The great majority of writers are in favour of its veracity and I have also been of that opinion, although I have not believed in a long voyage. I have expressed the opinion that Hanno did not get further than southern Morocco, because of the difficulty of return to the north already outlined above. But I have now been convinced that Hanno's Periplus is a forgery from the arguments of Tauxier and Germain.[1] My suspicion was awakened by the fact that no archaeological discovery of antique material has been

[1] H. Tauxier, *Rev. Afr.* 151 (1882), 15–37. G. Germain, *Hespéris*, XLIV (1957), 205–48.

made on the southern Moroccan coast and also because no one who knows the West African shores can recognize them in Hanno's descriptions.

In fact this text is a jumble of all that the ancients believed was to be found in that part of Libya, some facts being true, but most of them not. There is no mountain on the coast between the Anti-Atlas in southern Morocco and Kakoulima (Guinea) and Sierra Leone; no river flowing to the sea between the Draa and Seguiet el Hamra in the north and the Senegal in the south; no island between Mogador and Cape Blanco except Herne in the gulf of the Rio de Oro; no volcano other than the Cameroon mountains.

Hanno's Lixos can only be the river Loukkos of Larache, known under that name during the whole of antiquity, and Cerne, 3 days from it, is probably Mogador. The three islands dominated by high mountains exist nowhere on the African coast. No mountain 12 days from Mogador and no volcano 11 days further on. Not one word on the Sahara (his 2 days desert is far in the north between Lixus and Cerne), not one word on the difficulty of the return voyage. Those who have written on the problem have not, generally, lived on that coast. Those who know Port-Etienne for instance at Cape Blanco in Mauretania, which has the sad privilege of receiving the strongest winds in Africa, blowing all year long from the north, may easily imagine what would have happened to an ancient maritime expedition, with all sails lowered, even if it had fifty oars, trying to go northwards against the gale.

Tauxier's arguments are different. He studies the Periplus as a Hellenist and a historian, commenting that the first reference to it is not that of Aristotle, as commonly supposed. Aristotle's *Treaty of Marvels* is a composite work only begun by him but continued by several authors at different periods. One must wait for Eudoxus of Cyzicus (about 100 B.C.), probably also a forgery, copied by Cornelius Nepos (mid first century B.C.) and above all Pliny (A.D. 79) for the first mention of Hanno. The text that has come down to us is even later, probably dating from Byzantine times. Far from being the report of a Carthaginian admiral, this

Periplus, in its original form, is a bad compilation written by a first century B.C. Greek forger, and, in the form in which it is known today, a mutilation and an arrangement of that original text by a much later writer.

Germain, who did not know Tauxier's work when he wrote his study, arrives at almost the same conclusions. He shows the borrowings from Greek authors, chiefly Herodotus, and points out that the vocabulary is of a late period. Like Tauxier he thinks the author is a forger and hoaxer who amused himself by paraphrasing Herodotus. His conclusion is that the Periplus is a literary exercise and not a historical document and its author either a hoaxer or a naive person to whom a false document has been sold and who embroidered it.

One more argument strengthens the case for considering the document a forgery; the total absence of antique remains south of the island of Mogador. That island, without doubt Polybius's *Cerne contra Atlantem* has been excavated since 1951 and remarkable results have been obtained there giving evidence that the site has been occupied for many centuries—pre-Roman Carthaginian pottery, Roman pottery, coins of Juba II and of Roman times. The other islands more to the south (Herne, Arguin, Gorée, and others) have all been prospected in vain. Every square yard of Gorée, for instance—the type of small island near the coast the Carthaginians showed their liking for and settled in the Mediterranean, like Djidjelli, Algier's Admiralty island, Cherchell—has been excavated for foundations, digging of wells, burying of water pipes, and the planting of trees. Not one single ancient sherd has ever been found there, as would have been the case had the ancients navigated these waters.

The other sea voyages on the Saharan coast, by Euthymenes of Marseilles (not dated satisfactorily), Polybius (147 B.C.), Eudoxus of Cyzicus (if the account of his voyage is not a forgery), Juba II of Mauretania and sailors of Cadiz (first century B.C.) did not go very far. Some had at least one important result; the discovery of the Canary islands at the extreme end of the zone of variable winds, from whence it was possible for ships equipped with square sails and without rudders, to return northward. With the possible exception of the Phoenicians of Necho, the ancients did not navigate West African coasts further south than the Canary Islands and Cape Juby.

It is clear that external influences on West Africa during antiquity can be attributed only to land contacts across the Sahara, by the intermediary of Libyo-Berbers on the one hand, and of petty tribes living in the savanna between Meroe and Lake Chad on the other. Between the agricultural societies of the Mediterranean and of Negro Africa, they acted as an impoverishing filter for civilizing influences.

ARCHAEOLOGICAL REMAINS

Archaeological remains in the southern Sahara and savanna regions are plentiful. They can be divided into monuments, mostly graves, and rock pictures.

Monuments

The pre-Islamic monuments have been preserved by the desert climate so that they are to be found by the thousand in rocky regions. They are in the main tombs. To prevent corpses from being eaten by hyenas it was necessary to bury them deeply and to erect large cairns of stones over them, and for chiefs these cairns are often of considerable size, up to 50 m. in circumference and 4 m. in height.[1] Every hill shows at its foot or on its lower slopes some of these graves, grouped or in isolation. In some places, where grazing is still relatively abundant, as at the mouth of valleys in the plain, hundreds of monuments bear witness to the ancient presence of man.

It is difficult to date these tombs, but, in the present stage of our knowledge, they may have been first constructed at the end of Neolithic times, that is from the second half of the first millennium B.C. Had it been earlier, we should have found near the important neolithic villages of the Tichit-Walata cliff already mentioned, huge cemeteries of mounds corresponding to the density of the population. Nothing of the sort exists there and

[1] Full details of all monuments of the area together with bibliography can be found in R. Mauny, *Tableau Géographique de l'Ouest Africain au Moyen Age* (Dakar, 1961).

we still do not know where the inhabitants of these communities were buried—perhaps in the family compound itself.

On the other hand, immense cemeteries containing thousands of graves exist in the Fezzan where many have been excavated. The material they have yielded is pre-Islamic, dating from the first millennium B.C. to the end of the first millennium A.D.[1] The corpses were buried in a contracted position and the material produced by the excavations consists of pottery (some of it Roman), beads, Roman glass, leather, and cloth. The skeletons show that the predominant population throughout the period belonged to the Mediterranean race. After centuries of slave-trade from the south, the Fezzanese of today, extremely mixed, are predominantly negroid.

There are many different types of graves and they have been classified in different ways. The greatest living Saharan scholar, Monod, gave us a few decades ago a provisional classification that is still used today.[2] It has been followed and amplified by Reygasse for other parts of the desert.[3] Many of these graves are mere piles of stones covering a hole dug in the ground in which the body was placed. This type is known as a *basina* which is the word used for it in the language of the Berbers. A form derived from it is the *chouchet*, a cylindrical stone structure, sometimes with several stories, becoming smaller in diameter towards the top. When eroded they are often indistinguishable from a *basina*. Some of them are surrounded by a stone circle at some distance, with annexed galleries where the cult of the dead was probably celebrated. Some tumuli have two long extended arms, forming a V opening usually to the east. Others look like crescents and others show a combination of several of the previously mentioned types. Rectangular monuments are found, both in Mauretania and the Fezzan, pointing to a direct Mediterranean influence. Modern Tuareg tombs often follow some of these ancient models but the two stones marking head and feet and their orientation show that they belong to Islamic times.

[1] P. Bellair, *Bulletin de Liaison Saharien*, 35 (1959), 214.

[2] Th. Monod, *Inst. d'Ethnologie*, XIX (1932), 20–60.

[3] M. Reygasse, *Monuments Funéraires préislamiques de l'Afrique du Nord* (Paris, 1950).

Away from rocky areas this type of grave is no longer found, and the stones are replaced by earth or sand, the protection against predators being only thorn bushes, and after a few years surface indications almost vanish. But in the case of kings and chiefs, large mounds were erected, even after the Islamization of the country, and still survive today. The building of such mounds was described in A.D. 1067 by the Arab writer el Bekri as being still in use in the kingdom of Ghana. He describes how, when the king died, his subjects built a great dome of wood at the place chosen for the grave, put the corpse on a bed, placed his ornaments, weapons, dishes, cups, food, and drink beside him. Then they covered the funeral chamber with mats, burying inside a number of the palace servants whilst still alive, and then threw earth on it until it looked like a hill.

Although such mounds have not so far been found in the vicinity of Kumbi Saleh (probably the site of the capital of the state of ancient Ghana), scores of them are known in the region of the bend of the Niger west of Timbuctoo, in the Goundam-Niafunke region. This is in the great inner delta of the Niger and the mounds appear as small hills on these flat plains. Some of them, as at Kouga, are 15 m. high and the diameter of the base is 150 m. Their remarkable state of preservation is due to a special technique used to reinforce them. The external crust is as hard as pottery and of the same consistency, for it has been made of damp clay baked in small pits, some 2·5 m. deep, over a fire. The fire hardened the clay into a brick-like consistency, thus affording a remarkable protection against rain and erosion. The charcoal from the bottom of one of these pits has given a radio-carbon date of 950 ± 150 B.P., that is about A.D. 1000, just before the Islamization of the region.

Some of these mounds were excavated at the beginning of the century by Desplagnes. He succeeded in finding the funeral chamber and gathered numerous pots of very fine work with a red slip, copper and iron bracelets, weapons, ornaments and stone beads. The exterior of the mound produced other implements thrown in as sacrificial offerings. Other important mounds exist in Senegal near St. Louis and north of the Gambia, in Sine Saloum, and even in Nigeria near Katsina. For that region, let us recall that the Arab traveller Ibn Battuta, in the middle of the fourteenth century, speaks of a custom similar to that practised in Ghana for kings' funerals. Thirty people were placed alive in the grave of the ruler of Koubar (Gobir).

The western Sudan has also yielded a series of interesting Iron-Age megaliths from two main regions, Senegal and Gambia on one hand and the region west of Timbuctoo on the other. The Senegambian group, known since the end of the nineteenth century, roughly limited in the north by the Dakar–Niger railway, and in the south by the river Gambia, extends from Kaffrine to Tambacounda. Dozens of sites have been located composed of stone circles, most of which are graves. The site of Sine includes fifty-four circles with a total of more than 900 megaliths. These are hewn in laterite in the shape of huge cigars up to 3 m. high, but with an average of 2 m. Some of them, 'lyre stones', so called from their shape, are very carefully carved. On the eastern side of the circles, several bigger megaliths are placed, including lyre stones, and these may represent, like the forked poles on some modern graves in Guinea, either some deceased person or the spirit of good protecting sanctuaries from the spirit of evil.

Some of these stone circles have been excavated and yielded large pots turned upside down, remains of skeletons and very poor grave goods. Had it not been for the poverty of the contents, these tombs would have been plundered many centuries ago, for no modern tribe of the area recognizes them as being of their ancestors, and the country is now Muslim.[1]

The Malian group is chiefly represented by a large site at Tondidaru. Two groups of megaliths exist there, some of them phallic in shape, from 2 to 3 m. high, carefully carved in sandstone. Known since the beginning of the century, they have been much damaged by previous investigations, but what remains has now been declared a Historical Monument and it is hoped that there will be no further damage. It is difficult to give a date

[1] P. Ozanne, 'The Anglo-Gambian Stone Circles Expedition', *W. A. Archaeol. News-letter*, 4, (1966), 8–18.

for Tondidaru. It is unquestionably pre-Islamic (pre-eleventh century in this area) and earlier than the mounds in the vicinity of which we have already spoken, but it is post-Neolithic and a date about the fifth century A.D. would seem plausible. A carbon date is badly wanted for this unique site, and excavations carried out there could be of great importance for all the western Sudan for we are here at the extremity of the western trans-Saharan caravan routes of antiquity.

An important new megalithic site on the western edge of the Tibesti mountains at Enneri Mokto was discovered by the helicopter of the Berliet-Chad Expedition in 1960. We know little of it for it has only been visited hastily and no excavations have been carried out there. The site consists of several groups of small megaliths, forming in some cases large circles made of two parallel lines of such stones standing about 1·5 m. high. They may represent a re-use of former pre-Islamic monuments. The material found nearby, pottery, beads, and pieces of vessels carved from volcanic rock, points to the period of transition between the Neolithic and the Iron Ages, perhaps at the beginning of the first millennium A.D.

Still in the republic of Chad are the numerous and important Sao sites, grouped in the lower Shari valley for a radius of 100 km. round Fort Lamy. These are ancient villages, built on artificial or natural hillocks on the banks of rivers. Some of them are half a km. long and nearby are smaller sites that seem to have been initiation sites or shrines. Several campaigns of excavation have been carried on there with spectacular results by J. P. and A. Lebeuf, resulting in the discovery of a medieval and post-medieval Chad civilization. The Sao in local legend are giants who ruled the country until the coming of modern populations. The material excavated consists of fine terracotta figurines, both human and animal, ornaments of stone, copper, and bronze, weapons, and many thousands of potsherds. Huge funerary pots were used. The villages were surrounded by defensive walls.[1]

The dating of this culture is a difficulty. Islam came gradually into the country from the eleventh century but mainly after the

[1] J. P. Lebeuf, *La Civilisation du Tchad* (Paris, 1950).

fifteenth century when Arabs from the Upper Nile swarmed into the Chad savanna after the fall of the Christian Kingdom of Nubia. Radio-carbon dates are also badly needed here, at least for the oldest of the medieval sites. As for the more recent sites, clay pipes excavated from them give a date of not earlier than 1600 since this would seem to be about the time of the introduction of tobacco in this part of Africa. Local tradition suggests that *Datura Metel* was smoked before tobacco, but this still requires to be proved.

Important excavations have recently been carried out at Daima in the extreme north-east of Nigeria in part of the area traditionally associated with the Sao. Study of the excavated material is still in progress and the writer is indebted to the excavator, Mr. G. Connah, for the most up-to-date information available at the time of going to press. Here the excavation of a settlement mound 11 m. high has yielded evidence of an apparently continuous occupation from the beginning of the sixth century B.C. until the end of the eleventh century A.D. It seems possible that a predominantly pastoral people equipped with polished stone axes and a range of bone tools and 'harpoons', lacking metals and building mainly in wood were replaced by an iron-using predominantly cereal cultivating people with wider contacts and a tradition of mud building including the making of potsherd pavements. This replacement probably took place about the eighth century A.D. following the arrival of the earliest iron about the fifth or sixth century A.D. Certain late elements at the very top of the mound, including a few fragments of smoking pipes, are thought to represent sporadic reoccupation of the mound after its general abandonment. The basis of the chronological evidence from this site lies in a series of eight radiocarbon dates.[1]

Other ancient sites in the Chad area have recently yielded interesting remains, chiefly pottery with remarkable designs. Tungur and Maleidinga are the best known of these sites.[2] This is

[1] G. Connah, 'Radiocarbon Dates for Benin City and further dates for Daima, N.E. Nigeria', *J. Hist. Soc. Nigeria*, IV (1968), 313–320. See also above, pp. 9–11.

[2] *Bulletin I.F.A.N.*, B, XXV (1963), 435 ff., 442–51.

in the area of Koro Toro where Christian Nubian ceramics of a late period (thirteenth to fifteenth century) have been found in blacksmiths' villages.[1] Other discoveries have been made north of Lake Chad. These consist of ruins of fired brick at several places, but they are not dated and many may be more recent than is commonly supposed. Thus from the Atlantic to the approaches of the Nilotic Sudan and from the centre of the Sahara to the rain forest, West Africa has proved to be a rich province for archaeological remains from the Iron Age, showing links with the Mediterranean and the Nile Valley.

Remarkable results have been obtained recently by a Dutch Mission, which has worked in the well-known Dogon escarpment at Segue, near Bandiagara in Mali, on a number of caves used for burials and ceremonial purposes by the Tellem, the predecessors of the Dogon. A number of skeletons was found and examined and radio-carbon dates ranging from A.D. 1055 to 1295 have been obtained.[2]

Rock Art

Rock engravings and paintings cover practically all the Sahara, except south-west of Lake Chad—with a few exceptions on the Bauchi Plateau in Nigeria. Here one leaves the steppe lands, the domain of the nomads, to enter the country of the sedentary agriculturalists. In north-west Africa rock art seems to be the property of the nomads.

Of the five groups of drawings encountered, two belong to a period prior to the one studied here: a naturalistic group of Neolithic times and a bovidian pastoralists' group of the end of the Neolithic. We are concerned here with two other groups: The latter part of the equine group (the whole group covering the period from about 1200 B.C. up to our era), and the Libyo-Berber group (about 200 B.C. to A.D. 700). The dessication of the Sahara during the Iron Age drove the bovidian pastoralists to the grassy steppes in the south and the Libyo-Berbers replaced the former Negro stock in the desert. Warriors and hunters are represented with shields and large spears that can only be made

[1] Op. cit., pp. 39–46.
[2] *Koninkl. Nederl. Akad. van Wetenschappen*, Series C, 70 (1967), 338–67.

of iron, and they are sometimes mounted on horses. They have short or long clothes, probably made of leather, and feathers on their heads. They hunt giraffes and antelopes on horseback and their two-wheeled chariots with one, two, or four horses cross the desert.

The Libyo-Berber group follows the equine with no apparent racial change in the population, but Libyan inscriptions appear and the camel gradually replaces the horse. The armament is the same but a dagger worn on the elbow becomes common. One can see the progressive decadence of rock art as drawings become more schematic and slipshod, probably because, after the Neolithic, the nomad lost the mastery of stone engraving. At the end of the period, the animal shown everywhere is the camel, mounted by warriors or hunters after ostrich and antelope, and they are sometimes represented by the score on the same site.

The peopling of some parts of the south Sahara at the period by Libyo-Berbers is shown by the presence of numerous sites showing the work of the equine or Libyo-Berber groups, whereas in that region drawings of the bovidian pastoralists are very rare. The conquest of the south savannas by Saharan nomads is thus attested by rock art from Mauretania to the borders of the Nilotic Sudan.

THE GREAT WEST AFRICAN EMPIRES

The western Sudan enters history with the arrival of the Arabs. We have texts showing that as early as A.D. 666 an expedition led by Oqba ben Nafi reached the Kawar Oasis just north of Lake Chad; and a second, in A.D. 734, crossed the Sahara from Morocco to southern Mauretania, bringing back a considerable amount of gold.

Many archaeological sites of the region fall into the period after the arrival of the Arabs and this includes those associated with the great empires of the western Sudan.

Ghana

The first mention of Ghana occurs about A.D. 800 when the astronomer Al-Fazari, as transmitted by Masudi, makes the following laconic statement: 'Ghana the land of gold'. We know little about the beginnings of this state, but according to local tradition codified in the sixteenth and seventeenth-century chronicles, the *Tarikh el Fettash* and *Tarikh es Sudan*, the kingdom was founded before the Hegira. It was powerful and wealthy until the eleventh century, for all the gold from the western Sudan, which in the Middle Ages was the greatest gold produc-ing country in the world, went through it before crossing the Sahara and reaching the Moghreb and Egypt. We have infor-mation about it and its capital, which must be the ruined site at Kumbi Saleh in south-east Mauretania, from el Bekri (A.D. 1067) who describes it 10 years before its destruction by the Almor-avids, as a well-organized pagan state with powerful army and great riches. The capital, he tells us, was divided into two parts, one inhabited by the king, his court and soothsayers, and the second by rich Muslim traders. The Almoravids, fanatical Berbers of Mauretania, who had already seized and plundered the great town of Awdaghost in 1054, took Ghana in 1077, caus-ing the pagan rulers to flee to the south. Such was the end of the only big state which attempted to oppose the Islamic invasion.

Excavations have been carried out at Kumbi Saleh in 1914, 1939, 1949–51, giving us important information on this medieval commercial city. The ruins have been dated by radio-carbon to 1210 ± 150 A.D. Other excavations are in progress on the site of Tegdaoust, that is probably el Bekri's Awdaghost, by the University of Dakar and several campaigns have already taken place since 1960 producing early and late medieval material, the upper levels being still more recent, showing an occupation during the seventeenth century of which we have no written record. A radio-carbon date of A.D. 810 ± 80 has been obtained from the lower level.

Mali

The second of the famous western Sudan empires was Mali. Its origins are as obscure as Ghana's and it is only in the eleventh century that we have, from el Bekri, the first mention of it in which he gives an account of the king's conversion to Islam. It became powerful during the thirteenth century under the real founder of the state, Sundiata. A series of military victories resulted in the extension of his dominions especially after the defeat of his Susu enemies at Kirina in about A.D. 1235.

Sundiata's successors were equally successful and the peak of the dynasty's power was reached when Mansa Musa made a spectacular pilgrimage to Mecca in A.D. 1324, passing through Cairo. He left so much gold in Egypt that its value fell considerably for years in the Middle East. He returned with lawyers, traders, and an architect poet, es Saheli, who built residences for him in Arab style. The city of Timbuctoo began to become famous as a place of learning at this time.

During the rule of one of his successors, Mansa Suleiman, the great Moroccan traveller Ibn Battuta visited the capital of Mali in 1352. A decline came at the end of the fourteenth century with civil wars caused by rivals for the throne, and with the rise of the Songhai state, and after a century of continual decay, the great empire of Mali shrank to its original province on the upper reaches of the Niger, around Kangaba and Niani. Excavations have been made recently on this last site by a joint Guinea–Polish expedition to try and locate the fourteenth-century capital.[1] Discovery of the site has been very difficult as there are no stone buildings as at Kumbi Saleh, but only mud buildings which time has largely worn away. Much further work is needed before the archaeological problems of Mali's capital are solved.

Songhai

Songhai's beginnings, like those of its forerunners, were modest. Some time around A.D. 700–800 a little kingdom existed at Koukia, downstream from Gao, and its chiefs were converted to Islam about A.D. 1000. We have little information about it until the beginning of the fourteenth century, apart from the discovery in a cemetery at Sane near Gao, of marble tombstones made in Almeria and dated from A.D. 1100 to 1150.

The Songhai kingdom was tributary to Mali till the middle of

[1] W. Filipowiak, *Africana Bulletin*, (Warsaw, 1966), 116–27 and *Archaeologia Polona*, X (1968), 217–32.

the fifteenth century when the greatest man of the dynasty, Sonni Ali (A.D. 1464–92), liberated his country and founded the empire. A usurper, Askia Mohammed Touré, seized power from Sonni Ali's son, restoring the Islamic faith which had been suppressed by his predecessors. His pilgrimage to Mecca in 1496 is described in detail in the *Tarikh el Fettash*. Under his rule the Songhai empire extended from the Hausa states of northern Nigeria to the Atlantic. We have descriptions of it by the traveller Leo Africanus who visited it in 1513, at the peak of Askia Mohammed's reign. Some of his successors maintained the power of the state but civil wars between princes wanting to become kings enfeebled the empire, which became an easy prey to the Sultan of Morocco who, employing a small army composed chiefly of Spanish renegades armed with muskets, succeeded in beating the Askia at Tondibi in 1591.

The Portuguese on the Coast

Meanwhile the Portuguese who had been trying since 1424 to discover the coast south of Cape Bojador, the then limit of navigation in the Atlantic, doubled that famous cape in 1434. The tenacious effort of Henry the Navigator brought his compatriots to Cape Blanco (1441), Cape Verde (1444), and Sierra Leone was reached by the time of his death in 1460. The Portuguese settled in many places on the coast and up the rivers and began the traffic that was to degenerate in the sixteenth century into the slave trade. Our knowledge of the coastal areas, non-existent in earlier periods, begins with the accounts of Zurara (1453–68), Cadamosto (1455), Diego Gomes (about 1495), Duarte Pacheco Pereira (about 1507) and above all Valentim Fernandes (about 1508). West Africa had definitely left the prehistoric Iron Age to enter history.

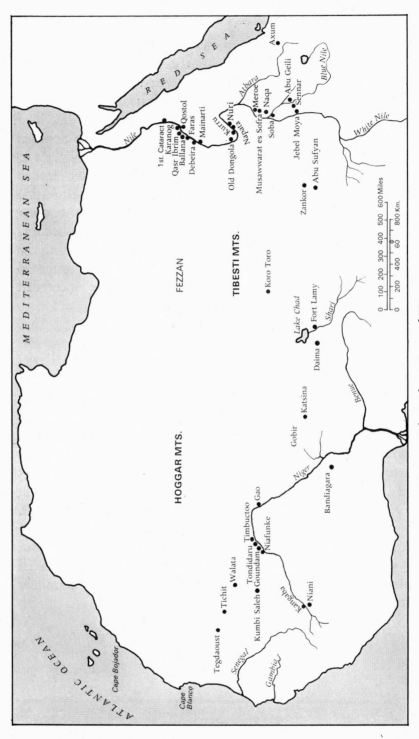

MAP 5. The Sudan—East and West.

4

THE SUDAN

by

P. L. Shinnie

THE Nilotic Sudan, or at least that northern part of it in which archaeological work has been carried out sporadically for a little over a hundred years, differs in a great many respects from the other areas treated in this book. Of the southern part of the country, which for our purpose may be considered as all that territory within the frontiers of the Republic of the Sudan which lies south of about 13° North, nothing is known and no archaeological work has been attempted. It would be possible to speculate on the course of events in that vast area but, in the absence of any archaeological material, consideration of it will be excluded from this chapter. North of 13° the situation is different and an attempt will be made to summarize what is known and to pay special attention to some of the work which the construction of the High Dam at Aswan has inspired.

In comparison with the countries to south and west the Sudan is historically much better known. Geographically it lies close to Egypt and the Near East and has benefited from the interest which the world of scholarship has long shown in the ancient eastern Mediterranean. Its ties with Pharaonic Egypt have provided a chronological framework and a general historical story, which stands in marked contrast to the comparative obscurity of sub-saharan Africa in the past. We are, therefore, in a far better position to understand human development, to study technological innovations, and to place them in their proper historical perspective.

Unlike most of the rest of Africa, during much of the period under review the civilization of the Sudan was literate—but for the earlier period the language of most of the inscriptions (Meroitic) cannot be understood. For the succeeding centuries when Old Nubian was the language of the country, the few texts known are almost exclusively theological in content, and this makes them of little value for understanding either the history or the material culture of the time. From the Arab invasion of Egypt in the seventh century A.D. onwards there are a number of works in Arabic which give information about historical events but they too throw no light on changes and fashions in objects of art or daily life. So to construct a picture of the life of the Sudan in the period from about 650 B.C. to A.D. 1300, which are the limits this chapter intends to cover, it is necessary to use the methods of the archaeologist and to treat the material remains of the culture in the same way as the remains of non-literate, and therefore by normal terminology, pre-historic, communities described in other sections of this book.

Another advantage that the archaeologist in the Sudan has over those in other parts of tropical Africa lies in the dry climate and the consequent preservation of archaeological materials. The northern part of the area, and the best known, is almost rainless and the desert virtually borders the Nile on either bank. Here Iron-Age man had to live close to the river and thus not only are his remains well preserved[1] but the area in which he lived is clearly defined and limited, and the surface indications of his existence are easier to see than amongst the vegetation of tropical forest or savanna.

South of about 17° North human habitation is not confined to the river banks for here annual rainfall, even if erratic, allowed man to cultivate his crops and pasture his animals away from the river. Even here the vegetation is comparatively thin and

[1] The white ant causes considerable destruction and this is the reason why even in dry areas organic materials are rare.

discovery of ancient sites comparatively easy. Preservation is not so good as it is further north but material remains are still plentiful.

The proximity of a number of cultures whose antecedents are known, which can be set in order, and in which the archaeological material has been studied and dated, to vast areas whose chronology is scarcely yet established, should be of value for the chronology of Africa as a whole. In fact the known cultures of the Sudan have not, so far, been of assistance in dating material further south and this arises from the easily observable fact that nearly all archaeological work in the Sudan has been in the north, where the glamour of Ancient Egypt has imposed an Egyptological bias. The most southerly site of the Iron Age so far excavated is at Jebel Moya[1] only about 150 miles south of Khartoum, but once sites up the White and Blue Niles and to the West of the Nile have been investigated we may hope for evidence that could help us to probe deeper into Africa.

The emphasis on work in the North has been reinforced in recent years by the flooding caused by the Aswan dam. This has resulted in the fullest possible archaeological exploration of an important part of the northern Sudan and has given a great deal of extra information of value, but it does not yet help very much with the problems of the chronology of southern and non-riverain areas, although the rather precise dating now available for the pottery of medieval times should be of value. When archaeologists turn their attention further afield, there is the possibility that known and dated material may be found in association with unknown local objects, thus providing a chronological anchor for the unknown and immediately giving it a significance in an otherwise chronologically unidentifiable context.

The general historical and chronological outline of the Iron Age in the Sudan has been given by Arkell[2] and a detailed study of the evidence made by Wainwright[3]. It need not be repeated

[1] F. Addison, *Jebel Moya* (London, 1949).

[2] A. J. Arkell, *A History of the Sudan to 1821* (London, 1961), pp. 138 to end, and more summarily in *Current Anthropology*, 7 (1966), 451–2.

[3] *Sudan Notes and Records*, XXVI (1945), 5–36.

here in detail. There seems little doubt that the Sudan received its knowledge of the use and presumably also the technique of smelting iron from Egypt where it first becomes common in the seventh century B.C. Egypt with its conservative traditions came late into the Mediterranean Iron Age where the Hittites, at least, had been using iron since the second millennium B.C., and the usually accepted view is that it was the Assyrian military contacts with Egypt, culminating in their invasion of that country in 671 B.C., which first introduced iron weapons in significant quantity to the Nile Valley. It should be noted that the rulers of Egypt at that time were from the Sudan (Kush to use the ancient term) whither they retreated in the middle of the seventh century B.C. to maintain themselves at Napata, having launched their original occupation of Egypt from there some 60 years before.

The use of iron weapons and tools by the Assyrians is well attested but it seems improbable that the Egyptians learnt of the technique of iron working only from a military expedition, and the existence of Greeks in large numbers in the Nile Delta at this time is probably of greater significance. These Greeks, coming as mercenary soldiers and traders, established a number of towns of which Naukratis is the best known. They were certainly making iron, and presumably making the weapons which the troops of the Pharaoh Psammetichus, many of whom were Greeks and Carians, used during their Sudan campaign in 591 B.C.

It can be assumed that the Sudanese learnt of the use of iron in the seventh century and in part from their first contacts with the Assyrians, and the inferiority of their own weapons of copper may have been one factor in their military defeats. But when they themselves started to work the metal is not certain. Wainwright[1] has listed the occurrences of iron in Kush and from this it can be seen that the first iron implements at Napata occur in the sixth century B.C., and the first of the royal tombs to contain iron is that of Harsiyotef whose date is conventionally given as 404–369 B.C. or 416–398 B.C. (let us say that he reigned at about

[1] Op. cit.

the beginning of the fourth century B.C.). In his tomb at Nuri, near Napata, the miniature tools in the foundation deposits are of iron, while in all earlier tombs of a line of rulers living between *c.* 750 B.C. and the reign of Harsiyotef these are of copper. From Harsiyotef's time onwards iron is sporadically found but is not common in either royal or commoners' graves until well into the first century A.D. Iron was not entirely unknown even before Harsiyotef and a few fragments have been found in earlier tombs. Particularly noteworthy is the iron spear head found in the tomb of Taharqa (690–664 B.C.). This spear head was wrapped in gold, an indication of the value attached to it. As late as the time of Queen Amanishakhete, in the second half of the first century B.C., iron was still regarded as sufficiently precious to be used for jewellery, but since all the royal tombs have been badly robbed, evidence from them may not be conclusive.

The conclusions to be drawn from this are not absolutely clear. A number of iron smelting centres are known of which the most important is at Meroe itself, but the history of iron working at this site is not fully understood. The town itself, to which the ruling house of Napata moved in perhaps the early sixth century B.C., was occupied from at least the time of Piankhy, *c.* 750 B.C., to as late as the fourth century A.D. and perhaps later. It contains a large number of mounds of iron slag which have attracted the attention of all visitors and whose presence has given rise to the view that Meroe was the centre from which techniques of iron working spread through the African continent. The slag mounds visible on the surface seem, on present evidence, to date from not earlier than the third or fourth centuries A.D. but may be later. The top levels at Meroe have been badly eroded and nothing now remains of them but a scatter of pottery. The surface pottery, as a result of 1,500 years of erosion and human damage, is now very mixed but sherds resembling some of the pottery from Soba[1] suggest that occupation, and therefore iron working, may have gone on as late as the eighth century A.D.

Recent excavations show that previous views which suggested

[1] P. L. Shinnie, *Excavations at Soba*, Sudan Antiquities Service Occasional Papers No. 3 (Khartoum, 1955).

that iron only became common at Meroe from the first century A.D. must be revised. At the bottom of a recently excavated cutting iron was found in some quantity in association with pottery of Napatan type (Pls. I and II). A radio-carbon date for this level gives 514 B.C. ± 73 (Birm, 97). The evidence suggests that iron was being worked as well as being used at this time.

Whatever the precise date for the introduction of iron as a significant element in the culture of the Sudan, the civilization of late Napatan and Meroitic times was certainly that of an iron-using people and a description of that civilization can now be given. As already emphasized Meroitic culture is known in far greater detail[1] than is that of any part of ancient Africa further south. The general historical outline is also known and names of rulers, approximate dates, and even some events, mainly of a military nature, can be noted. Founded on the cultural traditions left by the Egyptians after hundreds of years of occupation of the northern Sudan, the Sudanese kings of Napata are seen as the rulers of a state of markedly Egyptian character. Contacts with Egypt were very close at the beginning of the period and the Napatan rulers controlled Egypt for a time as the group of kings known as the 25th Dynasty. After these rulers departed from Egypt, Napata continued to be their capital until they moved south to Meroe. Twenty-six kings were buried in pyramid cemeteries at Kurru and Nuri, close to Napata, until, at a date near to the beginning of the third century B.C., the main royal cemetery was established at Meroe where forty or more rulers were buried, the last burial being perhaps in the early part of the fourth century A.D. (Pl. III).

Attempts have been made to produce a precise chronology for these rulers and two versions are current.[2] It needs to be pointed out that these dates should be used with great caution—in the whole series of rulers spanning some thousand years only three are dated by external evidence apart from the six earliest who are known from Egyptian history. The other dates have been arrived at by averaging and then weighting the results according

[1] P. L. Shinnie, *Meroe—A Civilisation of the Sudan* (London, 1967).
[2] Op. cit., pp. 58–61.

PLATE I

Excavations at Meroe. Section of main trench showing grain storage bins of c. 500 B.C.

PLATE II

Excavations at Meroe. Bottom of main trench showing cache of Napatan pots of c. 500 B.C.

PLATE III

The Pyramids at Meroe.

PLATE IV

to the richness or otherwise of the burials—it being assumed that a ruler with a well-built tomb and rich grave goods would have ruled longer than one with poorer material. This method is not entirely satisfactory, and it gives merely an indication of date.

Meroitic culture is known from sites that range along the Nile from not far south of the First Cataract to Sennar on the Blue Nile. Few are known away from the river except in the grassland area between the Nile and the Atbara, the ancient Island of Meroe and the heartland of Meroitic civilization, and here some of the finest of Meroitic buildings are to be found. These are in the main religious and though many are now much ruined, at the two great sites of the Island of Meroe, Musawwarat es Sofra and Naqa, many temples are still standing. Egyptian artistic influence is much in evidence but Meroitic art contains also a distinctive indigenous element; the temples and pyramids and the sculptured reliefs associated with them are all of Egyptian inspiration but show interesting and important variations from the normal styles of Egypt as in a graffito of a royal head from Meroe (Pl. IV).

Many temple plans show Egyptian influence, and the Amun temple at Meroe, the largest known, is typically Egyptian in its lay out; but more truly Meroitic temples sometimes consist of small single chamber buildings with a colonnade surrounding them, as at the Sun Temple at Meroe, a plan showing departure from Egyptian styles and which may be of Syrian inspiration rather than indigenous. Of special interest is the unique complex of buildings at Musawwarat es Sofra. Its main feature is a central temple of the single chamber type just mentioned, but standing on a large platform and with an elaborate series of walls, ramps, and courtyards surrounding it. Excavations here over the last few years have produced striking results,[1] of which the most spectacular was perhaps the finding of a temple of the lion god Apedemek with all the blocks of one wall excellently preserved by the fortunate chance that they had fallen face downwards with consequent protection of the reliefs. This wall contained important religious inscriptions, as well as a representation, with his

[1] *Kush*, X (1962), 170–202; XI (1963), 217–26.

name, of king Arnekhamani, the builder. This discovery, by a comparison of the wording and calligraphy of the text with those of Ptolemaic Egypt, has enabled a much closer date to be given to this king, in the late third century B.C., and thus also for the temple, and it is now probable that dates can be given for the different parts of the Musawwarat complex which seems to have been in use for several centuries.

Buildings other than temples are little known since it is only very recently that attention has been paid to domestic sites. But over the last few years a number of houses have been excavated in the area between the first and second cataracts, and at Meroe a large number of houses of late Meroitic times has now been found. All these are built of sun dried brick and are of simple design, except for one at Gaminarti[1] which appears to have housed a complete community or an extended family.

The highly characteristic pottery of Meroe has been well known ever since the excavations at Karanog early in this century,[2] but it is only very recently that attention to stratigraphy has made it possible to begin to date the various styles. Adams[3] has made a first attempt at ordering this pottery but his examples come mainly from the northern region of Meroitic power, where perhaps a semi-independent province arose in the first few centuries A.D. The Meroe excavations will give further information from the southerly part of the realm and before long a proper analysis of Meroitic pottery should be possible.

What can be seen at present is that there are two quite distinct traditions present in the ceramic art. One that looks north for its inspiration, and one that springs from Africa. The pottery of northern influence is of a wide range of ware and decoration, the best known being the very fine painted wares which do not seem to be earlier than the beginning of the first century A.D. In addition, there are much coarser painted wares, which on the evidence from Meroe, are somewhat earlier in date, and there is also a common class of unpainted red ware of markedly Roman

[1] *Kush*, XI (1963), 11–27.
[2] Woolley and MacIver, *Karanog* (Philadelphia, 1910).
[3] *Kush*, XIII (1965), 126–73.

type found in the upper levels at Meroe and in royal tombs ranging from the first to the fourth centuries A.D.

In addition to this pottery there are black wares which contrast very strongly with the Mediterranean styles of the others. This pottery, built up by hand and not wheel-made as are the other wares, obviously belongs to an indigenous African pottery tradition and bears resemblances to much modern pottery both in the Sudan and other parts of Africa. Pottery of this type has a long history in the Sudan, appearing sporadically from as early as C-Group times (c. 2,000–1,500 B.C.), in those cultures least influenced by Egypt. Curiously it is rare in earlier Meroitic times and the first occurrence in the royal tombs is in tomb S.4 at Meroe which is to be dated to the early part of the third century B.C.

Although the presence of iron from the sixth century B.C. makes it legitimate to consider the Sudan culture from that time as being part of the Iron Age, iron implements have only been discovered in large quantities in tombs dating from the first century A.D. From this time on, notably in the large cemetery at Faras, iron arrow heads of the distinctive single barbed Meroitic style become common, and the number increases towards the end of the Meroitic sequence and into the succeeding one of the X Group people.[1] The late houses at Meroe produced sufficient fragments of iron to show that it must have been in common use.

Archaeological evidence shows a cultural change in the fourth century A.D. which is usually taken to coincide with the end of the Meroitic state. The new element is shown by the presence of large numbers of tumulus graves, particularly in the region round the junction of the Blue and White Niles northwards to the point where the river Arbara joins the Nile, and also much further north where, just over the present frontier with Egypt, the tombs of chiefs at Ballana and Qostol, and in the Sudan at Firka show material of remarkable richness. These are the burial mounds of the people known as the X Group.

[1] The curious terminology of A, C and X-Groups used by archaeologists of the Sudan goes back to the days of the Archaeological Survey of Nubia when Reisner faced with a number of previously unknown cultures gave them letters of the alphabet as a handy designation.

In the southern tombs, many of which are on the outskirts of the town of Meroe and therefore presumably of people living in it, the difference is marked by a new type of pottery consisting of large jars, usually, and probably correctly, known as beer jars. These are of coarse hand-made fabric, shaped like gourds or baskets, and frequently bearing the impressions of the mats on which they were made. The northern cemeteries of all social classes show a wheel-made pottery deriving from the late Meroitic wares. Other material consists of iron weapons, crowns of silver, jewellery of considerable splendour, elaborate horse and camel trappings, and many luxury objects imported from late Roman Egypt.

The origins of the X Group and their possible identity with the people of the smaller tumuli and poorer grave goods further south has been much argued. Two peoples known from classical writers have been seen as possible bringers of what might be called the Ballana culture; the Nobatae coming from the oases of the Western Desert, whence Diocletian is said to have brought them in A.D. 296 as mercenaries to defend the Nile Valley from the other, the Blemmye people of the eastern desert and the Red Sea hills, possibly the ancestors of the modern Bega. Perhaps the view that the rulers buried at Ballana and Qostol are to be identified with the Nobatae has more to commend it, though there is no reason to suppose that the majority of the population was not the same as in Meroitic times. Similarity of the name Nobatae suggests that they may be the same people as those called Noba. Aezanes, in an inscription at Axum of about A.D. 350, describes a military campaign in the Island of Meroe against the Noba, in whom it is tempting to see the people of the late tumulus graves. Further resemblances to the name Nubian, that of the language spoken along the Nile today from well into Egypt to a little way below the fourth cataract, also suggest that they were the bringers of that language and that it displaced Meroitic. From the present distribution of languages related to Nubian it could be inferred that the speakers of it came from west of the Nile. Archaeology has nothing to add to this at present since no investigations, other than the most casual, have been carried out away from the river, and it is not possible to say even whether or not the tumulus graves are found to the west.

Something must be said about the now widely held view that iron-working techniques spread to large parts of Africa from Meroe. This view, first stated in detail by Wainwright,[1] has received great currency and is now frequently held to be an established fact. Since Meroe was working iron in quantity at a time when its use seems not to have been known further south or west, there is certainly a possibility that the knowledge was diffused from there—but there is as yet no archaeological evidence to support such a view. Meroitic culture belongs to the Nile Valley, and, with the special exception of the Island of Meroe, no objects or monuments of the culture have been found away from the river other than a group of bronze bowls found at Axum. Meroitic culture reached up the Blue Nile at least as far as Sennar; whether or not it extended south similarly up the White Nile is not yet known, though there is a group of mounds which has been examined by Arkell who considers that pottery found on the surface shows Meroitic characteristics. Further investigation of these mounds as well as exploration further south may throw light on the problem of the spread of cultural developments from Meroe.

The view that Meroe was a centre from which diffusion of techniques started has led to the supposition that it was also a source of less tangible influences, such as state organization and the concept of divine kingship. These are not matters on which to express an opinion in a predominantly archaeological context and I have discussed them elsewhere:[2] here let it just be said that no properly attested archaeological material whether from Meroe or from Pharaonic Egypt has been found to suggest wide-scale diffusion of techniques, material, or concepts.

The site of Jebel Moya in the southern Gezira has produced material, probably of Meroitic date, of rather different type.

[1] *Uganda Journal*, 18 (1954), 113–36. An important paper by B. G. Trigger, 'Meroe and the African Iron Age', *African Historical Studies*, II (1969), 23–50, appeared too late to be used.

[2] In *The Legacy of Egypt* (in the press), and in 'Meroe and West Africa', *W.A. Arch. Newsletter*, 6 (1967), 12–16.

Here a large cemetery shows an iron-using people with a distinctive pottery—much of it decorated in a very unusual way by scratching after firing—and a number of characteristics of markedly African type. These include lip plugs, found in vast number, and such traits as extraction of the lower incisor teeth. The people themselves seem to have been Negroid. There has been considerable argument about the date of this cemetery but the consensus now is that it is Meroitic and shows a local variant of that culture.[1]

Recent work has revealed many more sites of Meroitic and X Group people between the First and Second cataracts but these have not added much to our knowledge. Mostly cemeteries, they repeat time and again the material already well known. They do however show that the area was heavily populated from about the first century B.C. onwards following a long period which has left very little archaeological material and can therefore be presumed to have had a very small population. It is clear that Nubia was far more prosperous during the Iron Age than at any time since the Egyptian New Kingdom and its population was greater than at any previous date and perhaps no less than in modern times. The reasons for the increase of prosperity and population—since there seems to have been little, if any, climatic change—is most likely to be due to the introduction of the *saqia*, the ox-driven water wheel, which, introduced from Egypt at this time, transformed agriculture by enabling far larger areas to be irrigated.

The Ballana culture begins to change during the sixth and seventh centuries at a time when the coming of Christian missionaries from Egypt and Byzantium caused a change in religion and brought the country within the influence of eastern Mediterranean Christian culture. The period from mid-sixth century A.D. to the final disappearance of Christian rulers with the coming of Arabs and Islam in the fourteenth Century is normally described as the Christian Nubian period and provides a considerable range of material. The early stages do not show any break in the cultural tradition and pottery and house types are clearly derived from those in use in Ballana times. There is no

[1] *Kush*, IV (1956), 4–18.

evidence of any ethnic change and it is likely that the language of Christian times, Nubian, was being spoken before the coming of Christianity.

As with earlier periods, our knowledge is mainly of the settlements along the river and we are very badly informed about the archaeology of other areas. A patchy history of Christian times has been compiled[1] and recent work has made possible a detailed chronology of the material remains. The pottery can now be used as a fairly precise means of dating[2] and a chronology of churches has also been established.[3] Until the recent excavations in Nubia, churches were virtually the only buildings known, but now, with the excavation of towns at Debeira and Mainarti[4] as well as numerous smaller sites, a wealth of information about domestic buildings and daily life has been acquired.[5]

The known history of Christian times shows that on the ruins of Meroitic power three kingdoms arose, of which at least the ruling houses were quickly Christianized. These were Nobatia, on the extreme north, Makuria in the Dongola stretch of the Nile, and Alodia much further south in the region of Khartoum. By the eighth century the two northern kingdoms had come together, perhaps by military conquest, to form the kingdom of Dongola with its capital at Old Dongola, now being excavated by a Polish expedition. By this time, on the evidence of the large number of churches, the population must have been largely Christian.

What is known of subsequent history derives mainly from accounts from Arab sources, of varying encounters with the Muslim rulers of Egypt, at times with Nubian success as in c. A.D. 745 when they invaded Egypt and may have reached Cairo, or defeat as in A.D. 1173 when Turan Shah, brother of Saladian, occupied Qasr Ibrim. Arab and Muslim pressure increased, though there was never a rapid occupation of the country as in North Africa in the seventh century, and Arabic tombstones

[1] Monneret de Villard, *Storia della Nubia Cristiana* (Rome, 1938).

[2] *Kush*, X (1962), 245–88.

[3] *Journal of the American Research Centre in Egypt*, IV (1965), 87–139.

[4] *Kush*, XI (1963), 257–63; XII (1964), 208–17, 222–39; XIII (1965), 148–76, 190–4.

[5] A useful summary of recent work is to be found in *Journal of African History*, VI (1965), 263–273.

from the tenth century A.D. onwards at sites in the Red Sea Hills and in the region of Wadi Halfa attest to Arab penetration of a peaceful kind, probably as part of trading activities. By the fourteenth century the northern Christian kingdom was in an advanced state of decay and by exploiting rivalries in the royal family Muslims gained control. The southern kingdom of Alodia, or Alwa, may have survived later, and have come to an end in the early sixteenth century, though it has been suggested that, like Dongola, its fall also came during the fourteenth.[1]

The material culture of Christian Nubia is now well known so far as the northern part of the area is concerned and a great deal of archaeological activity has been carried out on sites of the period during the last few years. The material found consists of buildings, both ecclesiastical and lay, church frescoes, and a range of small artefacts, again both religious and lay. The depredations of white ants have made the finding of organic materials rare and it is only at a few favoured sites, such as Qasr Ibrim (which since it is in Egypt strictly lies outside the scope of the chapter though culturally it belongs with the rest of Christian Nubia), that cloth, wood, paper and so on, have been found.

The religious buildings of the period range from the magnificent cathedrals at Faras, Qasr Ibrim, and Old Dongola to small parish churches, many of them made of sun-dried brick. Adams lists 154 (including those of Egyptian Nubia) and has made a detailed chronological study showing them to range in date from the early seventh century up to the end of Christian times in the fourteenth or fifteenth century. There are variations in style and building material, but the majority are basilican in plan and there is no doubt that the type was introduced from Egypt at the very beginning of Christian times.

Parallels with the churches of Coptic Egypt are close in the early period, but later variations in Coptic church plan were not always reflected in Nubia, and certain characteristics of later styles in Nubia, particularly the small churches of very late date with a central dome, point to Syria as their place of origin and suggest that there were other influences at work in Nubia in

[1] Bulletin School of Oriental and African Studies, 23 (1960), 1–17.

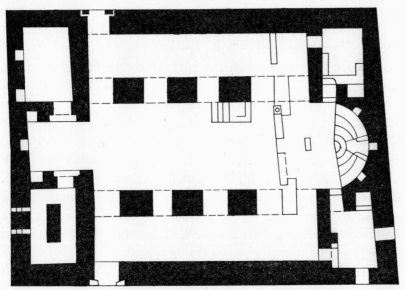

A   The basilican church at Debeira West

0   1   2   3   4   5 Metres

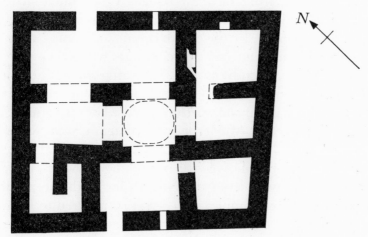

N

B   The domed church at Serra East

FIG. I.

addition to those of Coptic Egypt. Similarly the frescoes at
Faras do not seem to derive from Coptic originals, but seem more
directly inspired by Byzantine or Syrian models. Since Greek

8

remained in use, at least for grave inscriptions, up to the end of the twelfth century it seems clear that Nubia had retained, or re-established, links with the Byzantine world which one would have expected to be broken after the Arab conquest of Egypt in A.D. 639.

Domestic architecture is now also comparatively well known. Buildings are of sun-dried brick, many of them roofed with the so-called Nubian vault, which makes the proportions of the rooms necessarily narrow, as can be well seen at Debeira. There were also flat-roofed buildings, often with steps up to the roof. Unlike modern Nubian villages which are spread out in a line parallel to the river, the medieval villages and small towns clustered closely together with little conscious planning. Some houses were of two stories but this was rare.

Of the artefacts of the time the most striking and the best studied is the pottery. It is of a range and richness not otherwise known in Africa, except for the Meroitic pottery with which it has obvious affinities. Starting with plain red, wheel-made, wares certainly derived from those of Ballana times and much influenced by late Roman pottery—(some of it being an obvious copy of *terra sigillata*), by the eighth century a painted ware of great elegance comes into use and continues with varying styles to the end of the eleventh century. Thereafter there is a decline, as part of the general decay of Christian Nubian culture, until we reach the crude hand-made ware of the very late settlements. As with the fine pottery of Meroe, the painted 'classic' wares of Christian Nubia are obviously of Mediterranean (and perhaps Persian) inspiration and owe little or nothing to Africa, nor did the style spread away from the Nile Valley with the possible exception of a few examples which will be referred to later.

Other objects are not found in great number—churches are unlikely to contain them and, generally speaking, town and village ruins contain only broken fragments since in most cases on the abandonment of these settlements the inhabitants took most of their portable property with them. Graves, normally the source of so much archaeological material, in Christian times contain only bodies, though the gravestones that go with them often give valuable chronological information. But a small range of domestic and decorative objects in stone, glass and metal have been found, and in a few cases of wood.

Archaeological investigation has so far been confined almost entirely to the area to be flooded by the Aswan dam and most of the information we have of the material culture comes from that area. Further south we are dependent on surface collections except for the monastic site at Ghazali[1] where a large church as well as associated monastic buildings has been excavated, and at Old Dongola where excavations are now in progress. For the southern region the only excavated site is Soba, the capital of Alodia where, together with painted pottery of the type known from the north, several distinctive local styles have been found. Amongst these is a burnished black ware which has been found at a number of places in the Gezira, the area south of Khartoum between the White and the Blue Niles. Here there is also a number of sites covered with fragments of red brick which may be of Christian times.

The culture of medieval Nubia, like that of Meroe, was a literate one and seems to have been multi-lingual. The main spoken language of the time, as of much of the area today, was Nubian and a number of documents are known written in that language with the Coptic form of the Greek alphabet. Evidence for the use of Greek and Coptic is to be seen in the many tomb-stones written in those languages. The Arabic tomb-stones already mentioned, as well as graffiti at Faras and invocations on the walls at Debeira, show that that language was also to some extent current.

From the above description of the Sudan in the Iron Age it can be seen why our information is closely tied to the river and how it comes to be concentrated on the area to the north close to the Egyptian frontier. On the areas to east and west we know very little and that virtually only by surface observation. To the east a few sites of probably medieval date have been observed of which the most important is the ruined town of Aidhab,

[1] P. L. Shinnie and H. N. Chittick, *Ghazali—A Monastery in the Northern Sudan*, Sudan Antiquities Service Occasional Papers No. 5 (Khartoum, 1961).

once a commercial port of importance, and from which collections of Islamic and Chinese pottery have been made. Tombs of uncertain date have been found at many places and south of Port Sudan, towards the frontier of Ethiopia, are sites which may have been occupied in Ptolemaic times.

In the western Sudan (Darfur and Kordofan) Iron-Age sites have been visited at Zankor[1] and Abu Sufyan.[2] Zankor consists of a number of mounds covered with red brick and stone fragments. Partial excavation showed that there were buildings, and a group of distinctive pots with some resemblances to known types from Soba were found. At Abu Sufyan is a mound covered with red brick fragments but nothing more is known about it. Further west a number of sites are known in Darfur, but are mainly of late date, some of them of the eighteenth century. Perhaps the most interesting is that of Ain Fara where red brick ruins of some complexity stand on a hill. Originally thought to date from the sixteenth century and to have been an outpost of the Bornu empire, more recently it has been suggested that they are of medieval date on the evidence of two potsherds of medieval Nubian type. The details of the finding of these sherds are not absolutely sure and recent work has not produced any of this pottery from the site. Precision must wait on further investigations, and it would be wise not to rely too heavily on this evidence in proposing medieval Christian influence in the area. There are, however, other fragments of information, mostly in unchecked oral tradition, of Christianity in the west; and at Koro Toro in Chad sherds have been found which seem certainly to be from the Nile Valley and of medieval times, probably twelfth or thirteenth century. The use of red brick at many of these sites in the west, together with some in Chad and as far west as those of the Kanuri in Bornu may indicate that there was contact along this route which runs throughout just south of the desert. A medieval date for westward influences from the Nile would be more acceptable than a Meroitic one; it has the merit of some archaeological evidence to support it and could in part explain persistent stories in Nigerian oral tradition of people coming from the east.

Although this account of the Iron Age in the Sudan is necessarily patchy, it is possible to give an historical outline at least for the riverain areas and to describe the main features of the succeeding civilizations and it can be seen that from the time when a distinctive Meroitic culture first emerged there was a strong cultural unity until the coming of Islam. This can best be observed at Mainarti, the only site which shows the whole range of development without a break. For periods later than the coming of Islam, the archaeological record has not been investigated and we are unable to identify material of the period, except for that from the Fung site at Abu Geili.[1]

The immigrants, partly nomads, may well not have had a material culture which would leave evidence, much of their equipment being of leather and cloth; but the life and culture of the riverain cultivators must have continued in much the same way as before even though they changed their religion, and in many places, their language, under the powerful influence of Islam and Arabic. The paucity of descriptions by travellers before the nineteenth century is a barrier to fuller understanding. It does seem that there was a shift of dwelling sites and the villages of Christian times were, in the main, abandoned, though no attempt has been made by archaeologists, even in the areas now flooded, to see if present villages overlie earlier ones. On the whole this seems unlikely, and the dwellings of the people of the fifteenth to seventeenth centuries are unknown. When outside travellers, such as Bruce in 1772 and others later, provide information the settlement pattern seems much as now and this shift from the old village sites must have happened during those centuries for which we have no evidence.

[1] O. G. S. Crawford, *Abu Geili* (London, 1951).

5

THE COAST OF EAST AFRICA

by

H. N. Chittick

FOR some 2,000 years ships from Arabia and north-western India have been sailing to and from the East African coast, taking advantage of the alternating régime of the monsoons, which for nearly half the year blow from the south-west, and during four months from the north-east. These coasts were the most southerly region known to the ancients; consequently in this part only of equatorial Africa do we have any historical knowledge going back to before the fifteenth century. It is a history linked more to the other lands bordering the Indian Ocean than to the interior of the continent; the sources are meagre, often corrupt, often half-myth. Nevertheless they can provide us with some framework of the pattern of events— a framework which needs to be verified, supplemented, and, as we shall see, sometimes modified by archaeological evidence.

Though the northern part of the coast was the most easily accessible to the early voyagers, it was the region lying south of the equator which offered the greatest potential attraction to the traders and settlers from the hot, dry lands of the north Indian Ocean; an attraction dramatically demonstrated in the nine-teenth century by the transfer by Sayyid Sa'id bin Sultan of his capital from Muscat to Zanzibar. From the Horn of Africa to the latitude of Mogadishu, the coast is barren, poor in harbours, and with an arid hinterland. The stretch from Mogadishu to a little south of the equator, near the present border of Kenya and Somalia, is known as the Banadir coast; as its name shows, it is broken by useful harbours, but is still somewhat barren. From about 2° S there is a fair rainfall, and the coast is much indented by drowned valleys. There are many offshore islands, those with water offering secure homes for trading people. The islands afford protection to the adjacent coast, much of which is fringed with mangrove swamps. The mangroves are broken by stretches of steep sandy beach with an almost flat foreshore. Where the beaches are protected from the force of the ocean they provide ideal landing places; boats coming in on the high tide anchor and are left high and dry on their nearly-flat bottoms as the water recedes, when they can conveniently be unloaded. Offshore, in between the islands, a shallow-lying coral shelf affords a rich harvest of fish.

Before considering the archaeology of the coast, it will be helpful to summarize what is known of the history of the coast from written sources. Certain places in East Africa are apparently mentioned in Pliny's *Natural History*, published about 75 A.D.; but the names are recited without comprehension, and although the passage across the Indian Ocean (known to the Greeks and Romans as the Erythraean Sea) to India was well known after Hippalus brought back knowledge of the monsoons to the Mediterranean about 30 years earlier, Pliny's knowledge of Africa effectively ends with the Gulf of Aden. It is the *Periplus of the Erythraean Sea*, which, supplemented by Ptolemy, provides us with the first useful information about the East African coast. The *Periplus* is an anonymous work apparently written by a Greek merchant who lived in Egypt. Its date has usually been placed in the second half of the first century A.D.

The *Periplus* is a sort of merchant-adventurer's guide to the Indian Ocean, and provides us with more detailed information than we are vouchsafed for 1,000 years afterwards. Voyages down the East African coast, known as Azania, were made to obtain aromatic gums from the region of Cape Guardafui, and chiefly ivory from what is now the Swahili coast. Here the chief town was called Rhapta; the site of this is not known, but it perhaps lies under the mud of the Rufiji delta. The mouth of this river lies opposite the island of Mafia, formerly known as Manfia or Manfisa, in which we may recognize Menouthias, the only island named in the *Periplus* and by Ptolemy. In the *Periplus* however, the description of the position of the island fits better with Pemba or Zanzibar; only one island being remembered, probably the name was applied to all.

Azania, we are told, is subject to Charibael (probably Karib'il, ruler of Himyar—south-west Arabia) and had long been under the domination of whichever was the most powerful state in Arabia. However the people of Mouza (the port of Mocha) control the southern Azanian coast under the authority of Charibael. Men from the ships sent from Mouza know the language of the inhabitants and intermarry with them. The natives are described as piratical and very tall, which suggests they may have been Kushitic; there is nothing in the description or on other grounds to indicate they were Negro or Bantu.

Weapons and implements of iron constitute the primary import, and suggest that the inhabitants did not know how to work iron. Glass vessels were imported also. Besides the ivory, tortoise-shell, rhinoceros horn and coconut oil were exported; these goods are still traded at the present day, and no doubt have been throughout the last 2,000 years. Slaves were mentioned as being taken from the horn of Africa, but not from the region further south. Nor indeed are slaves mentioned as an export of the East African coast until quite recent times, not attaining a large scale until the eighteenth century. There must, however, have been a considerable trade in early times for it to have been possible for the Zanj slaves to revolt with a large measure of success in Iraq in the ninth century.

After the time of the *Periplus* and Ptolemy (whose work was probably revised in the early fifth century) we have virtually no information about Azania, or the land of the Zanj as it was known to the Arabs, until the tenth century. It is true that there are numbers of local chronicles which profess to give an account of colonization carried out under the first caliphs of Islam, but none

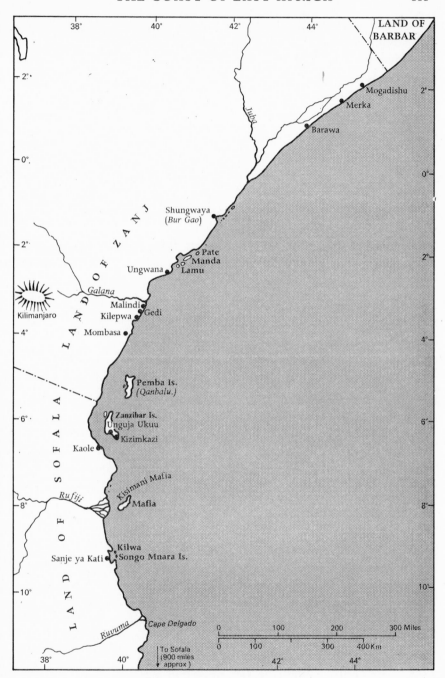

MAP 6. The East African Coast.

of these sources date back to before the nineteenth century. In all such literature there is a strong tendency to exaggerate the antiquity and illustriousness of one's forbears. 'Civilization' in Swahili is 'Ustaarabu', 'becoming like an Arab'; all local sources, early as well as recent, should be read bearing in mind that there is a tendency to over-emphasize the Arab element.

The Arab geographers provide us with a certain amount of information, but there continues to be extreme difficulty in identifying the places which they mention. Usually there is more than one reading, and in the Arabic script corruption, especially by the omission or misplacing of a *nukta* (dot) is very easy. Moreover, the interpretation is further complicated by the fact that most of the geographers believed, following Ptolemy, that the southern part of Africa trended round to the east, joining up with lands in the Far East. The land of Waqwaq for example, is sometimes thought of as being in Africa, sometimes as in Asia. There is also confusion between the islands of Indonesia and those off the south-eastern coast of Africa, which is possibly connected with the migration of Indonesians to Madagascar (and perhaps first to the mainland) which occurred in the early centuries of the Christian era.

There is also some information to be gained from Chinese sources concerning the East African coast, but that dating from before the fifteenth century is of little value and probably all learnt at second hand. In the first half of the fifteenth century, however, Chinese fleets sailed at least as far as the southern Somali coast, and traded there; the accounts they give of the towns there appear however to be very garbled.

The coast is usually divided by the geographers into three sections: that of Barbar (ending about Mogadishu), that of the Zanj, and the country of Sofala, whose northern boundary seems to have been in the region of the modern Pangani, between 5° and 6° S. Until the thirteenth century most of the settlements of the coast seem to have been pagan. The first Muslim towns appear to have been on the islands of Pemba and Zanzibar; in the tenth century Qanbalu (Pemba) had a mixed Muslim and pagan population. Barawa, Mombasa (referred to as the seat of the king of the Zanj) and Malindi as well as other unidentified towns on the mainland, are mentioned by al-Idrisi, writing about 1150, who indicates that they are all pagan. Mogadishu was probably developing at this time, for Yaqut 70 years later writes of it as the most important town on the coast, and the only one on the mainland which he states to have a Muslim population; the people are divided into clans each with its own chief. At the same time (c. 1220) we are told of a sultan in Pemba who is an Arab from Kufa (in lower Iraq); a bare mention is made of Kilwa. At the time of Ibn Battuta's visit in 1331 Mogadishu still seems to have been at least as important as Kilwa; it was ruled by a man with the title of Sheikh. Mombasa at this time appears to have been of comparatively little importance.

The Arab geographers tell us little of the racial characteristics of the Zanj. The original population lived by hunting and gathering, but though many groups of hunters probably survived until comparatively recently alongside other peoples (some are still in existence) they are not described by any of the early sources. It is generally accepted that the Bantu had arrived in the lands of the coast before the tenth century A.D. and this is supported by what appears to be a corruption of the Bantu root for king, and other Bantu words, in al-Mas'udi's account of the gold-producing country of Sofala and the Waqwaq. This, however, is difficult to reconcile with his statement that the Zanj are a type of Ethiopian (Ahabish) who have migrated southwards, and his description of them as cattle owners on a large scale who use oxen for riding and as a beast of burden. There is also some evidence that the Bantu who inhabited the Banadir coast before the arrival of the Galla (in turn displaced by the Somalis) were present at an equally early date. These Bantu, whose chief settlement was named Shungwaya, later spread south and west, and were the main ancestors of the north-eastern group of Bantu tribes, which includes among others, the numerous Kikuyu and Chagga, as well as various smaller tribes still living near the coast.

The Arab geographers write of the Zanj as being ruled by elected chiefs who had substantial bodies of armed men under

HUNT LIBRARY
CARNEGIE-MELLON UNIVERSITY

their control. They tell us also of the pagan preachers among them and their love of oratory. We have no other information about their social system.

Apart from recent compilations (the Chronicles of Pate and Lamu, the *Kitab az-Zunuj* and others) which it has been suggested are highly suspect, there exist only two historical sources derived from the coast itself. Both are versions of a Chronicle of the kings of Kilwa, which was set down probably between 1520 and 1530. One is a copy made in Zanzibar in the last century; the other is transmitted by the historian de Barros in the middle of the sixteenth century, together with other information which he apparently derived from a second source. On these have been constructed the received history of the coast. Derived from de Barros is the story of the Emozaydij, heretics from Arabia who settled on the East African coast, apparently in the eighth century; this immigration is uncorroborated, and the story is regarded as of doubtful authenticity. A further emigration, from al-Hasa on the Persian Gulf, is recorded by de Barros, but is considered to be a variant of the story of the coming of the Shirazi. The latter is presented in the Kilwa Chronicle as the main event of the history of the coast. The sultan of Shiraz, named Hasan or Husain, with his six sons, is related to have sailed to the African coast in seven ships, each of which stopped at a different place. The sultan himself is said to have disembarked in the Comoros, and a son named 'Ali at Kilwa, where he established himself. This Shirazi immigration has usually been interpreted as a movement of people from the Persian Gulf; the story cannot be related to the history of Shiraz and is certainly largely mythical. Based on regnal years, chiefly those given in de Barros' version, which records several more sultans than the Arabic version, the event has been assigned to the second half of the tenth century A.D. However, as a result of recent evidence from excavations at Kilwa, and a re-examination of the Chronicle, it appears probable that it should be really dated some 200 years later, perhaps as late as 1200. The writer also considers that the movement was rather of people from Mogadishu and the Banadir coast southwards; people whose remoter ancestors came from Persia and the Gulf, and hence already called themselves Shirazi.[1]

Mafia was at least as important a place as Kilwa at this time, and the sultans seem to have divided their time between the two islands. About the middle of the century there was fighting between Kilwa and the people of Shanga (probably the island of Sanje ya Kati), who twice deposed the sultan, but were finally vanquished.

Towards the end of the century there was a change of dynasty, recorded only in the Arabic version, and then only cursorily. But the archaeological evidence shows a marked change in culture, as we shall see; and it is very probable that there occurred a considerable immigration from Arab lands at this time. The succeeding years, covering the first quarter of the fourteenth century, were probably those during which Kilwa gained control of Sofala and the trade in gold, and also of Zanzibar and Pemba and parts of the mainland. This gold, obtained from the regions of Rhodesia with which we associate Zimbabwe and the Monomatapa, was from now on the foundation of Kilwa's wealth.[2]

The third ruler of this dynasty, al-Hasan ibn Sulaiman, was visited by the great Arab traveller, Ibn Battuta in A.D. 1331; the name he records, and that of his successor, agree with those given in the Chronicle. This invaluable confirmation ensures that the Chronicle from this time onwards is at least in outline accurate. But we learn little of value from its account of the remainder of the fourteenth and fifteenth centuries; we may note that the Great Mosque of Kilwa was restored during the reign of Sulaiman ibn Muhammad (c. 1421–42). In the latter part of the century there were numerous dynastic quarrels, in which the

[1] G. S. P. Freeman-Grenville, *The Mediaeval History of the Coast of Tanganyika*, Oxford, 1962, analyses the Kilwa Chronicle at length; the writer's proposed chronology is set out in 'The Shirazi Colonization of the East African Coast', *Journal of African History*, VI, No. 3 (1965). The latter serves as the basis of the historical summary now set out.

[2] This expansion, and the transformation of Kilwa from a town built of wood to one almost entirely of stone is ascribed in the Portuguese version of the Chronicle to two rulers not recorded in the Arabic who on the hitherto received chronology are held to have ruled in the middle of the twelfth century. The writer considers, however, that their names are a duplication of those of the beginning of the fourteenth century.

wazirs, who are first mentioned some decades before, took a prominent part. These dissensions facilitated the conquest by the Portuguese; in 1505 Sofala, Kilwa and also Mombasa were all overrun, and a fort, soon to be abandoned, built at Kilwa. Within a few years the Portuguese were dominant over all the important centres of the coast, which entered a period of economic and cultural decline which was particularly marked in the south.

It should not be thought that the dominance of Kilwa amounted to anything that could be called an empire, a term which has often been used. Up to the time of the establishment of the dynasty of Abu'l-Mawahib at the end of the thirteenth century, Kilwa, in association with Mafia, was just one trading town among many, though the most prosperous. After 1300 she controlled Sofala and at times the off-shore islands and parts of the mainland, especially of what is now Mozambique; but all the towns of about the position of the present Dar es Salaam were probably independent.

Local sources, however, tell us little that can be relied on about the early history of these towns. The story of the immigration of Syrian Arabs at the end of the seventh century in the reign of the caliph 'Abd al-Malik ibn Marwan recounted in more than one of these recent chronicles may well have a common mythical source; to these are ascribed the foundation of towns on the coast as far south as Kilwa and the Comoros. This cannot be credited, but there may have been some settlement of individuals or small groups as minorities on the pagan mainland. The only foreign source to indicate emigration tells us of two brothers who fled with their followers to the land of Zanj in the reign of the same caliph, but this account is also comparatively recent and its accuracy is suspect.

The most important and longest of the recent Chronicles is that of Pate, which treats mostly of the history of the Nabhani dynasty, derived from Oman, on the island of that name in the Lamu archipelago. This puts the establishment of the dynasty in A.H. 600 (A.D. 1203–4), a date that is certainly too high. Archaeological evidence shows that the town was non-existent or of little importance before the fourteenth century and the Nabhani may not have taken over from the preceding Batawi dynasty until about 1700. Accounts of the conquest by Pate of all the places of importance on the coast are wholly uncorroborated and are certainly mythical. The period of Pate's prosperity began in the latter part of the fifteenth century, growing after the arrival of the Portuguese.

The Chronicle of Lamu tells us little of that place before 1700, though we know from an Arabic source that it was in existence before 1383. The Chronicle of Mombasa tells us nothing of interest for the period with which we are concerned. As to the northern towns: there is evidence that there was a Sirafi community in Merka which it has been maintained arrived there at the time of, or before the partial destruction in about A.D. 976 of Siraf, the greatest port of the period in the Persian Gulf. Recent excavations at Siraf have, however, shown that the town continued to exist, though in decline, until much later.[1] At Mogadishu a record dating back to about 1700 tells us of the replacement of the original federation of tribes each under its own sheikh by a sultanate, the first ruler of which was Abu Bakr ibn Fakhr ad-Din, of South Arabian origin. That this change of system indeed occurred is confirmed by a comparison of the record of Yaqut with that of Ibn Battuta; it probably took place about the middle of the thirteenth century. By the time of the latter author the ruler already spoke 'Maqdashi' (?Somali) so that the immigrants seem to have already been assimilated to the earlier inhabitants. Otherwise the records of Mogadishu are remarkably meagre, considering the importance of the place.

Artefacts of Middle and Later Stone Age date have been found at a number of places on the coast; these no doubt are the relics of hunting, nomadic peoples. It is remarkable that no settlement sites are known which date to before the Islamic era; the pottery from every place which has yielded such has included imported Islamic wares. Were it not for the historical evidence,

[1] Interim reports on the excavations at Siraf are published by David Whitehouse in *Iran, Journal of the British Institute of Persian Studies*, VI (1968), 1–22 and VII (1969), 39–62.

one would equate the beginning of the Iron Age with the arrival of the first Muslim traders.

There have been a number of reported finds of Ptolemaic and Roman coins which have been adduced as material evidence of the trade of which the *Periplus* informs us. Most of these finds are unsatisfactorily documented. The most notable is a large collection from Port Durnford (Bur Gao) in the extreme south of the Somali coast. This is supposedly the site of Shungwaya, in the nuclear area of the north-eastern Bantu. The collection included coins from Ptolemy II onwards, the latest being of Egypt under Ottoman Turks, all apparently supposed to have been found in one location. Some doubt has been expressed about the accuracy of the reputed circumstances of finding;[1] and it is noteworthy that the discoverer made no mention of the coins in his original description of the site and what he found. A further group of coins recorded as having been dug up in a mound at Kiomoni near Tanga in 1896 has recently been traced by the writer in the Museum für Völkerkunde in Berlin and includes two coins of Roman Emperors (Constans and Carus), but the remaining four include two of Umayyad Caliphs and one probably Fatimid (11th century A.D.) so that it seems unlikely that the coins came to East Africa in the time of the Romans. The same is true of the Bur Gao find, even if this is genuine. A few sherds of Roman pottery would be more exciting than all these finds; so far the sites of the earliest trading settlements are quite unknown.[2]

Excavations have been carried out at numbers of sites on the coast, first by the pioneer archaeologist of this region, Mr. James Kirkman, since 1948, and subsequently, since 1958, by the writer. The results of this work enable us now to present a tolerably complete picture of the cultural development and the way of life of these towns, and to amplify, and in some cases propose modifications to, the historical records.

[1] Grottanelli, *Pescatori dell'Oceano Indiano* (Cremonese, Roma, 1945), Appendix III. No reference was made to the discovery of the coins in the original description of the journey concerned which took place in 1913, the find being referred to only in a different account written twenty-two years after the event. The question is examined by the present author in the appendix to 'An archaeological reconnaissance of the southern Somali coast', *Azania*, IV (1969), 115–130.

[2] A single small sherd from the basal level of Kisimani Mafia appears to be a Nabataean painted ware of the first centuries A.D., but all other material found at this site is Islamic.

The earliest site of importance to be examined is that of Manda, which lies at the northern coast of Kenya. Here recent excavations by the British Institute of History and Archaeology in East Africa have brought to light the remains of a town which was established in the ninth century A.D., and which was a place of much wealth from its inception. It has a long history, declining in later times; but we are here concerned only with the earliest period of the town.

The lowest strata are dated by the imported pottery; this is mostly Islamic but includes a small proportion of Chinese wares. The latter, including green-glazed Yüeh stoneware and white-glazed porcelain, are dated to the ninth and tenth centuries, and thus present evidence of the import of Chinese goods at a date much earlier than hitherto attested. Islamic and white tin-glazed earthenware bowls imitating the Chinese porcelain, are also found in these strata. The predominant Islamic glazed pottery consists however of large jars with incised and moulded decoration under a blue-green glaze, of a type whose origins go back to Sassanian and Parthian times, and which has been referred to as 'Sassanian-Islamic' ware. In addition to the glazed wares, a large proportion (about 15 per cent of the whole) of unglazed jars were imported; these are precisely similar to the vessels found in the recent excavations at the port of Siraf, on the eastern side of the Persian Gulf, near where these jars are thought to have been manufactured. The total proportion of imported wares, about 30 per cent of the whole, is higher than at any later site, and imported glass, much of which is similar to that from Siraf, is also comparatively common.

Building in stone was carried out at Manda, though the majority of houses were probably of wattle and daub. In addition to masonry of coral rubble in lime mortar, similar to that found in later periods, sea walls were constructed of massive blocks of coral, weighing up to a ton each, and fitted together without mortar. This type of construction has been observed at no other site.

Among the locally made pottery, the most characteristic type is a shallow bowl with carinated rim, decorated with grooves

9

and red paint or graphite. Lamps are of a triangular, boat-like type, while an imported example is blue-glazed and nearly circular in plan.

Massive bowl-shaped lumps of slag, apparently from the base of furnaces, attest the smelting of iron, probably on a considerable scale, at Manda. This may be related to the puzzling reference by al-Idrisi at a rather later date (twelfth century) to iron mines near 'Mulanda', which has usually been identified with Malindi, further to the south.

Other finds from Manda were few; glass beads were very rare indeed, but beads of marine shell, and, as at Kilwa, the grooved stones believed to have been used in their manufacture, were found.

It remains to consider the significance of Manda. It is evident that it maintained close trading connections with the Persian Gulf and probably with Siraf in particular. Though we have no direct evidence that there were Muslims in the town, the use of stone and lime mortar for building suggests that there was a substantial colony of immigrants, presumably of that faith. The very large amount of imports shows that its oversea trade was on a big scale. It is likely that its chief export was ivory; large numbers of elephants are present on the adjacent mainland to this day. Ivory is the most important of the products of the Zanj country mentioned by al-Mas'udi, and he mentions that the voyages made to this region were from Oman and Siraf. He himself sailed in a Sirafi ship to Qanbalu, the only place he mentions by name, and which was presumably even more important than Manda.

While Qanbalu (on Pemba island) was presumably the most important of the trading towns, its site has not been identified with certainty. It is, however, very probable that there was another important trading settlement of this period at Unguja Ukuu, 'Old Zanzibar', some 20 miles south of the present town. At this site quantities of sherds of the blue-glazed 'Sassanian-Islamic' pottery of the type described from Manda have been found, and a hoard of gold coins was accidentally excavated here a century ago. A dinar almost certainly from this hoard is dated the equivalent of A.D. 798, and was struck by Ja'far al-Barmaki, *wazir* of the caliph Harun ar-Rashid.

The lowest levels at Kilwa Kisiwani go back to the same period, but are very much poorer than the contemporary deposits at Manda. Extensive excavations have been carried out at this place, providing a cultural and stratigraphic conspectus extending from the earliest until recent times, which moreover can be related to the historical information given in the Kilwa Chronicle. The findings from Kilwa will therefore be described in some detail.

The site of the town of Kilwa, known as Quiloa to the Portuguese (which name is found on all except recent maps) lies on the north-western corner of Kilwa island, some 160 miles south of Dar es Salaam, facing onto the finest harbour of the coast. Where the town was later to rise was originally a low sandy expanse only a little above high water mark; now, by the accumulation of centuries of debris and fallen buildings the ground level is some 4 to 5 m. higher. On it are built the scattered houses of the present-day village, known as Kilwa Kisiwani.

About half the accumulated deposit at Kilwa dates from before the introduction of coins which is believed to mark the beginning of the Shirazi dynasty. This 'pre-Shirazi period' is believed to last from around A.D. 800 until the latter part of the twelfth century. The material culture during this long span is remarkably uniform, but on the basis of the introduction of certain new types of object it is divided into two phases, the second beginning about A.D. 1000 or a little earlier.

In the lowest strata occur sherds of the thick blue-glazed pottery of the type referred to above, and on this evidence the earliest remains are assigned to the ninth, or possibly the eighth, century A.D. Owing to the depth at which these lowest levels lie it has not been possible to examine a large area. The remains consist of debris cast out by people who lived largely on fish and shell-fish. No traces of structures other than post-holes dug into the sand have been found at this depth, and most of the post-holes are the relics of the bases of timbers of rather later structures, so the debris is either due to fishermen who dwelt in

light shelters, or the excavated areas are outside the main settlement of the time.

At a slightly higher level are the remains of the first wattle-and-
daub houses. These are rectangular, and probably similar in
character to those of the present day, with roofs of palm-fronds.
These were to remain almost the sole type of house until the
beginning of the fourteenth century. However, short lengths
of masonry wall, constructed of coral-stone, sometimes cut
roughly square and set in mud mortar in courses about 20 cm.
deep, do occur in strata assigned to the tenth century, and
dwellings may have been built of this material at a date as early
as this.

The characteristic pottery wares of this first period fall into
two classes: the red-burnished bowls on which food was no
doubt served, and the cooking-pots, commonly bag-shaped,
with decoration on the rim. These two wares continue in use
with little change until the latter part of the thirteenth century,
in the Shirazi period, and exemplify the cultural continuity of
this long span, though new types of pottery were added to the
repertoire. During the first phase of the pre-Shirazi period, up
to the eleventh century, the red-burnished bowls are commonly
decorated with patterns in graphite, sometimes very finely
executed, with pencil-thin lines; bands of a trellis pattern are the
favourite motif. Later, in the second phase the graphite decoration is almost absent (though to be revived in a different style in
the fourteenth century), but the most characteristic shape continues to be a bowl with a thickened, inturned rim. This type
of red-burnished bowl is found also as far afield as Pemba and in
the early levels at Gedi, south of Malindi, and at other sites in
Kenya. This is the only example of a locally made ware being
commonly used over a wide area, and almost certainly manufactured at more than one place. In subsequent periods each
zone had its own particular wares; even places as closely linked
as Kilwa and Mafia, separated by only 80 miles of sea, have
different types of pottery from the fourteenth century onwards,
and there was only a slight amount of interchange.

Apart from pottery, the commonest objects found on the

coastal sites are beads. In the 'pre-Shirazi' period at Kilwa, especially by the first phase, these are almost exclusively discs of shell, sometimes of the *Achatina* snail, sometimes of sea-shell. They range in diameter from 4 to 10 mm. Large numbers of grooved stone blocks are also found, and were apparently used for grinding smooth the edges of these beads, most but not all of which are so finished. These blocks are so plentiful as to suggest that the beads must have been manufactured for export; most of these grinders are of sandstone, but a few are of coral and occasionally a thick potsherd is used. Large (*c.* 8 cm) cigar-shaped beads were sometimes made in terracotta in the first phase.

Metal objects are no more uncommon than in later periods. Most are of iron, and include, from the first phase, fish-hooks. A few fragments of copper (rarely found at any period because of its value for reworking) have been found. Iron was smelted from the very earliest times, as is evidenced by both tuyères and slag. There is no iron ore in the modern sense known in these regions; probably ferricrete concretions which can be found on the mainland nearby were used.

What appears to be a handleless spoon, made from the dorsal part of a large cowrie shell, is a common object before about A.D. 1000. These were undoubtedly made locally, but it is of interest that similar spoons have been found in excavations in Madagascar. Money cowries are common throughout the pre-Shirazi period, and were no doubt collected to serve as trade goods. It is possible that they served as a sort of currency; it is notable that they became rare after the introduction of coinage.

Imports were very rare during the first phase of this period, but include glass vessels, which indeed are commoner in relation to the imported pottery than in later times. Sherds of the latter, however, are only of the order of 0.2 per cent of the whole assemblage. Besides the thick blue-glazed ware already mentioned, a ware with a similar yellow coloured body with a white glaze is found. All the fragments of these come from bowls; on some of the later ones (probably tenth century) the white is splashed with blue.

A fragment of slate-like stone on which Arabic letters have

been scratched attests that some at least of the inhabitants during the latter part of this phase were literate and hence no doubt Muslim, but it is probable that the great majority of the population was pagan.

The beginning of the second phase of the pre-Shirazi period is marked by the appearance of Islamic sgraffiato[1] ware as the characteristic import; it is thought that this occurred around A.D. 1000. There is however no cultural break, though the quality of imports increases. These now include a few steatite vessels, commonly finished by turning on the lathe, which seem to have been manufactured in Madagascar. New types of local pottery are added to the repertoire, and spindle whorls, virtually lacking in the earlier phase, begin to appear. Some of these are formed from a simple rubbed-down potsherd, others neatly made of clay with an incised design, commonly a star, on the upper face. They were fixed to the spindle by a hook of iron wire. The thread spun was probably of cotton, which we know from historical sources was grown on a considerable scale at a later period; no doubt it was also woven.

Within this period falls the earliest inscription on the coast. This famous monument, the only Kufic inscription in East Africa, is built into the mosque at Kizimkazi Dimbani at the southern end of Zanzibar island. It records the construction of a mosque by Sheikh as-Sayyid Abu Imran Musa ibn al-Hasan ibn Muhammad. The mosque in which it is incorporated was constructed in the eighteenth century, but on the foundations of an earlier building which was probably that built by Abu Imran Musa. The lower levels of the settlement site have yielded sgraffiato pottery, and are probably contemporary with the mosque. The inscription is dated 500 A.H. (A.D. 1107) and confirms that there were substantial Muslim settlements in the Zanzibar group of islands.

Oral traditions on the Tanzanian coast tell of a people called the Debuli who came, apparently in small numbers, before the

[1] A type of pottery in which the underglaze slip is partially cut away to a pattern. The glaze, applied subsequently runs into the incised lines; glaze colours are commonly variegated yellow-green and brown.

Shirazi. This name is probably connected with Daybul, on the Indus, the greatest port of Sind and the first to be conquered by the Arabs (in A.D. 711/12). It seems that though the main trading connections of the coast were with the Persian Gulf, some of the commerce was carried on, among others, by merchants from Daybul, who would in any case be expected to call at the ports of the north Indian Ocean on their way to Africa. It may be imagined that some of these merchants settled on the African coast, and would, together with other settlers, have provided a nucleus of Muslims at Kilwa and Mafia. Traditions of the Debuli are lacking on the Kenya coast, and are not mentioned in the Chronicles.

The close of the pre-Shirazi period is marked by the appearance of the first coins at Kilwa and at Kisimani Mafia, on the westernmost point of Mafia island. The earliest of these whose text can be certainly read are of copper with a diameter of the order of 2 cm., in which respect they resemble the later coins. They carry the name of ʿAli ibn al-Hasan written in one line on the obverse, with a rhyming phrase (Yathiku bi Mauliʾl-Minan, 'trusts in the Master of bounties') on the reverse. This pattern is followed in subsequent Kilwa coins, the reverse always expressing the reliance of the ruler on God.

These coins of ʿAli ibn al-Hasan have hitherto been ascribed to a sultan of that name who ruled towards the end of the fifteenth century, but recent discoveries make this attribution impossible. It is probable that he is to be identified with the founder of the Shirazi dynasty, whose name is variously given as ʿAli ibn al-Hasan or ʿAli ibn al-Husain.

At a still lower level than the coins described above, numbers of minute coins, mostly of copper but a very few of silver, have been found. These tiny pieces (those of copper weigh about 0·5 gm., those of silver less than 0·1 gm.) have superscriptions that cannot be read with certainty, but they are in the same style, and appear to carry the same text, as those certainly of ʿAli bin al-Hasan, though those of silver have only al-Hasan on the obverse. Their appearance is therefore thought to be contemporary with the establishment of the first dynasty of 'Shirazi' rulers. The span of this dynasty, thought to be from the latter part of the twelfth century until about 1300, is also a convenient archaeological era, its end being very clearly marked. Kilwa and Mafia were now certainly Muslim towns; there is some evidence that their rulers were of the Shi'a persuasion.

During this period the use of stone for building considerably increased, at least on the southern part of the coast. As was always the case, the stone used was coral, usually cut from the reefs out to sea at low tide. The masonry of this period is of roughly-cut blocks of stone, laid in courses and usually set in lime mortar. Stone was seldom used for dwellings, and no complete plan of a house has been recovered. The mosques conform to one type, with a flat stone and lime-concrete roof supported by wooden pillars, with doors at both the south end (opposite *gibla*, the direction of Mecca) and in the sides. The lime used was of a very high quality, burnt in pits in the ground, with tunnels running into them to induce draught—a more advanced system than that in use in Portuguese times or at the present day.

The earliest built graves are dated to the early part of this period, or the end of the preceding. They are solid stepped structures like an elongated pyramid, capped by a ridge of triangular section. They have only been found at Kilwa.

External trade increased considerably in this period. Chinese porcelain was imported on a significant scale for the first time, but was nevertheless rare in comparison with the fourteenth century and later. This should not, however, be thought to imply that the Chinese brought goods to these coasts. Though the Chinese ships are known to have reached as far as the region of Malindi in the fifteenth century this was an exceptional voyage. Merchandise would have been transhipped at least once and probably more, in Persian Gulf ports or on the west coast of India. Most of the glazed pottery continued to come from the Islamic world, and was still in the sgraffiato type, though declining in quality towards the end of the period.

There was at this time a greater interest in adornment of the person, and no doubt other refinements. Rods of copper, decorated with an incised design at the centre, were used to

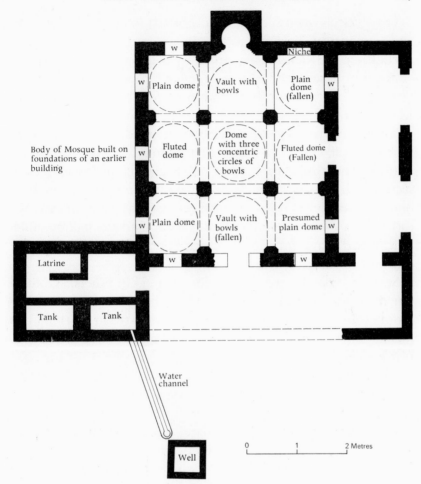

Body of Mosque built on
foundations of an earlier
building

FIG. 2. The small domed mosque at Kilwa.

apply black *kohl* (antimony) to the eyes.[1] Glass beads, and some
of semi-precious stones, began to be imported in quantity,
probably from India. These are predominantly of the 'wound'
type manufactured by winding a thin trail of hot glass round
a rod, and subsequently pressing into shape. The less attractive
cane beads, formed by snapping short lengths off a thin hollow
rod of glass and subsequently heating to round off the edges,
are rarer. Shell beads continued to be made during the first half
of this period, but manufacture had ceased before 1300.

[1] Similar rods have been found in medieval sites in Nubia and at Fostat (editor), and are
still used in some regions of the Orient at the present day (author).

Glass vessels continued to be imported; beside the large flasks and cylindrical beakers, little phials, some with moulded decoration, are found. They probably contained *kohl* and scents.

Steatite vessels, notably three-legged cooking vessels, were imported in larger numbers, and indicate substantial trade with Madagascar.

The same types of local pottery as were made earlier continued to be manufactured. Among new forms, the first lamps are notable. These are very shallow, nearly circular in shape, thick in section, with a simple pinched-out spout (sometimes more than one) for the wick. Ovens of burnt clay let into the floor (Swahili *gai*) were a new introduction, and were used for baking small unleavened loaves of millet or rice flour. Their use continued through all subsequent periods.

Spindle whorls are found in greater numbers. Conical crucibles, used for smelting or melting down copper are commonly found, and indicate a substantial industry in working this metal. Such crucibles have come to light at four sites from Dar es Salaam southwards.

The town at Kisimani Mafia, or Mafia as it was known, was at this time at the zenith of its prosperity, and probably of greater wealth than Kilwa. In Kenya the lowest levels of Gedi and Kilepwa are probably of this date; and Ungwana, near the mouth of the Tana River, whose origins go back earlier, was flourishing at this time. These sites have yielded red-burnished bowls with in-turned rims, as found further south, but other types of local pottery are different. At Ungwana, thin burnt bricks were used in building, laid over plastered rubble foundations. This, and a single brick found at Mafia and another at Manda, attest a mode of construction unknown at any other period.

Much must be awaiting discovery on the Somali coast, notably at the site of Shungwaya and at Mogadishu. At the latter place, three standing structures of the thirteenth century survive. Two of these are cylindrical towers which served as the minarets of mosques—a feature not otherwise found until the nineteenth century. Of these one, incorporated in the Friday

Mosque, rebuilt much later, is dated by an inscription to the equivalent of A.D. 1238. The third building is the mosque of Fakhr ad-Din, the main part of which seems to date from this period and an inscription incorporated in the (later) *mihrab*[1] dates from A.D. 1269. It is quite different in style from the earliest mosques of the Kilwa region, and relates rather to the architecture of the succeeding dynasty at that place. Notable also are two inscriptions mentioning persons from Persia, one dated the equivalent of A.D. 1217 on the grave of a man from Naysabur in Khurasan, and one of A.D. 1268-9 set up by a man from Shiraz. These are the only known inscriptions of Persians and lend support to the view that people of such origin first settled on the Banadir coast; some of their descendants, no doubt mixed with local blood, emigrating to places further south.

The turn of the thirteenth-fourteenth century is marked by a break in the cultural tradition, primarily on the southern part of the coast. This is most marked in the architecture, a wholly new style being introduced, but there is also a break in the local pottery and a greater diversity of material culture, with a very marked increase of imports of Chinese porcelain.

It is probable that this new era is related to the new dynasty of Abu'l-Mawahib at Kilwa, which the Arabic version of the Chronicle tells us was established at the end of the thirteenth century. It is likely also that it was at this time that Kilwa gained control of the port of Sofala, near the present Beira, and so acquired a monopoly in the gold trade. There are grounds for believing that this new dynasty and the new architectural elements are related to the arrival of immigrants from south-western Arabia.

The new order is dramatically exemplified by the great palace at Kilwa known as Husuni Kubwa. This huge structure, covering two acres and having well over a hundred rooms, combines the residence of the sultan with a great commercial establishment, nearly half the total area being given over to store rooms. Built outside the town—it is about a mile distant from the centre—it gives the impression of being a colonial establishment—a ruler

---

[1] The apse-like projection pointing towards Mecca.

isolated from his subjects, trading on a large scale on his own account. It was not, however, inhabited for long; on its abandonment the ruler presumably began to live in the town—a move which we may associate with the integration of immigrant people with the pre-existing inhabitants.

The residential part of Husuni Kubwa is arranged on an axial plan, and consists essentially of a number of dwellings disposed around sunken courtyards. Each dwelling is founded on a basic plan of two long narrow rooms, one behind the other, fronting on the court, with small bedrooms to the rear, an arrangement of rooms which was to be the foundation of the plan of houses on the coast. New elements and techniques include the use of domes and vaults and carved decorative stone blocks. The octagonal bathing pool, each side with an inset apse provided with steps, is an exotic form not later imitated. Husuni Ndogo, close to and probably contemporary with Husuni Kubwa, consists of a massive enclosure wall provided with towers, and is similarly unique. Monolithic pillars were used in the Great Mosque at Kilwa which was greatly extended at this time. Most of these elements, and indeed the general plan of the Husuni buildings, owe their inspiration to models in Arab lands, and the builder must have learnt his trade in those parts. The inscriptions from Husuni Kubwa, in Arabic and cut in stone, show a very high standard of workmanship, and impeccable grammar.

The fourteenth century saw an extended use of stone masonry not only at Kilwa but also on the Kenya coast, where the house plan follows that described above. The masonry itself is of the random rubble type, with finer coral stone for door jambs and decorative work; the coursed masonry of the earlier period is seldom if ever found.

The earliest 'panel tombs' date from this period. These are large graves, often designed to accommodate several interments; the face of the eastern end is divided into a number of plastered panels by cut stone frames. Many of these tombs, probably those of men, are surmounted by a tall pillar at the east, by reason of which they have also been called 'pillar tombs'. With a single exception, these tombs are only found north of the region of Dar es Salaam; no built tombs of the period are known in the Kilwa region. The significance of these facts is not known.

The imported pottery of this period is pre-eminently Chinese celadon of the Yüan and early Ming dynasties. The favourite was the small bowl with lotus petals carved on the exterior. A very little Chinese blue-and-white ware was imported in the fourteenth century, notably the large 'Mei-Ping' jars; Chinese stoneware, usually with incised decoration under the greeny-brown glaze, was also imported. The characteristic Islamic pottery is a poor-quality ware with a matt yellow glaze decorated with linear designs in black; this may have been made in Aden. It is common on the Kenya coast, but is rare (as are all Islamic wares in this period) on the southern part of the coast.

The locally made pottery is very diverse at this period. At Kilwa the most characteristic ware has a raised decoration of bands and strips; another ware, apparently locally made, was thrown on the wheel. On the Kenya coast the typical form is a carinated cooking pot with incised decoration on the upper part, a form which persists later. Lamps are common; those in the Kilwa area have a vertical side and a projecting spout, while on the Kenya coast they are of a plain boat shape. Spindle whorls of this period are plain discs of terracotta, without decoration.

Glass beads were imported in large numbers, the proportion of the cane type to the wound variety increasing with time. Beads of aragonite (cut from the giant clam) were made locally.

Four of the early sultans of the new dynasty at Kilwa minted coins, two of them in large numbers. These coins, however, did not circulate outside the region of Kilwa and Mafia. The only other coins known to have been minted at this period were struck in Mogadishu, in very small numbers; a single example there carries a date (the equivalent of A.D. 1322)—the only example of a dated East African coin before recent times.

There seems to have been some decline in the prosperity of Kilwa in the latter part of the fourteenth century, and with one doubtful exception none of the sultans of the time, nor of the following century, minted coins. There was, however, a revival of building work in the first half of the fifteenth century, and on the Kenya coast this was the time of greatest wealth. The architecture of the coast in this century displays a considerable degree of uniformity, and we can form a good idea of the aspect of a town at this period from Songo Mnara, six miles south of Kilwa, and from Gedi, a little to the south of Malindi, a large part of which has been excavated by J. S. Kirkman. Though not towns of the first importance, many houses have survived at these places. Both owe their preservation to the fact that since their abandonment there has never been a substantial settlement in their vicinity; elsewhere the stone has mostly been robbed, only the mosques being spared. The houses were built very close to one another, often sharing a party wall and sometimes linked together, suggesting a family relationship between the occupiers. The blocks of buildings were separated by very narrow lanes, though often there were gardens behind. The houses for preference faced north; or, if this was not possible, to the east; their courtyards being on one of these sides. They were of one storey, except in the largest towns, up to three being found at Kilwa. Roofs were flat, of stone laid on mangrove poles, usually squared; the weight of these massive roofs and the strength of the timbers restricted the width of the rooms, which is 8 ft. or a little less. In plan, the houses followed that established in the previous century. The main entrances into the courtyard of the larger houses were impressive, and in the Kilwa area ornamented with borders of recessed orders of cut stone, sometimes with herring-bone ornament—the commonest decorative motif at this period, employed also to frame the *mihrabs* of mosques. In houses in the Kilwa area there was usually a private retiring chamber set at right angles to the other rooms. At least one latrine, well constructed in cut stone was included in each house, with an adjoining 'bidet' for ablutions. Houses at Gedi were also provided with a special compartment for cooling water jars.

There were usually no windows, except in the façade facing

the courtyard, so the inner rooms must have been dark, but with their thick ceilings and walls (the latter usually a cubit of about 19 inches in width) would have been cool. The walls were plastered and never painted. Decoration of any sort was sparing. Ornamental niches in cut stone were on occasions set in walls or on either side of doorways, which were often beautifully assembled of cut coral. Some of the main rooms were decorated with either hangings, or with carved wooden friezes, as in the previous period, as is attested by rows of holes for pegs for suspension. But the decorative motifs in cut stone found in the previous century are almost lacking. Their place was to some extent taken by glazed bowls of Persian and Chinese wares which were inset in masonry, notably in the vaulted roofs (only found in the Kilwa area) of the private retiring chamber.

Each settlement had its congregational mosque (Jamiʻ) where the community assembled on Fridays. The larger towns had several smaller mosques in addition. All follow the same plan, a roofed rectangular hall, divided into aisles by rows of masonry pillars, with an area for ablutions to the south or east, and usually one or more side rooms, often added. In the Kilwa area the roof is usually domed, or barrel-vaulted, but the vaults are constructed wholly in lime concrete in contrast to the stone voussoirs with which the vaults of the fourteenth century were lined. Sometimes the vaults are decorated with inset bowls. Elsewhere the roofs were in almost all cases flat. Ornament is almost confined to the *mihrab*, which has a pointed arch executed in recessed orders, resting on a square capital which surmounts the supporting jambs. The whole is surrounded by a rectangular projecting frame, often with lamp niches in the pilasters which form its sides, and sometimes with bowls set in the spandrels.

The moveable objects of the period show changes in fashion rather than a drastic break. The import of Chinese porcelain continued, and in even greater volume; blue-and-white ware now equals celadon in quantity, almost entirely in the form of rather small food bowls, while celadon was pre-eminently the ware for large bowls and covered jars. At Kilwa the porcelain exceeds in volume the Islamic glazed wares; the latter consist almost entirely of bowls with a plain blue or green glaze, which was used in quantity everywhere on the coast. The better, decorated, Persian wares were imported primarily for the decoration of buildings, as has been described.

On the Kenya coast the first eating-bowls appear among the local pottery, showing that food was served, rather than eaten straight from the pot. Such bowls are found much earlier at Kilwa, but in the fifteenth century small bowls with ring bases, whose shape is probably copied from imported examples became common, and indicate that each of the company, at least in the middle and upper ranks had his own food-bowl. These bowls were painted with designs in red—the only painted pottery ware known on the coast. Red-burnished ware became common again; cooking pots were ornamented with diagonal weals worked up on the surface, sometimes very finely done. Portable stoves were introduced for the first time. These are vessels provided with 'horns' on which the cooking pot stood, charcoal being placed within the stove; though found both in the north and south, the forms are different. So also are the forms of the lamps, which in the Kilwa area have almost completely covered-in tops, while in the north they continue to have the basic boat shape.

Beads of this period are almost entirely of the cane variety; Indian red was the colour preferred in the south, green in the north. Massive bicones of aragonite up to 3 inches in diameter and 9 oz. in weight are common in the south, and seem to have been used as beads, perhaps as anklets. Small plugs of aragonite and discs of terracotta were probably used as ear- or lip-plugs.

Chinese coins were imported in small numbers in this period and in the previous century, apparently for use as ornaments; they are usually of far earlier date than the context in which they are found. The earlier local coinage continued to circulate at Kilwa; it may be that the old dies remained in use. Coins seem to have been minted in Zanzibar in this century, as also in large quantities at Mogadishu; considerable numbers from the latter mint circulated at Kilwa. Elsewhere on the coast all transactions must have been by barter; at Gedi cowries were used for this purpose, or for external trade.

Such are the bare bones of the archaeological picture. We can supplement it from two eye-witness accounts. Ibn Battuta early in the fourteenth century describes Mogadishu as a town of enormous size living by trade, with many rich merchants. He writes of a curious system under which one of these men would entertain any visiting merchant, who could only buy and sell through his host. The town was famous for its woven fabrics, which were exported widely. A highly developed court life revolved round the Sheikh, as the ruler was entitled. When Ibn Battuta went to the mosque in his presence, he was brought special clothes to wear. The Sheikh walked through the town with a four-tiered canopy or parasol of silk carried over him, and accompanied by a band of drums, trumpets and pipes. The people were obese, from eating to excess. He describes a meal brought to him from the Sheikh: rice cooked in ghee with a seasoned sauce of meat and vegetables over it, and, as side dishes, bananas cooked in fresh milk; also ginger, peppers and mangoes in sour milk.

Kilwa sounds from Ibn Battuta's description to have been rather smaller than Mogadishu. He says that it is built entirely of wood, though this cannot be altogether correct; he also says that it is on the coast, and mentions no island, so his memory was in any case here at fault. He is most struck by the piety of the sultan, who was being visited by numbers of ships from Hijaz. These descendants of the Prophet Muhammad were being maintained by the sultan out of booty taken in raiding expeditions against the pagan Zanj of the interior. The Zanj, at least those of Kilwa itself, tattooed their faces, as do the Makua and Makonde at the present day, though it seems unlikely that these tribes were in the area of Kilwa at the time.

At the beginning of the sixteenth century, the Portuguese were considerably impressed with what they found in the towns of the coast. They were most struck with the luxury of the adornment of the upper classes. Clothes were of rich silk as well as cotton, though slaves wore only a loin cloth; we read of much jewellery of gold and silver, earrings and bangles for both arms and legs, none of which have come down to us. We learn more of their agriculture; millet and rice were the grain crops, and we know from another source that rice was actually exported to Aden, and so must have been obtained in quantity from the mainland. Oranges, lemons, pomegranates and Indian figs as well as onions and other vegetables were grown in gardens watered from wells. Fat-tailed sheep, goats, cattle and hens were raised; of course fish also formed a large part of the diet. Bees were kept in cylindrical hives hanging from trees, much as on the mainland at the present day. The boats of the coast ran up to about 50 tons, built with planks sewn with coir cords and with matting sails. These vessels were evidently of the *mtepe* type in use until recently, and whose ancestry goes back to the time of the *Periplus*.

The population of Mombasa in 1505 is put at more than 10,000. Contemporary estimates for Kilwa vary between 4,000 and 12,000; it had probably been greater a century and a half earlier. The Portuguese distinguished white and black Moors (Muslims) and Africans; the governing class appears to have been the Swahili 'black Moors'. Indian traders seem to have been very few. The women were kept closely confined to their houses, and we are told were ill-treated, which led to a remarkable incident at Kilwa in 1502, many of them attempting to leave with the Portuguese ships and to become Christians.

In conclusion, an attempt should be made to evaluate the significance of the society which flourished on the eastern coast. There is little doubt that this civilization, at its zenith in the fourteenth century, was the highest in the material sense that has existed until recent times in Black Africa. How far it really belonged to that continent has been much argued, and with little perception. The impetus came from overseas—as indeed is the case with various other civilizations. It was primarily an Islamic culture, and a mercantile society—we may recall at this point that the Prophet Muhammad himself was a merchant. This does not mean to say that it was Arab; the immigrants were probably few in number, and intermarrying with the native

African women and those already of mixed blood, their stock was rapidly integrated with the local people. Probably in the second generation and certainly by the third they would have abandoned their spoken language for Swahili, though retaining Arabic for writing.[1] Some elements of the African culture survived and were incorporated in the whole, but always secondary to the Islamic framework. Materially, and especially in the architecture, the people of the coast evolved a civilization that was in many respects peculiar to themselves, a civilization which it is best to refer to as early Swahili. Because of the prestige of Arab or Persian ancestors, they tended to exaggerate the importance of these in their lineage, and to build up falsely illustrious myths about their forebears. Hardly anything is recorded about the African aspect of their ancestry.

At the same time the impact of this civilization on most of the mainland coast was slight, and on the interior none at all. The inhabitants of the hinterland were considered ignorant, *kafir*, without the faith; people from whom if possible one protected oneself by a healthy stretch of water. Trade with the pagan Zanj certainly must have taken place, but the goods (mostly ivory, apart from the gold from Sofala) must have been brought by them to the coast. There was a trade route from lake Nyasa to Kilwa in the early seventeenth century, which may well have been used by some Muslims, and considerable penetration took place further south; but otherwise it is unlikely that any Muslims went into the interior, save on warlike raids, dignified by Ibn Battuta as *Jihad*, holy war. Their religion never penetrated beyond the shore itself of the mainland, nor did their impressive skills in building have any influence on the hinterland. Buildings in stone and the burning of lime for mortar was unknown even five miles from the coast.

We should picture this civilization as a remote outpost of Islam, looking for its spiritual inspiration to the homeland of its religion, its authors building up a society and a culture that

---

[1] The Arabic script was also adapted for writing Swahili; it is uncertain when this was first done, but the earliest documents in Swahili which have survived date from the early eighteenth century.

owned much that was individual to itself; scornful of their pagan neighbours, but willing to compromise with them in the interest of profit, appreciating the luxuries of life, but contributing so far as we know nothing to the advancement of science or learning.

SELECT BIBLIOGRAPHY

History:

Gervase Mathew, 'The East African Coast until the Coming of the Portuguese', Chapter IV in Roland Oliver & Gervase Mathew *History of East Africa*, Vol. I (Oxford, 1963).

G. S. P. Freeman-Grenville, *The Medieval History of the Coast of Tanganyika*, Oxford, 1962.

The above set out the received history of the Coast.

The following article proposes considerable modifications to the history and chronology:

Neville Chittick, 'The "Shirazi" Colonization of the East African Coast', *Journal of African History*, VI, 3 (1965), 275–94.

Archaeology:

Neville Chittick, 'Kisimani Mafia', Occasional Paper No. 1 of the Antiquities Division (Tanganyika, 1961).

Neville Chittick, 'Kilwa: a Preliminary Report', *Azania*, I, 1–36.

Neville Chittick, 'Discoveries in the Lamu Archipelago', *Azania*, II, 37–68.

Peter S. Garlake, *The Early Islamic Architecture of the East African Coast* (London, 1966).

J. S. Kirkman, *The Arab City of Gedi: Excavations at the Great Mosque* (London, 1954).

J. S. Kirkman, *Gedi—the Palace* (The Hague, 1963).

J. S. Kirkman, *Men and Monuments on the East African Coast* (London, 1964).

J. S. Kirkman, *Ungwana on the Tana* (The Hague, 1966).

J. S. Kirkman, 'The Tomb of the Dated Inscription at Gedi', Occasional Paper No. 14 of the Royal Anthropological Institute (London, 1960).

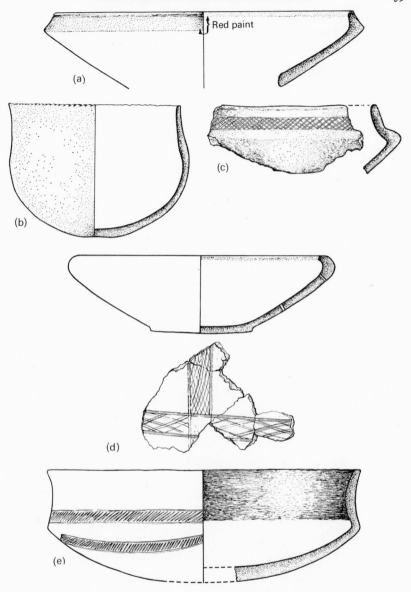

FIG. 3. (a) Bowl from Manda, ninth century. (b) Cooking pot from Kilwa. Type common in ninth/tenth centuries. (c) Fragment of carinated bowl from Kilwa. Type common in twelfth/thirteenth centuries. (d) Red burnished food bowl with graphite on rim; *below*, graphite decoration within base of similar bowl. Typically eleventh/twelfth centuries, from Kilwa. (e) Carinated bowl with incised decoration, graphite within rim, fourteenth century, from Kilwa.

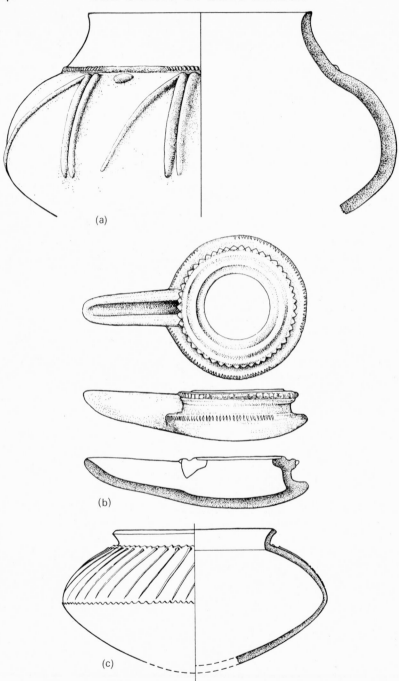

FIG. 4. (a) Jar with raised decoration, from Kilwa, fourteenth century. (b) Lamp from Kisimani Mafia, fourteenth century. (c) Wealed-ware cooking pot, fine example of type common in the fifteen/sixteenth centuries.

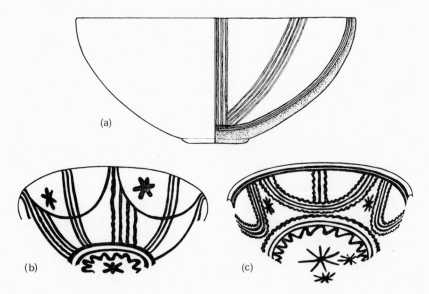

FIG. 5. Food bowls decorated in red paint, of type typical of fifteenth/sixteenth centuries, from Kilwa. (a) Shows the usual shape and commonest design, (b) and (c) less usual designs from the interior of such bowls.

6

THE INTERIOR OF EAST AFRICA

by

J. E. G. Sutton

THE view that iron must have diffused from the north, and in particular from Meroe on the Middle Nile—'the Birmingham of Africa', or variations thereon that have been quoted or misquoted—is commonly repeated in historical and archaeological works, both specialist and general, on eastern and southern Africa. The most detailed attempt to trace the line of diffusion has been Wainwright's. While admitting to being speculative, he postulated alternative routes from Meroe to Lake Victoria, the one to the west of the White Nile, the other to the east along the edge of the Ethiopian highlands. From Lake Victoria he argued further diffusion within East Africa.[1] Other writers, similarly conscious of the lack of firm evidence in the intervening regions, have suggested less direct routes of diffusion from Meroe, notably westwards to the region of Lake Chad or the 'Nok culture' of central Nigeria, and thence south-eastwards round or through the Congo forest to Uganda.[2] Now, as more Early-Iron-Age material is discovered both in East Africa and adjacent territories, and as more radio-carbon dates become available, the problem can be viewed more objectively, and the presumption of diffusion from Meroe is being seriously

[1] G. A. Wainwright, 'The Diffusion of -uma as a Name for Iron', Uganda Journal, XVIII (1954), 113–36. This article contains a wealth of historical, archaeological, ethnographic and linguistic information, but much of it is used uncritically.

[2] For example, S. M. Cole, The Prehistory of East Africa, 2nd ed. (1963), p. 301; B. M. Fagan, Southern Africa during the Iron Age (1965), pp. 48–9; M. Posnansky, Prelude to East African History (1966), pp. 87–90.

questioned.[1] Indeed, it begins to look as if much of East Africa may have obtained its first iron tools and iron-working from a southerly or westerly direction rather than a northerly one. The final picture will doubtless be more complex: it will not be a question of whether iron first arrived in East Africa from Meroe or the Zambezi, from West Africa, Ethiopia or the Indian Ocean, but of recognizing a combination of broad fronts.[2] But more than that: the obsession with origins becomes increasingly futile. More important is it to trace—as far as present evidence will allow—the processes by which East African peoples adopted an iron technology, and to discern the consequent economic and social effects.

The problem is complicated by the natural diversity of East Africa—the contrasts between the hot, dry plains of northern Kenya, and the lush margins of Lake Victoria; between the cool highlands with their montane forests and rolling grasslands, and the medium-altitude woodland-savannas that cover large parts of Tanzania. Each type of terrain has throughout the ages made different demands on human adaptation and settlement. Hence, culturally, economically and demographically, as well as historically and archaeologically, East Africa does not form a single unit. Some southern and western regions have much in common with Zambia and adjacent countries; whereas northern Uganda connects with the southern Sudan, and northern Kenya with the Ethiopian highlands and the plains of the Horn. The coast, moreover, has long been in contact with other lands bordering the Indian Ocean. This diversity is further borne out by the linguistic map, showing Bantu languages covering the south, the west and the coast, while in the north various Nilotic- and Cushitic-speaking groups predominate.[3] Whereas Bantu languages would have penetrated East Africa from westerly,

---

[1] R. Oliver, 'The Problem of the Bantu Expansion', *Journal of African History*, VII (1966), 361–76; J. E. G. Sutton, 'The Settlement of East Africa', in B. A. Ogot and J. A. Kieran (eds.), *Zamani: A Survey of East African History* (1968). See also M. Posnansky, 'Bantu Genesis—Archaeological Reflexions', *Journal of African History*, IX (1968), 11–22.

[2] Ethnographic evidence that might bear on the problem of the origins of East African iron-working is briefly discussed at the end of this chapter.

[3] J. H. Greenberg, *Languages of Africa* (1963); Sutton, in Ogot and Kieran, op. cit.

south-westerly and even southerly directions,[1] Cushitic languages have their centre of origin in Ethiopia, Nilotic languages
in the southern Sudan or the western edges of the Ethiopian
massif. One of the most interesting aspects of the East African
Iron Age is the acculturation and assimilation that has been
taking place between these various linguistic groups.

To understand this it is necessary to look back beyond the Iron
Age. More important than the coming of iron as a technological
change was the economic one, in which dependence on hunting,
fishing and gathering was supplanted or supplemented by food-
production, that is animal-husbandry and agriculture. In the
countries to the west and south of East Africa these two changes
went essentially hand in hand, the first food-producers being also
the first iron-workers. By contrast, in some parts of East Africa,
notably the highlands and rift valley of Kenya and northern
Tanzania, cattle and goats or sheep were being herded and types
of millet were presumably being sown and reaped during the
last one or two thousand years of the Late Stone Age. Evidence
for this comes from a large number of burials with their grave-
goods and a few occupation sites, some of them in rockshelters,
containing bones of domestic animals. Except for gourds, no
remains of cultivated vegetables have been found so far: however, the numerous grindstones and pestles, stone bowls and
pots, and on some sites ground stone axes, make it highly
probable that these people were cultivating grains. For sharp
tools, obsidian was worked by techniques derived partly from
the Kenya Capsian industries. The dating limits of this early
food-production are not precisely known, but so far there are
four radio-carbon dates in the early part of the first millennium
B.C. Skeletal remains indicate that these early herders and
farmers were mostly of Caucasoid physical type. They are
believed to have been Cushitic-speakers expanding from the
Ethiopian highlands.[2] Some of the more pastoral groups would

---

[1] See Oliver, art. cit.

[2] The arguments for this view are outlined in my article, 'The Archaeology and Early
Peoples of the Highlands of Kenya and Northern Tanzania', *Azania*, I (1966), 37–57; and
a paper to the Sixth Panafrican Congress on Prehistory, 1967, 'The Eastern African
"Neolithic" ' (publication forthcoming).

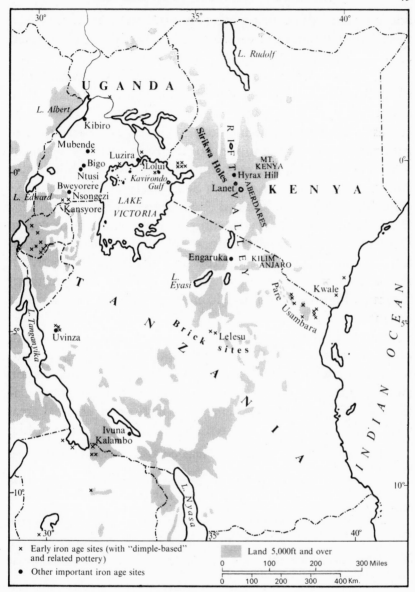

MAP 7. East Africa.

have occupied also the plains of northern and eastern Kenya. But neither in the plains nor in the highlands was food-production pursued to the exclusion of hunting, for bones of wild and domestic animals occur together on some sites. Maybe, groups specializing in hunting lived alongside others that concentrated on cultivating and herding.

The pottery of these Late-Stone-Age food-producers is quite varied, consisting of both coarse and fine wares. The shapes are always open-mouthed with simple rims. The decoration includes lines of dots and incisions, grooved and herring-bone patterns and filled-in triangles. For the most part this pottery is what has been called 'Kenya highlands Class A',[1] but it also embraces the early pottery from Site I at Hyrax Hill, Nakuru,[2] originally assigned to 'Class B'.[3] A suggestion that this pottery from Hyrax Hill can be compared with some Iron-Age ware in northern Malawi does not appear convincing.[4] In fact, it is difficult to see meaningful stylistic connections between the Late-Stone-Age pottery of the Kenya and northern Tanzania highlands and any Iron-Age pottery either local or distant.

There is little indication that food-production extended into other regions of East Africa before the Iron Age, either into southern or western Tanzania or into the Lake Victoria region and Uganda. The reasons for this are unclear, but lack of population pressure must be one. The more fertile and wooded areas would have been less attractive to people with a pastoral bias

[1] J. E. G. Sutton, 'A Review of Pottery from the Kenya Highlands', *South African Archaeological Bulletin*, XIX (1964), 27–35.

One of the best collections of this late stone age pottery comes from the cremated burials in the Njoro River Cave—M. D. and L. S. B. Leakey, *Excavations at the Njoro River Cave* (1950).

[2] M. D. Leakey, 'Report on the Excavations at Hyrax Hill, Nakuru', *Transactions of the Royal Society of South Africa*, XXX (1945), 302–12.

[3] Sutton, art. cit., pp. 29–30. The other 'Class B' pottery—the internally scored basket-decorated vessels (sometimes known as 'Gumban A')—are probably not connected and may be modern: see J. Brown, *Azania*, I (1966), 71–2.

While 'Class B' will have to be abandoned, Classes 'A' and 'C' apear to remain valid categories in the western highlands and rift valley of Kenya. 'A' is a very general class comprising the pottery found on most early pastoral-agricultural Late-Stone-Age sites; whereas 'C' belongs to 'Sirikwa holes' and some other Iron-Age sites of the second millennium A.D., and seems to be connected with Kalenjin-speaking populations. These are discussed below.

[4] K. R. Robinson, 'A Preliminary Report on the Recent Archaeology of Ngonde, Northern Malawi', *Journal of African History*, VII (1966), 187; and, B. Sandelowsky, 'The Iron Age of Northern Malawi: Recent Work', *Azania*, III (1968), 131.

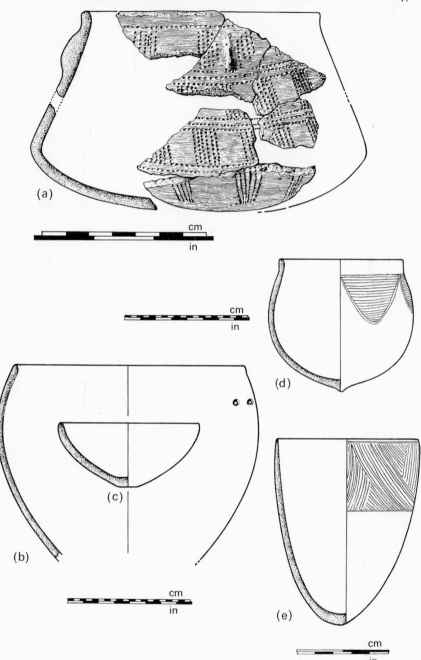

FIG. 6. Late-Stone-Age pottery from the Kenya highlands. (a)–(d) Njoro River Cave; (e) Hyrax Hill (site I).

and lacking iron axes, iron hoes and suitable crops like bananas. Elsewhere, shortage of good grass or the presence of tse-tse fly may have discouraged expansion. However, the negative archaeological evidence does not rule out the possibility of some extension from northern Tanzania into the southern highlands, or similarly up the Nile into northern and even western Uganda. Both regions possess fair rainfall and good grazing that might have attracted early grain-agriculturalists and stock-raisers. Linguistic evidence might be adduced to support these hypotheses.[1]

Nevertheless, it is certain that large parts of East Africa remained sparsely populated by hunter-gatherers until the Iron Age; and indeed, that the use of iron and the food-producing techniques associated with it spread very unevenly through East Africa. Whereas in some areas agricultural iron-using groups were settled by the middle of the first millennium A.D., various bands of hunter-gatherers have persisted till very recently, even to the present day, generally without metals, save for the odd iron tool or arrow-head obtained by exchange. Some have obtained pots in the same way, or have borrowed the art of potting from food-producing neighbours. But food-production, especially agriculture, can support larger populations whose tendency is to expand in search of new lands. Hunter-gatherers are thus placed at an economic and social disadvantage, and their numbers are now exceedingly small. Those who have not been absorbed within food-producing societies either maintain a symbiotic relationship or have been forced into those types of country which are least attractive for cultivation or herding. Nevertheless, skill and prowess in hunting have continued to be respected by most East Africans; and the noble hunter figures frequently in the myths of origin of chiefdoms in Tanzania and of the interlacustrine kingdoms. Many present-day peoples, moreover, appreciate a variety of wild foods if they can be obtained — fruits and vegetables, honey, game-meat and fish, both from the

---

[1] C. Ehret, 'Cattle-keeping and Milking in Eastern and Southern African History: The Linguistic Evidence', *Journal of African History*, VIII (1967), 1–17; Sutton, 'The Eastern African "Neolithic".

sea and from inland waters.[1] Apart from fish, only very rarely do such foods provide a substantial part of the diet.

Though numerically insignificant, latter-day hunter-gatherers are important historically. Some of them appear to be remnants of populations that inhabited East Africa before the beginnings of food-production. There is fairly good evidence that people of Bushman-type once occupied much of the southern and central regions. Firstly, Bushmanoid features have been noted in a few of the Late-Stone-Age skeletons from northern Tanzania and Kenya, as well as from shell-mounds on the eastern shores of Lake Victoria which probably overlap with the Iron Age.[2] Secondly, the Sandawe presently living in north-central Tanzania speak a Khoisan language which relates them to the Bushmen and Hottentots of southern Africa;[3] and, while essentially Negroid, some observers detect Bushmanoid traits in this tribe.[4] The Hadza (or Tindiga), further north by Lake Eyasi, may be a similar remnant, but there is some dispute on whether their language should be classified as Khoisan or Afroasiatic.[5] Whereas the Hadza continue to live as hunters and gatherers, the Sandawe have mostly changed to agriculture and stock-raising in this century. Their country is quite fertile, and there is archaeological evidence that it has been inhabited by agricultural peoples at certain periods in the past, notably in the Early Iron Age.[6] It also appears from recent excavations in rock-

[1] This remark might be qualified by noticing the existence of prohibitions against various wild animal and vegetable foods, which are doubtless of great socio-historical significance. Some of them presumably reflect the cultivator's or pastoralist's deep-rooted contempt for people who live by trapping, foraging, collecting or hunting. The Masai herdsmen, for instance, despise not only vegetables, whether wild or cultivated, but also game-meat, although their country abounds in it. The small bands of hunters in Masailand, known to Masai as 'Dorobo', they regard as 'primitive'. Hunter bands and castes are similarly despised by many of the 'Highland' Nilotes and Cushitic peoples, but this need not involve a refusal to touch game. Almost universal among Cushitic-speakers, however, is a taboo on fish. It extends to many Nilotic- and Bantu-speakers who have absorbed or been influenced by Cushites in Kenya and northern Tanzania.

[2] Cole, op. cit., pp. 218, 334–6.

[3] Greenberg, op. cit.

[4] J. C. Trevor, 'The Physical Characters of the Sandawe', *Journal of the Royal Anthropological Institute*, LXXVII (1947), 61–78.

[5] Sutton, in Ogot and Kieran, op. cit. If it should prove to be Afroasiatic (alternatively known as 'Erythraic'), presumably it should fall in the Cushitic division.

[6] See below; and Sutton, 'Archaeological Sites in Usandawe', *Azania*, III (1968), 167–74.

shelters and graves in Hadza country that food-producers inhabited that region at some time in the Late Stone Age, keeping cattle and goats or sheep and probably cultivating grains.[1] It is possible that these former food-producing peoples lived side by side with hunter-gatherers ancestral to the Sandawe and Hadza. On the other hand, the populations of north-central Tanzania may have shifted around, among other things in response to movements of tse-tse fly.

Perhaps the work of the ancestors of the Sandawe and Hadza are the hunter rock-paintings of north-central Tanzania, some of which occur in their present territories. In view of the thick Late-Stone-Age deposits in certain of the painted rockshelters, some of the surviving paintings (or at least the painting tradition) may date back several millennia, but others may belong to recent centuries.[2] Comparisons of the art and lithic industries at a very general level with those of southern Africa might support the view that Bushman-type hunter-gatherer popula-tions extended from East to South Africa before the beginnings of food-production, the coming of iron and the spread of Bantu languages. Besides the Sandawe (and perhaps the Hadza) as relatively unassimilated remnants, stories of hunters who have now vanished or been absorbed are told by a number of the Bantu tribes in Tanzania.[3] These may refer to similar groups that persisted till a century or two ago.

It is unlikely that all the hunter-gatherers that existed in East Africa in the Late Stone Age and all the remnants that continued into the Iron Age were of Bushmanoid stock. In fact there is little to show that specifically Bushmanoid types ever extended north of the equator in eastern Africa.[4] In western Uganda, in the highland forests bordering Ruanda and the Congo, there are

[1] Finds in National Museum, Dar es Salaam; brief report from Kyoto University group in *Tanzania Antiquities Department report for 1967.*

[2] See R. Inskeep, 'The Age of the Kondoa Rock Paintings, in the Light of Recent Excava-tions at Kisese II Rock Shelter', in G. Mortelmans and J. Nenquin (eds.), *Actes du IV Congrès Panafricain de Préhistoire,* II (1962), pp. 249–56.

[3] For example in Ukimbu—A. E. M. Shorter, 'Rock Paintings in Ukimbu', *Tanzania Notes and Records,* 67 (1967), 50.

[4] In view of the re-evaluation of the skull from Singa on the Blue Nile—Cole, op. cit., pp. 175–7.

people of pygmy stock; whilst in Kenya and northern Tanzania, again in highland forests, there are memories, which may or may not be reliable, of dwarfs until recent times. In Kikuyu country they are spoken of as 'Gumba'; and one can still see in places on the slopes of the Aberdare Mountains occupation sites with potsherds and obsidian flakes and tools that are ascribed to the 'Gumba' and known archaeologically as 'Gumba pits'. [1]

Another instance of Late Stone Age hunter-gatherers apparently continuing well into the Iron Age is provided by the excavation of Magosi Rockshelter II in north-eastern Uganda. Here a radio-carbon date of about A.D. 1240 was obtained for a 'Wilton' industry with pottery,[2] suggesting (as for 'Gumba pits') some form of contact with food-producers. It has also been argued that the occupation in very recent centuries of rockshelters on the north-western side of Lake Victoria by people with pottery known as 'Entebbe ware' indicates the late and gradual absorption of hunter-gatherer-fishermen.[3] Alternatively, they may be descendants of Early-Iron-Age populations that have concentrated on fishing or reverted to this way of life.

Finally, there still exist, mainly in the northern parts of East Africa, numerous bands and groups of hunter-gatherers speaking Cushitic, Nilotic and occasionally Bantu languages. Sometimes it is an archaic tongue, sometimes that of their present neighbours—or they may be bilingual. Certain of these groups are essentially independent, but others live in contact, if not actual symbiosis, with food-producing communities. Though they may in part descend from an aboriginal stock of hunter-gatherers, most of them must be of mixed origin. Some probably include remnants of early food-producing (or semi-food-pro-

[1] D. R. F. Taylor, 'The Gumba and the "Gumba pits" of Fort Hall District', *Azania*, I (1966), 111–17; Sutton, *ibid.*, pp. 45–7. A recent excavation is briefly reported in *Azania*, III (1968), 210. This yielded a somewhat perplexing radio-carbon date as early as the fifth century B.C.

'Gumba' and 'Gumba pits', it should be added, have nothing to do with what were formerly called 'Gumban cultures'.

[2] Information Professor M. Posnansky.

[3] R. M. Brachi, 'Excavation of a Rock Shelter at Hippo Bay, Entebbe', *Uganda Journal*, XXIV (1960), 62–70; M. Posnansky, 'Pottery Types from Archaeological Sites in East Africa', *Journal of African History*, II (1961), 195.

ducing) populations, that have resisted assimilation by numerous or more powerful iron-using food-producers by retreating into remote places. The Sanye of the Tana valley and the Asa-Aramanik in Tanzania Masailand, who are southern Cushitic-speakers, and the Teuso (or Ik) in north-eastern Uganda, with a language distantly related either to Cushitic or more probably to Nilotic, might fit such an explanation. The Okiek or 'Dorobo hordes' who speak Kalenjin dialects[1] in scattered parts of the Kenya highlands and Masailand, include numbers of Kalenjin, Masai and Kikuyu who in recent times, after losing their land or cattle or being rejected by their kinsmen, have sought refuge in the forest or the bush. Besides exchanging honey, game-meat and other natural products, they may perform crafts that their neighbours despise. Some Dorobo groups, for instance, supply pots to Masai; while the Ilkunono division or 'caste' of Masai undertake both potting and metallurgy.[2] These crafts are unlikely to have been developed by groups of pure hunter-gatherer descent. A comparable example further south would be the Bantu-speaking Wanyahoza (or Wakiko) fishermen in the Malagarasi swamps of western Tanzania, whose women make and trade pots to their Nyamwezi and Ha neighbours;[3] and one might instance other small fishing communities or divisions of tribes occupying lake-shore environments.

The earliest proven archaeological indications of Iron-Age occupation in East Africa are the 'dimple-based' and related pottery wares. The term 'dimple-based' is not entirely satisfactory, firstly because, although a depressed or dimpled base is a notable feature of many of these pots, it is by no means universal: there are 'dimple-based' pots, both individuals and whole collections, without dimple bases. Moreover, there is a tendency for the term to be used too broadly for a number of Early-Iron-

---

[1] The Kalenjin languages belong to the 'Highland' division of Nilotic, see p. 173.

[2] A. C. Hollis, *The Masai, Their Language and Folklore* (1905), pp. 330–1; information Professor A. H. Jacobs.

Groups of craftsmen, sometimes relying partly on hunting and despised by their neighbours, similarly exist in some regions of Ethiopia and the Horn.

[3] C. Macquarie, 'Water Gypsies of the Malagarasi', *Tanganyika Notes and Records*, 9 (1940), 61–7.

Age pottery collections, which while obviously related are certainly not identical. The most detailed analysis so far is Soper's,[1] in which he compared the 'dimple-based ware' from the Lake Victoria region,[2] with the 'Sandawe-type' in north-central Tanzania,[3] and with the collections of 'Kwale ware'[4] recently obtained in north-eastern Tanzania and south-eastern Kenya.[5] From this he concludes that the 'Sandawe-type' is inter-mediate between the Lake Victoria 'dimple-based' and the 'Kwale ware', though in fact closer to the latter.[6] Related to these East African Early-Iron-Age wares are those from a number of sites in Rwanda and Kivu,[7] and from one site far to the west on the Kasai.[8] Some of the Rwanda collections, though called 'dimple-based', contain some apparently atypical vessels.[9] The few pots from the Kasai sites, on the other hand, have fairly typical decoration and examples of dimples. Also related are the 'channel-decorated' wares of Zambia,[10] as well as variants south

[1] R. C. Soper, 'Early Iron Age Pottery Types from East Africa: Comparative Analysis', paper to the Sixth Panafrican Congress on Prehistory, 1967 (publication forthcoming).

[2] M. D. Leakey, W. E. Owen, and L. S. B. Leakey, 'Dimple-based Pottery from Central Kavirondo', *Coryndon Memorial Museum Occasional Papers*, no. 2 (1948); M. Posnansky, art. cit. (1961), pp. 183–5; id., 'The Iron Age in East Africa', in W. W. Bishop and J. D. Clark (eds.), *Background to Evolution in Africa* (1967), 631–4; id., art. cit. (1968); id. 'Terminology in the Early Iron Age of Eastern Africa with Particular Reference to the Dimple-based Wares on Lolui Island, Uganda', paper to the Sixth Panafrican Congress on Prehistory, 1967 (publication forthcoming).

[3] G. Smolla, 'Prähistorische Keramik aus Ostafrika', *Tribus*, N.F., VI (1957), 35–64; Sutton, art. cit. (1968).

[4] Named after a type-site in the Shimba hills near Mombasa—R. C. Soper, 'Kwale, An Early Iron Age Site in South-eastern Kenya', *Azania*, II (1967), 1–17.

[5] Two sherds, apparently of 'Kwale ware', have been found well to the north-west, in the forests of the Aberdare Mountains.

[6] It is expected that new names for these wares will be proposed in due course.

[7] J. Hiernaux and E. Maquet, 'Cultures Préhistoriques de l'Age des Méteux au Ruanda-Urundi et au Kivu' (part 2), *Mémoires de l'Academie Royal des Sciences d'Outre-mer*, N.S., X, 2 (1960), 1–88.

[8] J. Nenquin, 'Dimple-based Pots from Kasai, Belgian Congo', *Man* (1959), 242.

[9] Id., *Contributions to the Study of the Prehistoric Cultures of Rwanda and Burundi* (1967), pp. 257 ff.

[10] M. Posnansky, 'Iron Age in East and Central Africa—Points of Comparison', *South African Archaeological Bulletin*, XVI (1961), 134–6; B. M. Fagan, 'Early Iron Age Pottery in Eastern and Southern Africa', *Azania*, I (1966), 101–9; id., *Iron Age Cultures in Zambia*, I (1967), 29.

However, as Posnansky (art. cit., 1968) points out, 'channel-decorated' ware is not simply 'dimple-based' ware without the dimple. See also D. W. Phillipson, *Journal of African History*, IX (1968), 191–211.

of the Zambezi. The pottery from the Kalambo Falls site on the Zambia–Tanzania border provides a link between the 'channel-decorated' and 'dimple-based' wares to the south and north respectively, and includes the most southerly dimples yet discovered.[1]

Besides these variations from region to region and from site to site, single collections of Early-Iron-Age pottery in East Africa are liable to contain a wide range of shapes, sizes and decorative patterns. Broadly, there are two main types of vessel—open bowls, both straight-sided and saucer-shaped, and more globular pots. The latter often have slightly constricted necks and everted rims. The rim itself is commonly thickened and 'bevelled' or 'fluted'. 'Fluting' is commoner in the 'Kwale ware', where upturned rims also occur. If there is a dimple in the base, it may be a conspicuous depression, as is frequent in the Lake Victoria collections, or alternatively a slighter one which occurs more often among 'Kwale ware'. The vessels are of varying thicknesses, but are well-fired and sometimes bear a red or black burnish. Decoration is invariably by impression, and is usually concentrated in bands fairly close to the rim or on the neck and shoulder. It consists of grooving or 'channelling', most commonly roughly parallel and horizontal, or lighter hatching in diagonal, criss-cross, herring-bone, triangular and semi-circular patterns. From the 'Kwale ware' sites, lines of 'stamped' impressions, performed with a comb, are more frequent. There is also, as Soper puts it, a 'rich variety of elaborations and individual motifs', often of curvilinear or 'scroll' type, among the Lake Victoria collections.

Wherever they occur, 'dimple-based', 'channel-decorated' and related wares appear to be the pottery of the first iron-users and the first food-producers (except perhaps in the region of 'Kwale ware' which may partly overlap with the extent of earlier food-production in the Late Stone Age). It is true that on certain sites in Rwanda some pottery collections with 'dimple-based' affinities are reckoned to be associated with Late-Stone-Age industries of 'Wilton' type.[2] Similar situations do not seem

---

[1] Fagan, art. cit. (1966), p. 105.   [2] Nenquin, op. cit. (1967), pp. 58 ff.

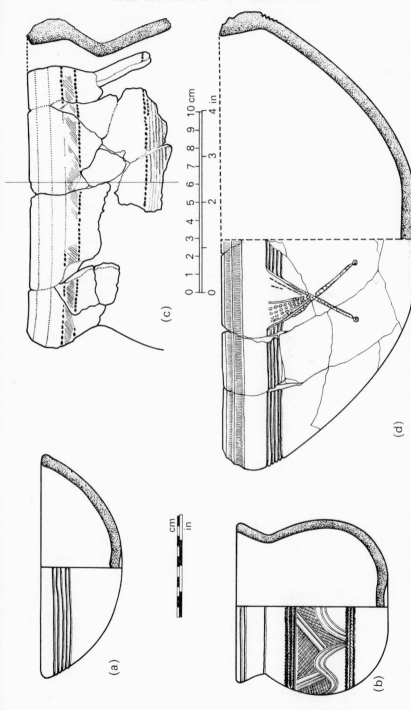

FIG. 7. Early-Iron-Age pottery: 'dimple-based' and 'Kwale wares.' (a)–(b), 'Dimple-based' vessels from Kavirondo sites; (c)–(d), Kwale.

to occur in East Africa. Where, as in south-western Uganda at the adjacent sites of Nsongezi Rockshelter[1] and Kansyore Island[2], both Late-Stone-Age remains and 'dimple-based' pottery occur, there is good reason to assume that the pottery is later than the stone industries and is thus Iron Age. In the Rockshelter this point is demonstrated stratigraphically. But iron finds are never plentiful, presumably because of corrosion, or because of the rarity of smelted iron and the need to reforge worn objects; so that on many sites an Iron-Age date has to be presumed from analogy and from the absence of a stone industry. However, at Kwale,[3] at certain of the Kavirondo sites,[4] and probably from those in south-western Uganda, the iron-ware consists of spear- and arrow-heads, pins and rings, and at one site in Kavirondo possibly a small hoe. Moreover, pieces of slag and tuyère indicating actual iron-working were recovered at Kwale and in Kavirondo.

Economy and domestic life are poorly illustrated. Again at Kwale and some of the Kavirondo sites, lumps or patches of baked or burnt clay have been recognized, but nothing firmly identifiable as a floor or structure. The continued use of rock-shelters, as at Nsongezi, is noteworthy, but should not be regarded as typical. In view of the metallurgy and the amounts of pottery, it can be assumed that the people were mostly settled and agricultural. However, no food remains have come to light, save for a few undescribed bones; and there is a grindstone from Kwale. One would guess that they were mainly dependent on millet crops. However, the occurrence of sites in wetter and more thickly vegetated regions to the north and west of Lake Victoria might be an indication that the banana was becoming known. Fishing was doubtless important also, in view of the position of so many of the settlements by rivers or on the shores and islands of Lake Victoria. Three sites recently discovered at

[1] S. Pearce and M. Posnansky, 'Re-excavation of Nsongezi Rockshelter, Ankole,' Uganda Journal, XXVII (1963), 85–94. (The captions to the pottery illustrations in this article—figures 4 and 5—were unfortunately transposed.)

[2] S. Chapman (née Pearce), 'Kantsyore Island', Azania, II (1967), 165–91.

[3] Soper, art. cit. (1967).

[4] M. D. Leakey et al., op. cit., fig. 8.

Uvinza[1] in western Tanzania were most probably connected with salt-working, for all were immediately adjacent to brine-springs that have been exploited in later times. This might imply trade, if only at the local level—as indeed might the evidence of iron-working at other sites. But none of these Early-Iron-Age sites has yielded evidence of developed or long-distance trade. There are no sea-shells or imported glass beads, not even on the Kwale type-site which is only 12 miles inland.

Few burials of this period have been recognized, though at Kalambo iron and dimpled potsherds were found in some pits thought to have been graves.[2] Skeletal remains were found on Kansyore Island, but they could equally well belong to an earlier or a later period. On the same site there is a 'Wilton' industry, as well as pottery of a distinct type, named 'Kansyore ware'. Chapman[3] believes that this ware is Iron Age, con-temporary with or slightly earlier than the 'dimple-based ware', and Posnansky[4] also argues that it is a local variant. This conclusion is based on the stratigraphy on Kansyore Island, which, though badly disturbed, seemed to indicate that 'Kansyore ware' was somewhat earlier than 'dimple-based', and on the occurrence of one sherd of 'Kansyore ware' in Nsongezi Rockshelter, in the same layer as the 'dimple-based' pottery. But this single sherd could be a stray; and, in view of the markedly contrasting shapes with simple and tapering rims and the very distinctive texture, gritty surface and overall decor-ation of the 'Kansyore ware', the argument for contemporaneity sounds very weak. The 'Kansyore ware' could as plausibly be assigned to the Late Stone Age. Both Chapman and Posnansky recognize similarities to 'dotted wavy-line' and derived 'neo-lithic' wares of the Middle Nile and Sahara,[5] but are naturally cautious of pressing a connection because of the long distances

[1] J. E. G. Sutton and A. D. Roberts, *Azania*, III (1968), 45–86.
[2] *Journal of African History*, VIII (1967), 522.
[3] Art. cit.
[4] In Bishop and Clark, op. cit., p. 632.
[5] A. J. Arkell, *Early Khartoum* (1949); id., *Shaheinab* (1953); id., 'The Distribution in Central Africa of One Early Neolithic Ware (dotted wavy line pottery),' in Mortelmans and Nenquin, op. cit., pp. 283–7.

involved and the lack of comparable finds in the intervening regions. However, the occurrence of rather similar pottery in at least one rockshelter on the eastern side of Lake Victoria,[1] and at some sites on its southern shore,[2] from certain sites near Lake Eyasi in northern Tanzania,[3] as well as the famous decorated sherd from a low layer in Gamble's Cave in the Kenya rift valley,[4] provide at least an argument for an extension of

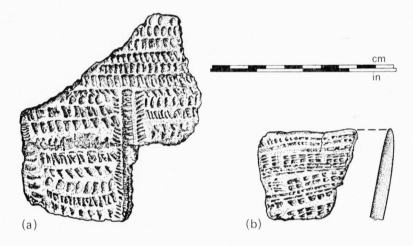

(a)   (b)

FIG. 8. 'Kansyore ware'.

advanced Late-Stone-Age hunter-gatherer-fisher peoples from the Middle Nile region into the northern and north-western parts of East Africa some time in the last three millennia B.C.[5] Though probably not food-producing themselves, the art of potting was doubtless derived from early food-producing societies in north-eastern Africa. (This would have been anterior to the period of Late-Stone-Age food-producers discussed

[1] In the National Museum, Nairobi.

[2] R. C. Soper, *Azania*, III (1968), 179.

[3] Smolla, art. cit.

[4] L. S. B. Leakey, *The Stone Age Cultures of Kenya Colony* (1931), pp. 103–4, 120–1; Sutton, art. cit. (1964), p. 31; id., 'The Eastern African "Neolithic" '.

[5] Recent work on the southern side of Lake Victoria and a radio-carbon date of the first millenium B.C. bear out this argument that 'Kansyore ware' is not Iron Age. See R. C. Soper and B. Golden, *Azania*, IV (1969).

above in the Kenya and northern Tanzania highlands and rift valley. The pottery of the latter, which would include that from a higher layer in Gamble's Cave,[1] is quite different).[2] On Kansyore Island it might be argued that certain selected decorative motifs of the 'Kansyore ware' were copied by the makers of the otherwise distinct 'dimple-based' pottery. Whether this could be taken as evidence of continuity or of connection between the first iron-using people and their Late-Stone-Age predecessors it is not possible to say.

Also confused by evidence from Nsongezi Rockshelter is the question of the dating of the 'dimple-based' and related Early-Iron-Age wares. Until very recently there were no radio-carbon dates available for the Early Iron Age in East Africa. However, at Nsongezi a date of about A.D. 1000 was obtained for the end of the Late Stone Age, just below the 'dimple-based' pottery layer. This suggested that the Iron Age in that region did not begin till the second millennium; whereas a number of sites with 'channel-decorated' and related wares in Zambia and Rhodesia were indicating that the Iron Age began there early in the first millennium A.D.[3] Not unnaturally, the earlier view of the diffusion of iron from the north into East Africa and thence into southern Africa began to be seriously questioned; and more than that, Oliver[4] put up a strong case for deriving the earliest Iron-Age peoples and 'dimple-based' pottery of East Africa from the south or south-west. Though this view may be basically correct, it is probably too sweeping. Firstly, it is dangerous to rely heavily on a single radio-carbon date: and, in the case of that from Nsongezi, the circumstances of the collection of the sample

[1] Leakey, op. cit., pp. 172 ff.

[2] See above. The early pottery from Site I at Hyrax Hill (Leakey, art. cit., 1945) might, in fact, include certain parallels for 'Kansyore ware' and other comparable collections. Moreover, several minor points of resemblance, but no direct connections, have been noted between the late stone age pottery of the Kenya highlands and Middle Nile wares (Sutton, art. cit. (1964), pp. 33–4). There may be some interesting possibilities here, but on present evidence this is all very tenuous.

[3] For these and other radio-carbon dates, see the lists prepared by Fagan in *Journal of African History*.

[4] Art. cit. (1966). For further comments see Posnansky (art. cit., 1968); and J. Hiernaux, 'Bantu Expansion: the Evidence from Physical Anthropology Confronted with Linguistic and Archaeological Evidence', *Journal of African History*, IX (1968), 505–15.

suggest that no reliability should be placed on it.[1] Secondly, further dates recently obtained from Early-Iron-Age sites in East Africa (as well as Ruanda and Kivu) fall within the first half and middle years of the first millennium A.D. These include dates of the late third and fourth centuries from sites in Kavirondo, of the fifth and sixth centuries from two of the Uvinza brine-springs, five dates of the first to third centuries for 'Kwale ware', one of the fourth century for a presumed grave with dimpled sherds at Kalambo, and two of the third century in Rwanda. It should be borne in mind that most radio-carbon dates in the first millennium A.D. may be calculated a little too early;[2] nevertheless, the emerging picture is of the first iron-using peoples spreading rapidly and colonizing a large part of eastern and central-southern Africa, extending to the Kenya coast, Lake Victoria and Kivu in the north, and to the Limpopo in the south, during the early or middle part of the first millennium A.D. Clearly, these settlements were sparse, but the blank areas on the distribution map—for instance southern Tanzania and the south-eastern Congo—may merely reflect insufficient fieldwork. In fact, the latter area, to the west of Lake Tanganyika, appears, from the known distribution of sites of 'dimple-based', 'channel-decorated' and related wares, to have been the centre of this Early-Iron-Age activity. If this was so, it becomes possible to avoid certain awkward questions that have been troubling historians and archaeologists—did migration take place from East Africa to the Zambezi or in the opposite direction?; were the 'channel-decorated' pottery wares the prototypes from which the more elaborate 'dimple-based' forms developed, or have the former merely devolved from the latter? The ultimate origin of these wares (and of the iron-working activity that was apparently an important factor in the spread) remains unclear. Arguments for connections with the Sudan[3] sound uncritical, being based on selected traits.

[1] However, it might be argued that the 'dimple-based' pottery from Nsongezi is a relatively late variety, in view of the types of decoration and the presence of slip—Posnansky in Bishop and Clark, op. cit., p. 630.

[2] *Journal of African History*, VIII (1967), 513.

[3] H. Straube, 'Die Historische Wurzeln der Ostafrikanischen Bodendellen-Keramik', *Kölner Ethnologische Mitteilungen*, IV (1965), 231–86.

Posnansky thinks a connection with wares in Nigeria at least as conceivable.[1] Influences deriving from the Indian Ocean, either its nearer or its further shores, have not been recognized in the pottery.

Whether or not it should ever prove possible to trace outside connections for 'dimple-based' and 'channel-decorated' pottery wares, what matters much more is their actual development, spread and differentiation. While there is much still to be learnt on all this, it is clear that it took place in Bantu Africa. A number of writers have hinted that these Early-Iron-Age sites indicate the expansion of the first Bantu-speaking peoples. This view has been most confidently advocated by Oliver,[2] who, following Guthrie's comparative study of Bantu languages,[3] argues that the centre of the Bantu expansion was around northern Katanga. When more information becomes available, it will, of course, prove necessary to amend or amplify the details of the Bantu spread; nevertheless, the overall view and the connection with the Early Iron Age sound entirely reasonable. Particularly significant is the linguistic evidence for the antiquity of iron and iron-working among Bantu, and also of their early association with boating and fishing.[4]

Until more sites are investigated and more dates obtained, it will be difficult to tell how long the 'dimple-based' and related wares continued to be made. In general, they probably belong to the first millennium A.D. This would be in keeping with the picture emerging further south. For instance, in southern Zambia 'channel-decorated' wares were being replaced by those of the 'Kalomo culture' in the middle and latter part of the first millennium,[5] while in northern Katanga the Kisalian wares of the late first millennium appear to derive partly from the

---

[1] Art. cit. (1968).   [2] Art. cit.

[3] M. Guthrie, 'Some developments in the prehistory of the Bantu languages', *Journal of African History*, III (1962), 273–82.

[4] Oliver (art. cit.) further argues that this view of early Bantu expansion is not necessarily inconsistent with that of Greenberg (op. cit., p. 38), who would place the ultimate origin of the Bantu languages in the region of eastern Nigeria and the Cameroons. See also the arguments of Posnansky (art. cit., 1968) for a much greater time-depth for any conjectural West African connections.

[5] Fagan, *Iron Age Cultures*, I, pp. 18 ff. It now appears that the earlier pottery at 'Kalomo culture' sites belongs to the general Early-Iron-Age complex. Phillipson, art. cit., 201.

'channel-decorated' and 'dimple-based' tradition.[1] At Kalambo on the Tanzania border the end of the 'channel-decorated' sequence is thought to have been about 1000 A.D.[2] In north-eastern Tanzania, moreover, new developments and new pottery types appear to supersede the 'Kwale ware' by the end of the first millennium.[3] To some extent these new developments may be attributable to new groups of people, or at least to new contacts. However, the Early-Iron-Age cultivators who made the 'dimple-based' and 'Kwale wares' must have formed a significant element of the stock of Middle and later Iron-Age populations of the Bantu regions of East Africa. They may have continued longer, relatively undisturbed, in the more remote woodland and waterside areas. In the Lake Victoria region, Posnansky argues that many features of the 'dimple-based' wares continue well into the second millennium influencing later pottery types, especially on Lolui Island.[4] Sherds with 'dimple-based' features have been picked up on Late-Iron-Age settlements by the Victoria Nile between Lakes Kyoga and Albert.[5] But these sites have not been excavated, and the association remains conjectural.

The middle and later periods of the Iron Age show much more regional differentiation. That said, it must immediately be added that the geographical limits of each culture, feature and influence remain hazy, and that the chronological sequences region by region are mostly very sketchy.

In north-eastern Tanzania, in and below the Pare and Usambara mountains, Soper,[6] enlarging on Fosbrooke's earlier work,[7] has located a number of Iron-Age sites, which he had grouped

[1] J. Nenquin, *Excavations at Sanga: the Protohistoric Necropolis* (1963); Posnansky, review of same, *Journal of African History*, V (1964), 140.

[2] *Journal of African History*, VIII (1967), 522-3, where it is suggested that the latest date, which can be alternatively read as fourteenth or sixteenth century, should be disregarded for stratigraphical reasons.

[3] R. C. Soper, 'Iron Age Sites in North-eastern Tanzania', *Azania*, II (1967), 19-36; and see below.　　　　　　　　[4] Art. cit. (1968). See also id., art. cit. (1961), 195.

[5] B. M. Fagan and L. Lofgren, 'Archaeological Sites on the Nile-Chobi Confluence', *Uganda Journal*, XXX (1966), 201-6.　　　　[6] Art. cit., *Azania*, II (1967), 19-36.

[7] H. A. Fosbrooke, 'Early Iron Age Sites in Tanganyika Relative to Traditional History', in J. D. Clark (ed.), *Proceedings of the Third Pan-African Congress on Prehistory* (1957), pp. 318-25.

according to pottery types as A, B, C, etc. All of them are reckoned to be later than the 'Kwale ware' in the same region. One site close to the sea at Tanga has produced a surprisingly early date of the fourth century A.D., but Soper notes that the pottery from this group—'incised ware'—might have possible connections with certain coastal wares of the end of the first millennium or the early part of the second. Some of the South Pare sites were definitely in contact with the coast, as is indicated by the finds of cowrie-shells and a few glass beads. There were also beads of stone and ostrich-eggshell, presumably made locally. Two such sites, lying side by side in South Pare, have yielded dates in the late ninth century, which is not necessarily too early for such trading activity in view of evidence now appearing on the coast.[1] It may, however, be somewhat perplexing that these two sites with almost identical dates have distinct pottery types. This might indicate different groups of people in the region—Bantu and non-Bantu, conceivably. On the other hand, one of the dates may be faulty. There is no direct evidence of the volume and content of trade—ivory *inter alia* one might guess. From the pottery and domestic animal bones it appears that these were occupation sites. Other old settlements in and around these hills are clearly of later date, and in some cases their pottery compares with that of the present tribes.

Not only in Pare, but also extending westwards and southwards over a large part of central Tanzania, through the Masai Steppe to Irangi, Singida, Ugogo and Pawaga (lower Uhehe, south of the Great Ruaha river) are numerous Iron-Age sites conspicuous for what are often referred to as 'burnt bricks'. These are, in fact, not bricks but lumps of burnt daub from house walls, and particularly the footings which are commonly preserved in place. The normal house-shape is rectangular, but circular examples are also known. It is not certain whether heat was applied to the footings deliberately by the builders in order to strengthen the construction, or whether the houses were burnt by accident or during warfare. Many of these sites contain

[1] H. N. Chittick in *Azania*, I (1966), 4 ff.; II (1967), 45 ff.; and chapter in the present volume.

grind-stones and potsherds. The latter may not be many centuries old, but they vary from one locality to the next, and are generally unlike those used by the present inhabitants of these regions. The latter tend to ascribe the sites to former peoples, remembered by different names from district to district. The problem is doubtless a complex one, involving perhaps not only Bantu but also Cushitic-speaking peoples, who are known to have been more extensive in these regions till recently. It will need to be tackled by a combination of archaeological and oral historical methods.[1]

In another direction from Pare, towards the north and north-west, lie the fertile regions of the highland Bantu. On either side of the Kenya–Tanzania border these highlands consist of mountain groups, such as Pare itself, Taita, Kilimanjaro and Meru, separated by expanses of drier plains. Further north in Kenya are more extensive highland masses occupied by Kamba, Kikuyu and related tribes. Bantu penetration and settlement of the highlands has been a long process, which on both linguistic and historical grounds must go back at least to the early part of the present millennium.[2] A large element of the highland Bantu probably moved inland from the coastal regions of northern Tanzania, Kenya and southern Somalia over a period of many centuries.[3] Some migrated further still and eventually joined up with other Bantu groups to the east of Lake Victoria.[4] This involved crossing the rift valley and the western highlands that have generally remained non-Bantu territory to the present day.[5] In and around the eastern highlands too there have been (and still are) numerous small non-Bantu populations. Some of these are

[1] The information on these sites is derived from Fosbrooke, art. cit., and a number of unpublished notes and reports, as well as some preliminary fieldwork by the present writer.

[2] H. E. Lambert, *The Systems of Land Tenure in the Kikuyu Land Unit*, part I (1950) (Communications of the School of African Studies, Cape Town), ch. 2–3.

[3] A. H. J. Prins, 'Shungwaya, die Urheimat der Nordost-Bantu', *Anthropos*, L (1955), 273–82. However, to suggest that all the hinterland and highland Bantu derive from the sixteenth century dispersal from Shungwaya on the southern Somali coast, which was partly occasioned by pressure from pastoral Galla groups, would be a gross over-simplification. See, J. F. Munro, *Journal of African History*, VIII (1967), 25–8.

[4] Sutton, art. cit. (1966), p. 50.

[5] Discussed below.

vaguely recorded in the highland Bantu traditions,[1] and may include Nilotic and Eastern Cushitic-speaking groups of no greater antiquity in the region than the Bantu themselves. But there has also been an important degree of absorption of earlier— probably Southern—Cushites by highland Bantu in general. This is indicated by various lines of evidence, particularly ethnographic. These Cushites would descend from the Late-Stone-Age food-producers of this part of eastern Africa. But a new development that may not have begun on an extensive scale till the coming of iron-using Bantu was the penetration into the forested and most fertile regions of the highlands, such as the southern and eastern slopes of Mount Kenya, the Aberdares and Kilimanjaro. However, the archaeological side of these processes of settlement, assimilation and 'Bantuization' during the Iron Age remains very poorly known.

In the more purely Bantu regions of southern and western Tanzania, the archaeological record of Iron-Age developments is even thinner.[2] The most productive sites investigated so far are connected with salt-working, at Ivuna[3] in the south-west and Uvinza[4] in the west. Early-Iron-Age pottery with 'dimple-based' affinities in the lowest levels at Uvinza has already been noted. Above this were found two other pottery groups. In both of these decoration was mostly done with a knotted grass or cord roulette, which, by analogy with the Lake Victoria region, was an innovation of the first half of the second millennium. A radio-carbon date of the late twelfth century has been obtained for the lower group of roulette decorated pottery at Uvinza. This is earlier than expected. In the middle group at Uvinza the roulette-pattern was more widely spaced and tastefully executed than in the later: this is similarly in keeping with Lake Victoria and western Kenya. The latest of the Uvinza

[1] Lambert, op. cit., ch. 4.

[2] There are, of course, a number of surface finds; and recent occupation and refuge sites are known—e.g. Sutton, 'Habitation Sites on the Liganga–Maganga ridge', *Azania*, II (1967), 199–200.

[3] B. M. Fagan and J. E. Yellen, 'Ivuna: Ancient Salt-workings in Southern Tanzania', *Azania*, III (1968), 1–43.

[4] Sutton and Roberts, art cit.

pottery groups was associated with intensive settlement and salt-industry by the brine-springs, such as the Vinza people are known to have been undertaking in the nineteenth century for trade both near and far in all directions along the caravan routes.

The sequence from the Ivuna salt-pans was more restricted. Four radio-carbon dates all fall between the thirteenth and fifteenth centuries. The pottery belongs to two main groups, neither of which bears any relationship to 'dimple-based' or 'channel-decorated' wares, thus tending to confirm a second millennium dating. The later group has some resemblances to modern wares in the locality, suggesting that it may be younger than the radio-carbon dates indicate. Salt working has continued at Ivuna to the present. In this context it seems highly significant that oral historical studies in southern, central and western Tanzania are beginning to demonstrate the importance of trade in rare but essential commodities such as processed salt and smelted iron, notably in the form of hoes, in the development of inter-tribal and inter-regional contact, and in the establishment of chieftancies in some parts. This, coupled perhaps with hunting expeditions and the prestige of ivory trophies, gradually evolved into longer-distance trading that brought ivory and other interior products to the coast, particularly that of southern Tanzania, and carried cloth, cowries, glass beads, wire and other currency and trade goods into the interior during the last two centuries.[1]

For it was not till the late eighteenth and nineteenth centuries that regular trade-routes linking the interior with the coast and the wider world began to develop in East Africa.[2] This is in marked contrast with both Ethiopia to the north and the Zambezi region to the south. It is known that merchant vessels were visiting the East African coast almost 2,000 years ago, and

[1] See A. D. Roberts (ed.), *Tanzania before 1900* (1968), especially the chapters by A. E. M. Shorter and A. D. Roberts; I. N. Kimambo and A. J. Temu (eds.), *A History of Tanzania* (1969), chapter by E. A. Alpers.

[2] This remark can be qualified for southern Tanzania, where the routes linking the Kilwa (and northern Mozambique) coast with the Lake Nyasa region were opened up a century or two earlier by Yao traders—see Alpers, in Kimambo and Temu, op. cit.

that Swahili harbour-towns were being established more than 1,000 years back,[1] but these were more concerned with trade up and down the coast, and from the ninth or tenth century A.D. with ivory, gold and other products from further south. Hence the interior behind the harbours and cities of the East African seaboard remained virtually unaffected. Some Pare sites[2] do admittedly indicate contacts extending a short distance inland, but otherwise the only imported objects or local substitutes found on pre-nineteenth-century sites in the interior are a few sea-shells and glass beads, which had an ornamental as much as a monetary value, and clay smoking pipes. This is not to deny that various food-crops and other cultural influences from overseas have percolated through East Africa during the Iron Age; but these do not demand the existence of trade-routes, but merely of contact, migration perhaps, and, especially, local adaptation.

This point is best illustrated in the interlacustrine region to the west and north of Lake Victoria, where a number of organized kingdoms have arisen in the last half-millennium or so. In the case of the most densely populated, and by the nineteenth century most bureaucratic, of these kingdoms, Buganda, the economy was based very largely on the cultivation of bananas, in origin a south-eastern Asian crop, but one that has been remarkably developed and diversified in the Lake Victoria region and other fertile parts of East Africa. And yet, in contrast to kingdoms in many parts of Africa, long-distance trade played virtually no part in maintaining the economic or political systems of Buganda and the other interlacustrine kingdoms until the nineteenth century.[3] Nevertheless, local trade, particularly in salt and iron, was important. The salt-industry at Kibiro on Lake Albert extends back several centuries;[4] while Buganda has tended to look to Bunyoro and other neighbours and its own western

[1] See the chapter by H. N. Chittick.

[2] Discussed above.

[3] The scant evidence for early outside contacts is discussed by Posnansky in a paper to a conference on 'East Africa and the Orient' held in Nairobi in 1967—to be published, H. N. Chittick and R. I. Rotberg (eds.).

[4] J. Hiernaux and E. Maquet, *L'age du fer à Kibiro* (1968).

provinces for its iron-workers, if not for its actual iron, be it in the form of tribute or trade[1]—and for its potters too.

The early history of the interlacustrine kingdoms can be reconstructed in outline by using archaeology alongside oral traditions.[2] The latter tell of a great kingdom or 'empire' of Kitara about five or six centuries ago, that was ruled by a somewhat legendary dynasty remembered as 'Chwezi'[3] with the centre of its power in the grazing lands of western Uganda. Some writers have argued that the Chwezi, as well as the possibly related pastoral aristocratic Hima castes that still exist in the western kingdoms, were of Ethiopian origin. While this remains an open question,[4] it is certain that the 'Chwezi empire' and the later kingdoms of the interlacustrine region were essentially those of Bantu populations. Some extensive sites in western Uganda surrounded by earthworks are said to have been the royal capitals and cattle-kraals of the Chwezi. The most famous of these is Bigo,[5] where radio-carbon dates of the mid-fourteenth to early sixteenth centuries seem to confirm the traditional history. Near by at Ntusi are earthworks of a different type, also attributed to the Chwezi, that can only be interpreted as reservoir dams. Their purpose was presumably to supply water not only for cattle, but also perhaps for a large settlement, which is indicated by a wide scatter of pottery. These works must have required considerable labour organization; which might support the view that the social stratification between the pastoral aristocracy and the cultivators in this region dates back to the Chwezi period.

[1] J. Roscoe, *The Baganda* (1911), pp. 5, 170, 378 ff.; Wainwright, art. cit., pp. 113–14.

[2] The best summary and discussion of the history of these kingdoms is by Oliver in R. Oliver and G. Mathew (eds.), *History of East Africa*, I (1963), pp. 180–91. For further comments, see Posnansky, 'Kingship, Archaeology and Historical Myth', *Uganda Journal*, XXX (1966), 1–12.

[3] Or 'Bachwezi', if one wishes to add the local Bantu prefix.

[4] See my paper, 'Ethiopian Echoes in East Africa', to the Third International Conference of Ethiopian Studies, 1966 (publication forthcoming).

[5] E. J. Wayland, 'Notes on the Biggo bya Mugenyi', *Uganda Journal*, II (1934), 21–32; E. C. Lanning, 'Ancient Earthworks in Western Uganda', ibid., XVII (1953), 51–62; P. L. Shinnie, 'Excavations at Bigo', ibid., XXIV (1960), 16–28. Further excavations at Bigo have been undertaken by Posnansky.

About the sixteenth century the interlacustrine region was invaded from the north by groups of Nilotic-speaking Lwoo, who were apparently possessed of superior military organization. The 'Chwezi empire'—if it ever really was a single unit—broke up, and was superseded by a number of smaller kingdoms to the north and west of Lake Victoria. Some of them, notably Bunyoro, were ruled by Bito dynasties who were of Lwoo origin, but who, as far as can be seen, took over the essence of the local Bantu political and social system. However, the ruling lines of certain of the southern kingdoms are probably of Chwezi, or at least non-Lwoo, descent. In several of these kingdoms, successive capital sites are known. Though never so extensive as the great Chwezi capitals, some of these later ones consist of sizeable earthworks. One such royal enclosure or *orurembo* at Bweyorere is remembered as having been used by at least two kings of Nkole, one eight generations ago, the other twelve. Excavations—and two rather ambiguous radio-carbon dates—tend to support the traditions.[1] Bones of long-horned cattle are prominent among the finds, as one might expect in this pastoral country. In fact, most of the famous royal earthworks of western Uganda, both of the Chwezi and of later times, are situated in the lush grasslands. This does not presuppose that the kingdoms were exclusively or even predominantly pastoral: all of them included fertile land and agricultural populations as well. Nevertheless, the royal, aristocratic, religious and emotional attachment to cattle in the western interlacustrine kingdoms is illustrated in many ways, notably in the oral literature, as well as by the model iron cattle in the royal treasure-house of Karagwe.[2]

There may be a lacuna in the archaeological record as at present known to the north and west of Lake Victoria, between the sites with 'dimple-based' pottery mostly close to the lakes and rivers, and those associated with the kingdoms in the mid and

[1] M. Posnansky, 'Some Archaeological Aspects of the Ethnohistory in Uganda', in Mortelmans and Nenquin, op. cit., pp. 375–80; and, *Uganda Journal*, XXXII (1968), 165–82.

[2] J. H. Chaplin, 'Rock Drawings from the Lake Victoria Region', *Antiquity*, XLI (1967), 146–7, Pl. XVIII–XIX.

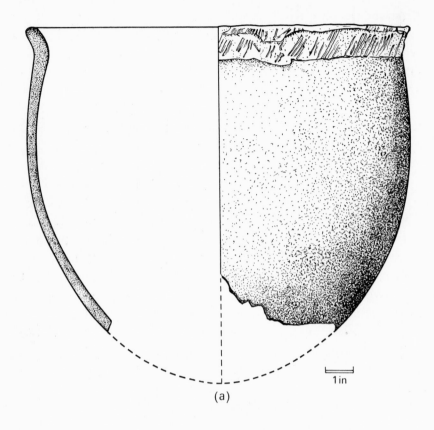

(a)

1 in

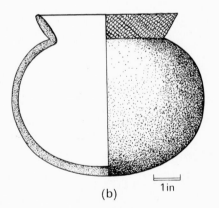

(b)

1 in

FIG. 9. Pottery from Bigo.

late second millennium. The pottery from these later sites is quite different.[1] At Bigo it divides into coarse and fine wares, some of the latter being painted or burnished. Particularly distinctive is the rouletted decoration on the rims, necks or shoulders of many pots. Both rouletting and graphite-burnishing occur at Bweyorere. Some of these finer wares are believed to have a royal connection. Also prominent at Bweyorere are gourd-shaped pots, which perhaps bear out the importance of cattle and milk-drinking. The range of pottery types in the interlacustrine region is probably richer than anywhere else in East Africa. There are, moreover, peculiar forms from religious centres, such as Mubende Hill.[2]

Also of religious significance, perhaps, are the terracotta objects found in Uganda. They include the famous figures from Luzira and Entebbe in Buganda,[3] and further west the decorated 'maces' from Ntusi,[4] Masaka and Nsongezi Rockshelter.[5] From their associations they should date to the Middle or Late Iron Age.

The introduction of rouletted decoration on pottery during the second millennium is a feature of many of the north-westerly regions of East Africa.[6] Besides on the Bigo wares, it occurs on the 'B' or 'Renge' ware of Rwanda,[7] on the 'recent' (i.e. post-'dimple-based') pottery of the Uganda–Tanzania border,[8] and further south at Uvinza after the Early Iron Age.[9] Rouletted decoration is not confined to Bantu regions: in the western Kenya highlands it was a marked feature of the pottery

---

[1] Posnansky, art. cit. (1961), pp. 187 ff.

[2] E. C. Lanning, 'Some Vessels and Beakers from Mubende Hill', *Man* (1953), 283; id., 'Protohistoric Pottery in Uganda', in Clark, op. cit. (1957), pp. 313–17; id., 'Excavations at Mubende Hill', *Uganda Journal*, XXX (1966), 153–63.

[3] E. J. Wayland, M. C. Burkitt and J. H. Braunholtz, 'Archaeological Discoveries at Luzira', *Man* (1933), 29; Posnansky, in Bishop and Clark, op. cit., pp. 632–4; Posnansky and Chaplin, 'Terracotta figures, from Entebbe', *Man*, N.S., III (1968), 644–50.

[4] M. Trowell, 'The Rosette Cylinder from Ntusi', *Uganda Journal*, X (1946), 151–2.

[5] Pearce and Posnansky, art. cit., p. 91, fig. 7. On these terracottas, see also Cole, op. cit., pp. 323–6.

[6] It also occurs on modern pottery in other regions.

[7] Hiernaux and Maquet, art. cit.; Nenquin, op. cit. (1967), pp. 272 ff.

[8] Pearce and Posnansky, art. cit., pp. 89–90; Chapman, art. cit.

[9] See above, p. 165.

of the Nilotic-speaking Kalenjin and their 'Sirikwa hole' sites dating from the middle of the second millennium at the latest. This pottery, variously named 'Gumban B'[1], 'Lanet ware'[2] and

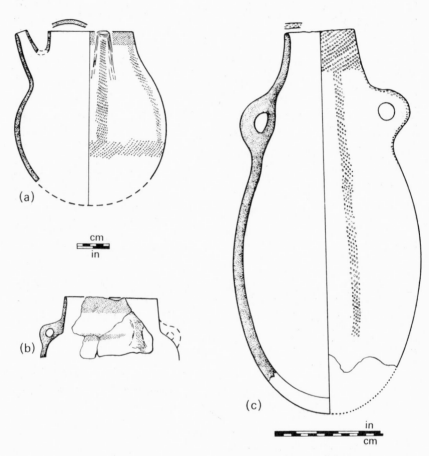

Fig. 10. Pottery from 'Sirikwa holes'. (a) Hyrax Hill (site II); (b) Mau Narok; (c) Lanet.

'Kenya highlands Class C',[3] is characterized by gourd shapes, sometimes with a square-cut rim with rouletted decoration along the top (as also occurs on some pots in western Uganda), handles

[1] L. S. B. Leakey, op. cit., p. 204; M. D. Leakey, art. cit., pp. 361–3, 372.
[2] Posnansky, art. cit. (1961), pp. 185–6.
[3] Sutton, art cit. (1964), pp. 30–1.

and occasionally spouts. The decoration is normally in bands round the rim and down the vessel in imitation of gourd-straps. It is possible that rouletting was introduced to East Africa by Nilotes, though this suggestion would need much ethnographic and archaeological research to confirm it.

The Nilotes are divided linguistically into three branches.[1] The 'Highland' Nilotes, who include the Kalenjin peoples, were the first to enter East Africa from the north, arriving with iron probably during the first millennium A.D., and absorbing numbers of the pre-Iron-Age Cushitic populations of the Kenya highlands.[2] Later, and in the lower country to their west, the Lwoo peoples, belonging to the 'River-lake' branch of the Nilotes, were settling in northern Uganda by the middle of the second millennium. Some of these Lwoo infiltrated into the Bantu kingdoms to their south,[3] while from the sixteenth century others migrated south-eastwards to establish themselves on the north-eastern shores of Lake Victoria and the Kavirondo Gulf.[4] Save for defensive enclosures of dry stonework built by these Kenya Luo in the nineteenth century,[5] archaeology has so far contributed virtually nothing to the history of the Lwoo peoples. Lastly, the 'Plains' Nilotes have expanded from a region to the west or north-west of Lake Rudolf more recently. One group, the Masai, entered the Kenya highlands and rift valley, where they displaced many of the Kalenjin about the seventeenth century, and pushed on into northern Tanzania, everywhere searching for the finest pastures. Another group, comprising the Turkana, Karimojong, Teso and others, has come to occupy the poorer grazing lands of north-western Kenya and north-eastern Uganda and to press upon the more fertile edges of the

[1] For linguistic and tribal classification and terminology, see Sutton, in Ogot and Kieran, op. cit. The appendix to that chapter also discusses the term 'Nilo-Hamitic', which was formerly applied to two of the three Nilotic branches, but which is now deemed valueless and confusing.

[2] This is mainly based on linguistic evidence—see ibid., and also the chapter by C. Ehret in the same volume.

[3] See above, p. 169.

[4] B. A. Ogot, *History of the Southern Luo* (1967).

[5] H. N. Chittick, 'A Note on Stone-built Enclosures in South Nyanza, Kenya', *Man* (1965), 147; L. Lofgren, 'Stone Structures of South Nyanza, Kenya', *Azania*, II (1967), 75–88.

Kenya highlands and eastern Uganda. Archaeologically, northern Uganda and northern Kenya are both very poorly known. The same applies to north-eastern Kenya, which consists mostly of yet poorer grazing, roamed in recent centuries by Eastern Cushitic-speakers, notably Galla and latterly Somali.

Of these non-Bantu regions, the one that can be discussed further is the rift valley and the highlands on its western side. Reference has already been made to the 'Sirikwa holes' and their pottery. 'Sirikwa holes' occur in group after group on the hillsides of the western highlands of Kenya and in the elevated part of the rift valley around Nakuru. They were sunken defended cattle-enclosures with houses attached made by the Kalenjin, whose economy, formerly as now, was based on a combination of agriculture and stock-raising. Some 'Sirikwa holes' date as late as the eighteenth century or possibly the early nineteenth, but the first ones must be several centuries older. The only radio-carbon dates so far are of the late sixteenth century from Lanet in the rift valley and the mid-seventeenth century from Moiben on the Uasin Gishu plateau in the west; but these dates fall within uncertain limits.[1] It is unlikely, however, that the earliest 'Sirikwa holes' stretch back to the first millennium, to the beginnings of the Iron Age, and to the earliest 'Highland' Nilotic settlements; and yet, no earlier Iron-Age sites are known in this region. 'Dimple-based' or related pottery has not been found there: in fact, there is nothing to bridge the gap between the burial cairns and other sites of the Late-Stone-Age food-producers on the one hand and the Iron-Age 'Sirikwa holes' on the other. It is note-worthy that, besides a few iron objects from excavated 'Sirikwa holes' and remains of iron-working on a number of sites, stone flakes and tools are also found at times. Some of these may be stray pieces; but the fair number obtained in the excavation of two 'Sirikwa holes' and an associated mound at Hyrax Hill, Site II ('the north-east village')[2] at Nakuru suggests an incom-

[1] Sutton, art. cit. (1966); and forthcoming publication, *The Archaeology of the Western Highlands of Kenya*; Posnansky, 'Excavations at Lanet, Kenya, 1957' *Azania*, II (1967), 89–114. The Lanet date is not actually from a 'Sirikwa hole', but from below an earthwork associated with a large group of 'Sirikwa holes'.

[2] M. D. Leakey, art. cit., pp. 363–4.

plete transition from a lithic to an iron technology. The pottery from this site, moreover, though not atypical of a 'Sirikwa hole', does appear rather archaic, and might strengthen the argument for a least an early second millennium date for the first 'Sirikwa holes'.

Site I at Hyrax Hill[1] also deserves mention. Here there were occupation and burials at two periods, the first by food-producers of the Late Stone Age, the second in the Late Iron Age. The latter settlement is unique. The pottery, both in shapes and decoration, is a developed form of the 'Kenya highlands Class C' pottery of the 'Sirikwa holes', while the stone enclosures and hut-circles may similarly be developed from the 'Sirikwa hole' form. Moreover, the pottery pipe-bowls, perhaps the iron-work too, and particularly the imported glass beads, which are of eighteenth or nineteenth century type,[2] also indicate a recent date. Now, from about the seventeenth century, the Masai were moving into the rift valley grasslands and forcing the Kalenjin back into the western highlands. Hence 'Sirikwa holes' ceased to be made in the rift valley (and somewhat later in the western highlands too, perhaps because the Kalenjin needed to devise more effective methods of protecting their livestock from large-scale raiding.)[3] The late site at Hyrax Hill is certainly not a typical Masai settlement; but it could be that of a group of 'Dorobo' of Kalenjin extraction or of Ilkunono Masai, who undertake smithing and potting. It is significant that modern Dorobo pots and many of those used by Masai to this day are clearly derived from 'Kenya highlands Class C'—as are some modern Kalenjin pots too.

Whereas in Kenya the southern Cushites of Late-Stone-Age descent have been virtually entirely absorbed by Bantu and Nilotes during the Iron Age, in northern Tanzania several groups remain unassimilated to this day. The most important tribe is the Iraqw (or Mbulu) now inhabiting the fertile highlands west of the

---

[1] Ibid., pp. 274 ff.

[2] Reassessed by H. N. Chittick, 'The Description and Dating of the Glass Beads in Eastern Africa', paper to conference on 'East Africa and the Orient', 1967.

[3] Sutton, 'Sirikwa Holes, Stone Houses and Their Makers in the Western Highlands of Kenya', Man (1965), 101.

rift valley between Lakes Manyara and Eyasi. According to Masai accounts, Iraqw were a century or more ago living and cultivating further north, not only at the Iron-Age settlement of Engaruka,[1] but also beyond the Kenya border.[2] Engaruka is undoubtedly the most famous Iron-Age site in the whole East African interior. Yet, despite some recent excavations there,[3] it remains very much a mystery. Earlier accounts of it as a city containing many thousands of people can now be discredited. For, obviously, it was an agricultural settlement, largely dependent on the irrigation potentialities of the river that tumbles down the escarpment into the dry rift valley. There can be little doubt that the extensive abandoned field-systems still visible at Engaruka were mostly cultivated by irrigation, despite the fact that only in a few places can one now trace or conjecture the actual irrigation works and furrows. In the valley the fields are mostly divided by stone lines, while those on the lower part of the escarpment are terraced by means of dry-stone revetments. On the escarpment there are also numerous closely packed homestead-complexes on platforms that have been levelled and revetted with dry stonework. There are several small enclosures and other stone features in the valley, presumably for domestic or stock-penning purposes. A few glass beads and cowrie-shells were found during the excavations, but there is no indication of important trading activities or outside connections.

These remains at Engaruka, indicating a concentrated agricultural population, may well span a long period of time, or indeed several separated periods. This view might be supported by the somewhat varied pottery types found in different parts of the site. Rouletted decoration is decidedly rare. More common forms of decoration are crude horizontal lines, sometimes in patterns of filled-in triangles, and lines of dots or combing.

[1] L. S. B. Leakey, 'Preliminary Report on Examination of the Engaruka Ruins', *Tanganyika Notes and Records*, I (1936), 57–60.

H. A. Fosbrooke, 'Rift Valley Ruins', ibid., 6 (1938), 58–60, thinks that the Mbugwe, a nearby Bantu tribe, and not the Iraqw, may be intended. But this sounds less likely.

[2] Information Professor A. H. Jacobs.

[3] H. Sassoon, 'Engaruka: excavations during 1964', *Azania*, I (1966), 79–99; id., 'New Views on Engaruka, Northern Tanzania', *Journal of African History*, VIII (1967), 201–17. The following account is based on these articles and the present author's observations.

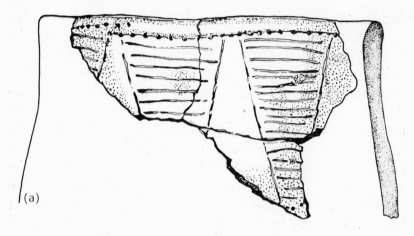

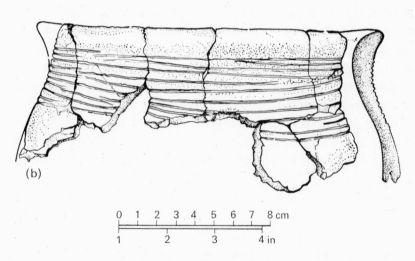

FIG. 11. Pottery from Engaruka.

Selected features in this pottery can be compared superficially with certain aspects of 'dimple-based' and 'channel-decorated' wares, or conversely of the Late-Stone-Age ('Class A') pottery of the Kenya and northern Tanzania highlands. Such observations are of little help; in fact, the pottery groups of Engaruka have more in common with one another than any of them have with other wares that have been described. Similar pottery has been picked up on at least one other, though much smaller, site in the same region. More perplexing than the pottery are the radio-carbon dates, which vary from the fourth to the nineteenth or twentieth centuries A.D. While it is not impossible that occupation or separate occupations covered so long a period, Sassoon has doubts both about the first millennium dates and about the most recent ones.[1] However, five of the nine dates so far obtained fall between the fifteenth and eighteenth centuries. Quite possibly these indicate the main occupation of Engaruka. This could fit admirably the contention that it was an Iraqw site; but that can only be verified by further archaeological field-work, as well as ethnographic and oral enquiries among the Iraqw and other peoples.

If Engaruka is really less important than it has been made to appear, the discussion of it does raise certain broader issues, such as the origins and cultural connections of irrigation and stone-building.[2] Irrigation is practised to this day by peoples of various linguistic groups in a large number of localities in the highlands of Kenya and northern Tanzania, both in the hills themselves and at the feet of escarpments where rivers run into the dry plains. The quality of the engineering is variable, but some of it is excellent. One might cite that of the Marakwet, a Kalenjin group on the Kenya rift escarpment, of the Sonjo, an isolated Bantu group of mixed ancestry living near to Engaruka, and of the large villages at the feet of the South Pare hills. It is possible that these practices derive from an ancient tradition extending back to the earliest Cushitic cultivators in these parts of East Africa and to their Ethiopian connections. Alternatively, they may have been developed independently in the East African highlands during the Iron Age, in response to local needs and conditions. Similarly inconclusive are discussions of pastoral

---

[1] Art. cit. (1967), pp. 208–9.

[2] Along with 'Azanian' and 'megalithic' theories: for example, G. W. B. Huntingford, 'The Azanian Civilization of Kenya', *Antiquity*, VII (1933), 153–65; B. Davidson, *Old Africa Rediscovered* (1959), ch. 8; G. P. Murdock, *Africa: Its Peoples and Their Culture History* (1959), ch. 25; Huntingford, in Oliver and Mathew, op. cit., pp. 71–4. These theories are discussed in my article in *Azania*, I, especially pp. 37–8, 45.

works, such as the reservoir dams in the fine highland pastures of northern Tanzania, and the wells in the poorer grazings such as the Masai Steppe and eastern and northern Kenya.[1] In the case of the wells, it is perhaps easier to argue for a long cultural tradition connecting with Ethiopia and the Horn, in view of their wide geographical extent and their ascription to a period beyond that of the present pastoral tribes.

Stone-building,[2] even more than irrigation, has been especially dear to the culture-diffusion schools. Stonework in East Africa depends in the first place on the local geology, on whether there are stones available on the surface or that have to be moved before building or cultivation can begin. For most of the features that are sometimes constructed of piled or dry stonework in the East African interior can be—and in stoneless country have to be —made of earth, trash or wood instead. This is true of field-terracing undertaken to conserve the soil in a few restricted localities in the Kenya and northern Tanzania highlands[3] (sometimes, but by no means invariably, connected with irrigation), and similarly of homestead and cattle enclosures. 'Sirikwa holes', for instance, may or may not be lined with stone-work, depending on whether the area is stony. Moreover, even at Engaruka, it is unlikely that houses were actually built of stone: we should probably imagine wooden houses with thatch roofs standing within the stone-circles and enclosures.

Finally, some ethnographic and sociological notes on the smelting and forging of iron in East Africa.[4] In the south-west,

[1] Ibid., p. 45; H. A. Fosbrooke, 'Prehistoric Wells, Rainponds and Associated Burials in Northern Tanganyika', in Clark, op. cit. (1957), pp. 326–35.

[2] For a fuller discussion, see my paper, 'Stone Building in the East African Interior', to conference on 'East Africa and the Orient', 1967.

[3] There are also references to ancient terraces in the southern highlands of Tanzania— G. E. H. Wilson, 'The Ancient Civilization of the Rift Valley', Man (1932), 298; P. M. Worsley and J. P. Rumberger, 'Remains of an Earlier People in Uhehe', Tanganyika Notes and Records, 27 (1949), 42–6. These reports are apparently based on misobservation of recent and modern ridging practices and dry season cultivations. See my article in Azania, IV (1969).

Reports of 'ancient roads', 'rock-constructions', etc. in the same region are mostly baseless.

[4] These summary notes are in no way an exhaustive treatment of the subject. Unreferenced material is based on private information including recent work by students in Tanzania. See Tanzania Zamani, No. 4 (January, 1969).

notably among the Fipa[1] and the Nyiha,[2] tall furnaces 3 or 4 m. high are built. Elsewhere furnaces are smaller,[3] and sometimes very low[4] or dug into the ground.[5] In the northern parts of East Africa bowl bellows, originating perhaps in the Nile region, are normally employed for maintaining an air current during the work, whereas bag bellows, more probably introduced from the Indian Ocean, are found in some parts further south.[6] However, archaeological evidence of methods used through the Iron Age is extremely thin: hence it is not possible to tell whether present or recent iron-working techniques in a particular region descend from the earliest iron-workers or are secondary innovations. The types of ore and methods of obtaining it vary considerably and may also influence smelting techniques. Information is now difficult to obtain, since, with the import of iron from overseas, smelters are few and scattered. And, though there are written accounts of smelting in several parts of East Africa, some of them are inadequate.

Until recently, iron-smelting was fairly well distributed throughout East Africa, but tended to be concentrated among particular tribes, sections and clans in areas of good ores. Expecially famous in Tanzania were the smelters of Pare in the north-east, of Makua in the south-east, of Nyiha and Fipa in the south-west, of Rangi in the centre, and of certain scattered localities in the west.[7] In Uganda, several western districts,[8] the Labwor in the north-east,[9] and the Samia by Lake Victoria on the

---

[1] R. C. H. Greig, 'Iron Smelting in Fipa', *Tanganyika Notes and Records*, 4 (1937), 77–81; R. Wise, 'Iron Smelting in Ufipa', ibid., 50 (1958), 106–11.

[2] B. and P. W. G. Brock, 'Iron Working amongst the Nyiha of South-western Tanganyika', *South African Archaeological Bulletin*, XX (1965), 97–100.

[3] For example, C. C. de Rosemond, 'Iron Smelting in the Kahama District', *Tanganyika Notes and Records*, 16 (1943), 79–84.

[4] A Galloway, 'A Note on the Iron-smelting Methods of the Elgeyo Masai', *South African Journal of Science*, XXXI (1934), 500–4. (It should be noted that the Elgeyo are not Masai, but Kalenjin.)

[5] As in western Uganda—J. Roscoe, *The Baganda* (1911), pp. 379 ff.; id., *The Banyankole* (1923), pp. 105–7; id., *The Bakitara or Banyoro* (1923), p. 220.

[6] Wainwright, art. cit., p. 125; Posnansky, op. cit. (1966), pp. 87, 90.

[7] Roberts, op. cit., pp. 101, 123.

[8] Roscoe, *The Baganda*, p. 170.

[9] P. and P. H. Gulliver, *The Central Nilo-Hamites* (Ethnographic Survey of Africa, East Central Africa, VII) (1953), p. 95.

Kenya border were outstanding. Among the Kalenjin, Masai, Kikuyu and other peoples of Kenya, there were districts that specialized in smelting, where particular clans or sections maintained a sort of monopoly.[1] Wrought iron, in such forms as bars and hoes, could then be traded within the tribe or to neighbouring peoples lacking good ores and smelters. Forging was a more widespread craft. For instance, the Chagga smiths on Kilimanjaro used iron smelted in Pare; the Lango of northern Uganda fashioned spear-heads from Palwo hoes in the nineteenth century.[2] Earlier, iron was exceedingly rare among the Lango; and in several other parts of East Africa, such as Ugogo in central Tanzania, the scarcity of iron before the further development of inter-tribal contact and caravans in the nineteenth century is well remembered.

As craftsmen possessing the skills and magic for supplying the necessary tools for cultivation and everyday life, as well as weapons for defence and war, smiths are highly respected in East Africa (even though among Masai and certain other peoples they may form a separate group regarded as 'unclean'). For smiths to aspire to chiefly or royal status was not so common. However, several instances of their attaining pre-eminence in the past are recorded in Bantu regions of Tanzania. The traditions of Pare tell of the leadership asserted by the Shana iron-working clan some sixteen generations ago;[3] while the history of near-by Usambara explains how in the eighteenth century a new ruling dynasty overcame the power formerly wielded by a smithing clan.[4] Among the Kimbu of western Tanzania, immigrants from the east in the eighteenth century managed to establish their superiority partly because of the iron they brought and their skills in working it; whereas in Ufipa the senior chiefly line, that was superseded politically by newcomers about the same time, was closely connected with iron-making.[5] But some

[1] For example, A. C. Hollis, *The Nandi, Their Language and Folklore* (1909), pp. 36–8; Galloway, art. cit.; Hollis, *The Masai*, pp. 330–1; J. Kenyatta, *Facing Mount Kenya* (1938), pp. 70–6.

[2] J. H. Driberg, *The Lango* (1923), pp. 30–1, 81, 87.

[3] I. N. Kimambo, *A Political History of the Pare People to 1900* (1969), pp. 5–6, 32, 47–51.

[4] Abdallah bin Hemedi, *Habari za Wakilindi* (1962), ch. 11.

[5] Roberts, op. cit., chapters by Shorter and R. G. Willis; Shorter, art. cit., pp. 53–4.

stories should not be accepted at their face value. For example, in the fertile country sloping down from Rungwe to the head of Lake Nyasa, the Nyakyusa have a myth that iron tools were introduced by a chiefly lineage from Ukinga three or four centuries ago.[1] Though it may have been scarce, it is most unlikely that iron was completely unknown till so late, especially in view of the discovery of Middle- and perhaps Early-Iron-Age sites just across the Malawi border.[2] Similarly, in western Uganda, some accounts would credit the Chwezi as having been clever smiths who introduced iron to the country;[3] while over the Tanzanian border in Karagwe, whose royal line claims Chwezi descent, king Ndagara in the early nineteenth century is remembered as a skilful blacksmith (though probably not a smelter) and a powerful magician.[4] Such traditions are doubtless idealizations, and are hardly consistent with the view that iron workers in western Uganda were of lowly class.[5] Moreover, the Early-Iron-Ages sites by Lake Victoria and further west show that iron was known long before the period of the Chwezi and the kingdoms.

Iron objects—hoes, spears, and in Karagwe model cattle—are frequent among royal or chiefly regalia and treasure-collections. This again does not necessarily indicate that the rulers are descended from blacksmiths. Yet it does emphasize the economic, political and military importance of iron, and the need for the ruling group to control its production and trade. An iron spear symbolizes power; an iron hoe, whether to be used in the field, to be forged into some other implement, or valued as currency or an heir-loom, symbolizes prosperity; an iron cow (or bull) may symbolically combine both.

[1] M. Wilson, *The Communal Rituals of the Nyakyusa* (1958), p. 1. This myth seems to be partly a rationalization from the fact that the Nyakyusa smiths were dependent for supplies of smelted iron on neighbouring districts, Ukinga especially. See J. Thompson, *To the Central African Lakes and Back* (1881), I, 272–3.

[2] Robinson, art. cit.; and, Sandelowsky, art. cit.

[3] Mrs. B. Fisher, *Twilight Tales of the Black Baganda* (1911), p. 39; Lanning, 'Ancient Earthworks', p. 60; A. R. Dunbar, *A History of Bunyoro-Kitara* (1965), pp. 22–4.

[4] J. Ford and R. de Z. Hall, 'The History of Karagwe', *Tanganyika Notes and Records*, 24 (1947), 8.

[5] Roscoe, *The Banyankole*, p. 105; id., *The Bakitara*, pp. 10, 217.

7

THE CONGO, RWANDA, AND BURUNDI

by

J. Nenquin

U NLIKE some other countries in Africa, the Rwanda–
Burundi–Congo area cannot boast of a long tradition in
organized archaeological research. One or two expeditions went into the field before 1940, but it is really only since
the Second World War that a certain effort was made to fill in the
all too extensive blank spaces on the maps alleging to show the
distribution of the Central African prehistoric cultures. This was
done by a more or less systematic investigation of geographically well-defined regions[1] and the formation of groups of
enthusiastic local workers;[2] with very few exceptions, however,
most people seemed to be interested in Stone-Age material only
and Iron-Age pottery or other relics of protohistoric culture-
groups were thought to be less important. Moreover, no comprehensive *corpus* of modern pottery has as yet been published,
thus making comparisons with older material much more difficult than would otherwise have been the case. It is not surprising
that with these handicaps, most of the available evidence consists
of scattered surface material, on which it is practically impossible
to build up anything like an overall picture of the protohistoric

---

[1] M. Bequaert in Kasai, A. Anciaux de Faveaux and J. Nenquin in Katanga, J. de
Heinzelin in the Ishango area, G. Mortelmans and H. Van Moorsel near Kinshasha and
Thysville, J. Hiernaux, E. Maquet and J. Nenquin in Rwanda and Burundi.

[2] As at Luluabourg and Lubumbashi.

cultures of the area under discussion. Pending many more excavations and a complete publication of the existing museum collections, one can only try to summarize here and classify geographically what is known of the metal- and pottery-using, protohistoric inhabitants of the Congo Basin and Rwanda–Burundi.[1] Evidence for relative and absolute age, such as it is, will be indicated in the appropriate paragraphs.

Roughly speaking, and for convenience's sake, three separate areas may be distinguished from which a certain amount of early pottery or other material is known:

1. To the East, and adjacent to the area covered in this volume: Rwanda, Burundi and part of eastern Kivu; with a so-called 'Neolithic' in Uele.
2. To the West and South-West: Kasai and the Stanley-Pool region, with the interesting caves near Thysville; and
3. Katanga, to the South-East.

Isolated sherds are known from the areas not mentioned in this very sketchy geographical distribution scheme, but the nature of this evidence is such, that no useful purpose can be served by describing it here.

1. RWANDA, BURUNDI AND EASTERN KIVU

Largely thanks to the work of J. Hiernaux and E. Maquet,[2] it is now possible to distinguish in this region three different types of pottery known as A, B and C ware.

(a) A-type pottery

Better known from other places in East-Central Africa as 'dimple-based' ware, it has been found in twenty different sites.

[1] A paper on the same subject is to be found in Bishop and Clark (eds), *Background to Evolution in Africa* (1967), 651–8.

[2] J. Hiernaux, et E. Maquet, 'Cultures Préhistoriques de l'Age des Métaux au Ruanda-Urundi et au Kivu. I,' *Acad. roy. Sciences colon.—Bull. des Séances*, N.S. II—1956-6 (Bruxelles, 1957), 1126–49. Id., Ibid., II. *Acad. roy. Sciences d'Outre-Mer, Mém. in-8°*, N.S. X, 2 (Bruxelles, 1960). See also J. Hiernaux, 'Le Début de l'Age des Métaux dans la Région des Grands Lacs Africains,' *Actes IVe Congrès Panafr. de Préhist. et de l'Etude du Quarternaire*, III (Tervuren, 1962), 381–9. J. Nenquin, *Contributions to the study of the prehistoric cultures of Rwanda and Burundi.* (Tervuren, 1967.) See specifically 257–87.

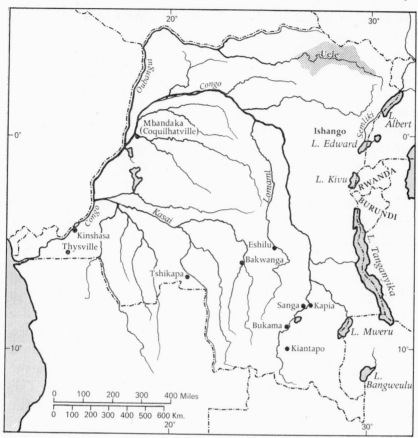

MAP. 8. The Congo, Rwanda and Burundi.

This type of ware needs no detailed description here,[1] and one illustration (see Fig. 12a) will be sufficient to show its similarity with the pottery from the famous Leakey–Owen–Leakey publication of the Kavirondo site.[2] It should be mentioned that the pot illustrated here was found, together with numerous others, by Mme I. Boutakoff about 30 years ago, in the Ruhimangyargya Cave near the southern tip of Lake Kivu.[3] Unfortunately, the

[1] See in this volume, pp. 152–156.

[2] M. D. Leakey, W. E. Owen, and L. S. B. Leakey, 'Dimple-based Pottery from Central Kavirondo, Kenya Colony', *Coryndon Memorial Museum Occasional Paper* (Nairobi, 1948).

[3] Mme. I. Boutakoff, 'Premières Explorations Méthodiques des Gisements de l'Age de la Pierre au Ruanda-Urundi. Abris Sous Roche, Ateliers et Stations en Plein Air', *Inst. colon. Belge—Bull. des Séances*, VIII—1937-1 (Bruxelles), 179–201.

description given of the different industries making up the cultural succession is not very clear; this much, however, seems certain, that a palaeolithic industry (no clear characteristics given) was followed by a sterile layer, on top of which were found the 'dimple-based' sherds mixed with a microlithic industry, of 'Wilton' type. The same author mentions similar ware, somewhat less well-made, from a number of rock-shelters grouped around the near-by site of Ruigega.

The same mixture of 'dimple-based' ware and 'Wilton' is found at several other sites, i.a. at Masangano, also in Rwanda. This Hiernaux[1] explains by suggesting the adoption of 'dimple-based' pottery by the 'Wiltonians', both cultures existing side by side. At five sites, on the other hand, it was seen that the 'dimple-base' level was overlying and clearly separated from a layer containing a microlithic industry on quartzite. A most tantalizing description has been given by Hiernaux[2] of a site near km. 150 on the Bukavu–Goma road in Kivu. There he discovered a large rockshelter in which were observed several stratified levels with different types of pottery, the whole overlying a lithic industry. Four pottery levels could be distinguished, the bottom one containing several 'dimple-based' sherds. This 'dimple-based' level was separated from the one with a lithic industry by a sterile layer of up to 40 cms. thickness.

What seems even more important regarding the introduction of metal-working in East-Central Africa, is the fact that in seven sites, 'dimple-based' ware was found associated with iron slag, fragments of tuyères, and plano-convex bricks. These bricks are hand-made and often decorated with rows of thumb-impressions, as was the case at Bishange,[3] where an iron-smelting furnace was discovered. As long as no radio-carbon dates are available, it remains difficult to say when and from where the

[1] loc. cit. (1962).

[2] loc. cit. (1962). More recently, E. Maquet and J. Hiernaux, 'Céramique ancienne en territoires Havu et Hunde', Africa–Tervuren XIV (1968), 111–116.

[3] J. Hiernaux, et E. Maquet, 'Un Haut-fourneau Préhistorique au Buhunde (Kivu, Congo Belge)', Zaïre (1954), 615–19. Also J. Hiernaux, 'Recent Research at Protohistoric Sites in Ruanda, the Belgian Congo (Katanga Province) and in Uganda (Kibiro)', in 'Discovering Africa's Past', Uganda Mus. Occ. Paper 4 (Kampala, 1959), 26–30.

makers of the 'dimple-based' ware arrived in Rwanda and Burundi. A number of carbon samples have indeed been taken at different sites there,[1] but no dates have as yet been published.

(b) B-type pottery

This type of ware is quite different from the 'dimple-based' pottery. It is much more roughly made, irregularly fired, and the paste contains large pieces of quartz. The most distinctive feature, however, is the heavy, thickened overhanging rim, squared at the top, and decorated with roulette- or cord-impressions, deep and irregular incisions, and sometimes wavy lines; the variety of decoration is greater than on the 'dimple-based' pots. An interesting feature is the occurrence of handles, which often show the same cord-impressed ornamentation.

Of the more than twenty sites where B-ware has been found, the collective burial at Ruli (Rwanda) is the most important one. Several bodies were discovered here, buried with a number of pots; one of these contained sorghum. Other indications of agriculture are the fragments of grinding stones found at Gikoma.[2]

No absolute dates are available for the B-type pottery in Rwanda and Burundi. It undoubtedly is later than the 'dimple-based' ware, as in several places it has been found overlying it. Thanks to the Ruli find, something is known of the physical type of the users of B-type ware: they seem to be rather similar to the present-day Hutu. Hiernaux[3] suggests that B-type pottery was used by the so-called 'Renge' (Abarenge), a group living in Rwanda before the arrival of the present population, and now extinct as an entity.

(c) C-type pottery

This pottery, although it has been found at ten separate sites, is not well known. It is much better made than either 'dimple-

---

[1] Oral communication by J. Hiernaux. See also J. Hiernaux and E. Maquet, *L'age du fer à Kibiro (Uganda)*, (Tervuren, 1968), 48.

[2] Hiernaux-Maquet (1960).

[3] J. Hiernaux, 'Note Sur Une Ancienne Population du Ruanda-Urundi: les Renge', *Zaïre* (1956), 4, 351–60.

based' or B-type ware. Here again the rim is the most distinctive feature: it is pointed, thickening towards the base; the decoration, mostly incised, consists mainly of fairly regular cross-hatching, but bird-bone impressions do occur.

Nothing is known about date or users of this type of ware. There are certain indications, however, that it is fairly recent. Indeed, it might be useful to compare a distribution map of the C-type ware and a map of the known residences of the Tutsi kings. On this subject some work has recently been published.[1]

Quite apart from these three pottery groups in Rwanda, Burundi and eastern Kivu, a number of isolated finds have been reported from the same area. De Heinzelin[2] mentions sherds of flat-bottomed vases at Ishango, associated with worked quartz. Between Lake Edward and Lake Albert in the lower Semliki valley, he reports having seen large heaps of iron slag (especially the valley of the rivers Sinda and Mohari), apparently in association with grinding stones, pottery sherds and quartz implements belonging to the usual atypical microlithic assemblage. The greater number of sherds seem to be fragments of perforated plaques used as salt filters, and other vessels used in salt extraction. The only older (?) sherds which were found belonged to a large, crudely made flat-bottomed pot, possibly of the same type as the Ishango ones. Hiernaux-Maquet[3] mention isolated surface finds from at least four other sites. One of these, at Nkarama near Butare, is a pot with a dimple in its base, but with modern type cord-impressed decoration of the shoulder. None, however, seem to be related to any of the known pottery groups.

2. KASAI AND THE STANLEY-POOL AREA

For Kasai, the evidence available does not even permit of an elementary classification into groups, as has been the case for Rwanda and Burundi; the material is too scanty for so large an area, and no absolute dates exist. There have been found in

[1] F. Van Noten, 'Tutsi Koningsgraven', Africa-Tervuren, XIV (1968), 57–62.

[2] J. de Heinzelin, 'Les Fouilles d'Ishango' (Bruxelles, 1957); id. 'Métallurgie Primitive du Fer dans la Région de la Basse-Semliki', Acad. roy. Sciences colon.—Bull. des Séances, N.S. V—1959–3 (Bruxelles), 673–98.

[3] Hiernaux-Maquet, loc. cit., (1960).

isolated places a certain number of pots and pottery sherds, which all one can do about is to describe them, hoping that sometime one may find a stratified site which it will be possible to excavate. The situation is somewhat better for the Stanley-Pool region, where Mortelmans[1] has proposed a working scheme for the typology of the pottery found in a number of caves near Thysville.

(*a*) Probably the oldest ceramics known from Kasai are four complete and typical 'dimple-base' pots found at Tshikapa some time ago and published some years ago.[2] The four pots, two of which have the dimple and the scroll/spectacle decoration, were discovered together; unfortunately it is not known whether evidence of metal-working was also to be seen at the site. This most interesting find shows the enormous extension towards the West of the 'dimple-base' ware, since Tshikapa is nearly 1,000 km. distant from the nearest known 'dimple-base' site in Kivu. The conservatism in style of decoration is also noteworthy, and seems to be an essential element of the 'dimple-base' cultural tradition.

(*b*) A practically complete pot was found near the Dibindi mine (diamond mines of the Forminière, near Bakwanga, Kasai), which lies approximately halfway between Kabinda and Luluabourg.[3] This pot shows a certain similarity in decoration with 'dimple-based' ware, and might possibly be included in this group.

(*c*) A third pottery find, but this time of a completely different type, is known from Sasatshie, in the same region.[4] It was found *in situ*, in gravels, and is flat-bottomed with a piriform body and a short cylindrical neck. Nothing is known about possible associated finds, or date.

(*d*) A considerable number of pottery sherds were collected

---

[1] G. Mortelmans, 'Archéologie des Grottes Dimba et Ngovo (Région de Thysville, Bas-Congo)', *Actes IVe Congrès Panafr. de Préhist. et de l'Etude du Quarternaire*, III (Tervuren, 1962), 407–25.

[2] J. Nenquin, 'Dimple-based Pots from Kasai, Belgian Congo', *Man* (1959), No. 242, 1–3.

[3] A more detailed description of this find is given in J. Nenquin's paper in Bishop and Clark op. cit. 653.

[4] See preceding note.

by M. Bequaert in the Tshienda Cave (Bushimaie, Kasai), together with metal objects (iron, copper) and fragments of skeletons. Fig. 12b–d gives an idea of this type of ware, which is probably not very old. All pots and bowls are round-bottomed, and have a constricted neck and outwards flaring rim; in the larger examples the rim is decorated with horizontal shallow grooves. The ornamentation on neck and shoulder very often consists of parallel lines or zigzag patterns impressed with a multiple-toothed comb; sometimes incised cross-hatching exists. In a few cases the inner face of the rim is also decorated with oblique comb-impressions (see Fig. 12c). Another element of decoration is a more or less vertical, unperforated 'handle', which however does not seem to have any functional purpose. This same element also exists with certain pots of Mortelmans Group III, to be described later.[1]

(e) Several pots which have never before been described, come from an old cemetery at Eshilu, somewhat to the South of Tshofa (25°10′ E.–5°15′ S.). As is the case at Tshienda, the Eshilu ware does not appear to be very old, although the cemetery was abandoned and the local inhabitants did not have any objection to the pots being taken away. Rather deep bowls are fairly common (Fig. 13a); some have a pronounced inner rim to take a lid, and one has a circular footring (Fig. 13d). A favourite shape seems to be a rather squat vase with a short cylindrical neck and a clearly indicated rim which is sometimes finely decorated with short oblique incisions (Fig. 13b). The ornamentation is quite rich and consists either of incised cross-hatching and parallel grooves, or of applied strips of clay which have been moulded into different shapes (rectangles, trapezes, festoons, etc.); irregular hollows have been made into these plastic bands (Fig. 13c). Sometimes both types of decoration are combined. It is mostly neck and shoulder which are ornamented in this manner, a technique which apparently is no longer used in this area.

(f). In a paper read by him at the Léopoldville session of the Panafrican Congress on Pre- and Protohistory, Mortelmans[2] described the possible succession of pottery types found in two

---

[1] G. Mortelmans, see note 1, p. 189; his Pl. IV, bottom centre.
[2] See note 1, p. 189.

caves near Thysville (Dimba/Tordeur and Ngovo/Langa), and distinguished six different classes. Stratigraphy could not be observed, but relative ages were suggested based upon the different degree of calcite deposition on the sherds, on the assumption 'thickest' calcite equals oldest pottery', a theory perhaps not wholly reliable. It has been possible to add to the material given by Mortelmans from the collections of the Musée royal de l'Afrique centrale at Tervuren, where a number of pots and sherds had been deposited by earlier workers, i.a. M. Bequaert, J. Heuts and N. Leleup. Although several new forms could be distinguished, it was thought to be more sensible to follow Mortelmans' classification before a complete study of the available material clarifies the situation.

The greatest part of his Group I consists of sometimes quite large (up to 50 cm. high) ovoid pots with pointed base, having frequently a small dimple or polygonal flattish surface (Fig. 14a). The rim is often squared, and decorated with radiating short incisions. The whole outer surface is covered with numberless parallel striations, the upper part often with additional oblique comb-impressions; numerous horizontal and more or less parallel deeper grooves complete the decoration.[1] Another not uncommon type is a deep bowl, wider at the shoulder than at the lip, which has the same overall-decoration: multiple striations, deep grooves and oblique comb-impressions; these last often fill hanging semicircular festoons (Fig. 14b). A very handsome type of ware is illustrated in Fig. 14c: a generally rather small pot with rounded base and short cylindrical neck. Here again the same elaborate decoration completely covers the outer surface of the vessel. Other types do exist, but in too small a quantity to warrant a separate category, at least at the moment. Some of the pottery from this group may be compared with the T4, T5 and T6a ware of Bequaert[2] excavated by him, also near Thysville.

[1] Without of course implying any degree of parentage, these ovoid pots might be compared—as regards the shape—with the much smaller ovoid beakers described by Mary D. Leakey in 'Report on the Excavations at Hyrax Hill, Nakuru, Kenya Colony, 1937–1938', *Transactions Royal Soc. South Africa*, XXX, 271–409, more specifically, Fig. 7 and Pl. XI.

[2] M. Bequaert, 'Fouilles à Thysville du Musée Royal du Congo Belge, en 1938', *Actes IVe Congrès Panafr. de Préhist. et de l'Etude du Quaternaire*, III (Tervuren, 1962), 323–50.

Mortelmans[1] finds in this type of ware a number of elements characteristic of the 'dimple-based' ware from the region of the Great Lakes. Without wishing totally to exclude this possibility, it is the opinion of this writer, however, that not nearly enough similarities exist to justify this hypothesis.

Group II is completely different, both in shape as in decoration. The not very numerous pots show a uniformity of type which is rather remarkable (Fig. 15b and c): deep vases with rounded base, vertical walls and slightly everted rim. The angular decoration is strangely reminiscent of woodcarving: 'entrelac' and 'Kerbschnitt'-motifs are exclusively used.[2] The probable influence of woodcarving has suggested to Mortelmans[3] the possibility that here one might have the pottery of the Kuba-population, which traditionally migrated from the coast towards Kasai sometime in the early sixteenth century, or shortly before. Another interesting fact is shown by the composition of the clay: it contains a certain amount of mica, which is not found locally. This might mean that this ware was imported from somewhere in the Monts de Cristal region. Both are possibilities which need investigating. Pottery of this group, as well as ware belonging to Group V, is also known from the Mbafu cave.[4]

It is not impossible that Group III is but a local imitation of Group II ware, although certain elements of ornamentation are similar to those found in the Tshienda Cave (see above, and Fig. 15a). Generally speaking, however, the same woodcarving designs are to be seen, but much less clearly executed; sometimes knobs and 'buttons' are added.

The black, thin, glossy ware of Group IV is quite different again, and its simple ornamentation consists mainly of wide,

---

[1] Mortelmans, loc. cit., 410–11; also J. Hiernaux in the Discussion, p. 422.

[2] See in this respect: M.-L. Bastin, 'Art Décoratif Tshokwe', *Museu do Dundo, Diamang, Publicações Culturais*, No. 55 (Lisbon, 1961), I–II; more specifically in Vol. II: Pls. 16, 44–8, 66–73, 225–9.

[3] Mortelmans, loc. cit., 413–14.

[4] G. Mortelmans, et R. Monteyne, 'La Grotte Peinte de Mbafu, Témoignage Iconographique de la Première Évangélisation du Bas-Congo', *Actes IVe Congrès Panafr. de Préhist. et de l'Etude du Quaternaire*, III (Tervuren, 1962), 457–86; see 479–80. See also P. Raymaekers et H. Van Moorsel, 'Lovo; Dessins Rupestres du Bas-Congo', Ed. Université de Léopoldville (1964); more especially p. 10 and photos 9–10.

channelled grooving, to which oblique comb-impressions are often added. Sherds of a few pots only have been found.

Pottery belonging to Group V is already known since 1935,[1] but from Kalina. It was again mentioned in 1938,[2] and Van Moorsel[3] illustrates ware of a very similar nature from the site of Konkobela, which was the capital of the Stanley-Pool region in the seventeenth century. All the sherds are yellowish-white in colour and are rather thin. The ornamentation is quite elaborate and consists of alternatively decorated and undecorated 'metopes' on the neck and shoulder, and 'cartouches' on the horizontal rim.[4] These are filled in with incised cross-hatching and oblique comb-impressions. Several sites where this ware has been found are known from near Kinshasa, Fig. 16a–c showing one sherd from N'Dolo, and another large fragment with a very sophisticated handle from Kingabwa. Although the decoration here is not quite similar to that on the Thysville pots, it may provisionally be classed within the same group.

The last group of ware found here, Group VI, includes a number of pots and sherds which are generally less well made and simpler in ornamentation, often only a small band of grooves or crossing comb-impressions under the slightly everted lip (Fig. 16d). This pottery is probably not very old.

A few iron objects (bracelet, fragmentary knife, etc.) were also discovered in the Dimba Cave. Unfortunately it was not possible to see to which pottery group they belonged, although certain signs indicate that Groups III or IV are the most probable.

Before leaving the Thysville area, mention must be made of a number of sherds found by M. Bequaert near the confluence of the rivers Congo and Pioka, at a place called Manyanga. The small cup (see Fig. 16e) which it was possible to reconstruct from

[1] J. Colette, 'Note sur la Présence de Nids Fossiles d'Insectes dans le Pleistocène Supérieur du Stanley-Pool', *Bull. Soc. belge de Géol., Paléontol. et Hydrol.*, XLV (1935), 319.

[2] M. Bequaert, 'Les Fouilles de Jean Colette à Kalina', *Annales Mus. Congo belge. D, I; Anthrop. et Préhist.*, I, 2 (Bruxelles, 1938).

[3] H. Van Moorsel, 'Esquisse Préhistorique de la Plaine de Léopoldville', *Acad. roy. Sciences colon.—Bull. des Séances*, N.S. II—1956-4, 582–95.

[4] See Pl. V, right, in Mortelmans, loc. cit.

these fragments, most probably belongs to Mortelmans Group II; although the everted lip and the inner rim are somewhat different, the incised decoration on neck and shoulder are quite characteristic of the 'woodcarving' style typical of this group.

(g) The last group of pottery sherds to be described from the Stanley-Pool area are a number of fragments found at Kingabwa near Kinshasa, and belonging to thick-sided, flat-bottomed pots with heavy, knob-like handles (Fig. 17a and b).These pots are quite heavy and squat, their sides being decorated with thick ridges of clay, nail-impressed or plain. Comb-decoration does occur, but this most frequently is a characteristic feature of the handles which, however, may also be decorated with deep incisions. These handles are sometimes shaped in the form of human figurines, and are quite handsome. Since they were found on the surface, unfortunately no date can be given for these most interesting objects.

As a separate group, at least in space, three pots must be described from a collection found near Coquilhatville on the Equator(o°o'–18°15'E.) unfortunately again under circumstances which allow of no dating. The first is the lower part of a globular pot, the rim of which is missing, and with a circular footring (Fig. 17c). The ornamentation covers the whole of the outer surface and consists of several horizontal rows of zigzagging incisions, a number of horizontal grooves and shorter oblique incisions. The second pot is rather smaller, and part of the everted lip has been retained (Fig. 17d). Again the outer surface is completely covered with zigzag incisions, horizontal grooves and fishbone-pattern incisions. The bottom is flat, and the lip is decorated with short incisions. The third vase (Fig. 17e) has a rather different shape, with a carinated shoulder and a short subconical neck. Body and shoulder are plain, the neck alone being decorated with numerous vertical short incisions in fishbone-pattern. The fact that here too the base is flat, makes this group of pottery quite outstanding amongst the other proto-historic(?) ware from Congo, where round-bottomed pots are much more frequent.

3. KATANGA

This is the last of the three areas about which a certain amount of pottery is known. Probably the youngest material comes from:

(*a*) Kiantapo Cave, which has been described by E. Pittard[1] and later, amongst others, by H. Breuil.[2] The main interest of this cave lies in the incised, very schematized human figures and other motifs which can be seen on its walls. The pottery which was excavated 'aux environs de la grotte'[3] was described as 'Vieux Bantou', and said to be of a type similar to modern ware, perhaps Luba. It was associated with glass beads, European faience, cowrie shells, iron objects and slag. No stratigraphy was observed, and, as has been said, the ware is probably quite recent.

(*b*) Of more importance for our present study are two pots which were found near Kapia, which is near Lake Kabamba, between Mwanza and Mitwaba; found probably in 1937, and at a depth of 1·20 m. (about 4 ft.). One large pot (Fig. 18a) has a hemispherical body and a high cylindrical neck of a slightly smaller diameter. The neck is decorated with groups of parallel grooves, alternatively left and right oblique. Together with this rather striking vase was found a second, more or less globular pot (Fig. 18b). The decoration is confined to a small band under the rim, again of shallow oblique grooves.

No dating evidence is available, but the pots are probably pre-Luba, as they are completely different from the present-day ware found in the same region.

(*c*) The protohistoric cemetery at Katoto near Bukama, on the river Lualaba, was partly excavated by Hiernaux and De Buyst in 1959.[4] This most interesting site produced 69 skeletons,

---

[1] E. Pittard, 'Gravures Rupestres (Qu'on Pourrait Peut-être Considérer Comme Capsiennes?) Découvertes dans le Haut-Katanga (Congo Belge)', *Archives suisses d'Anthropol. génér.*, VII (1935), 2, 163–172.

[2] Henri Breuil, 'Les Figures Incisées et Ponctuées de la Grotte de Kiantapo (Katanga)' (Tervuren, 1952).

[3] Breuil, loc. cit., p. 5.

[4] J. Hiernaux et J. De Buyst, 'Note sur une Campagne de Fouilles à Katoto (Région de Bukama, Katanga)', *Zaïre*, XIV, 2–3 (1960), 251–3.

about 300 pots and very numerous iron and copper objects. It was observed that frequently several individuals were buried together in the same grave. Complete skeletons of goats and dogs were also found. No description of the pottery has as yet been given, but from a photograph accompanying a short article by Hiernaux and De Buyst it seems to be quite different from anything else known from Katanga, several pots having short cylindrical necks and one, at least, seeming to show protuberant knobs. Although no copper 'croisettes' are known from Katoto, several other copper objects were found there such as bracelets and necklaces of a peculiar type. Interesting too are large shells which resemble the *kilungu* now worn by certain chiefs. radio-carbon dates for this cemetery have not yet been released, but it is understood that a complete publication is in preparation.

(*d*) The last site which must be mentioned is the large necropolis at Sanga, a village lying on the northern shore of Lake Kisale, which is but one of a string of lakes forming the Lualaba river in that area.[1] Since it was possible to excavate part of this cemetery in a methodical manner, a considerable amount of evidence is here available. It became apparent after a few days work at the site, that three different groups of ware could be distinguished which were named 'Kisalian', 'Mulongo' and 'Red Slip' ware.

The Kisalian pots have a remarkably uniform basic shape (Fig. 19a) and decoration, this last frequently being a half-moon or crescent motif, convex towards the opening, incised in the shoulder. The inwards turning lip is usually covered with incised cross-hatching, oblique comb-impressions or horizontal grooves. Several pots retaining the same shape have handles added (Fig. 19b), or have a more complicated ornamentation. Another distinctive shape is the shallow bowl, sometimes with

---

[1] J. Nenquin, 'Excavations at Sanga, 1957. The protohistoric Necropolis' (Tervuren, 1963); id. 'Inventaria Archaeologica Africana, CL 1–CL 11', (Tervuren, 1964); ibid. 'Une Collection de Céramique Kisalienne au Musée Royal du Congo Belge', *Bull. Soc. roy. belge d'Anthrop. et de Préhistoire*, LXIX (1958); 151–210; ibid. 'Notes on Some Early Pottery Cultures from Northern Katanga', *Jnl. African History*, IV, 1 (1963), 19–32. See also J. Hiernaux, 'La Deuxième Saison de Fouilles à Sanga (Katanga)', *Les Naturalistes Belges*, 40 (1959), 165–7.

spout (Fig. 19c), sometimes without, sometimes with triangular handle, sometimes without. Still another is the trilobate cup (Fig. 18c) of which quite a few examples of different sizes were discovered. Unique specimens are a rather nice vase (Fig. 18d) and a small vase with long neck, of which the upper part is formed by a horizontal disc modelled to represent a grotesque human face with eyes, nose, mouth and curly hair.[1] Equally important for the present study are the metal objects which were found in some abundance, both iron and copper. The copper 'croisettes' are not numerous, a few specimens having been discovered in two out of twenty-nine Kisalian graves only; tubular beads and pieces of sheet copper occur. It is in the copper necklaces, however, that the technical mastery of the Kisalian metal-workers is most apparent,[2] as is shown in one example (Fig. 20a) made of interwoven copper wire, and terminated by a loop-and-hook attachment. Others are made of very thin copper wire (about 0·2 mm. in section) which is first spirally wound to form a hollow tube of 2–3 mm. diam.; this tube is then again spirally wound to form the necklace proper, which is about 15 mm. in section and 150 mm. wide. Iron bracelets and anklets are mostly of the simple ring type, although some have pyramidal knobs at the ends. Belts consist of strings of iron beads, but one unique example (Fig. 20b) is made of five twisted iron bars, hammered together at one end into a single flat band with a loop. A last type of ornament to be mentioned here is the iron bells, examples of which were found in three graves (Fig. 20d). Iron knives, spearpoints and arrowheads were also found, as were iron axes (Fig. 19d); but only one iron hoe (Fig. 20c) was discovered, oval in shape and with a slightly raised central ridge.

In three instances the presence of separate human teeth in Kisalian graves was noticed: in two cases it concerns perforated incisors, probably attached to a copper necklace. In the third case, a complete human mandible was found fastened to a copper-

[1] J. Nenquin, 'Quelques Poteries Protohistoriques à Face Humaine Trouvées au Katanga (Congo)', *Jnl. de la Soc. des Africanistes*, XXX, 2 (1960), 145–50.

[2] J. Nenquin, 'Protohistorische Metaaltechniek in Katanga', *Africa-Tervuren*, VII (1961–4), 97–101.

chain belt by means of copper rings. It is further noteworthy that special care seems to have been taken of children's graves, the grave-goods there being especially rich and varied.

Two radio-carbon dates are fortunately available for Kisalian graves[1] (dates before 1960):

$$B\text{-}263 \quad 1240 \pm 120 \,(= \text{A.D. } 720 \pm 120),$$
$$B\text{-}264 \quad 1070 \pm 200 \,(= \text{A.D. } 890 \pm 200).$$

These seem to indicate that the time from the second half of the seventh century A.D. to well into the ninth or perhaps later, may be considered as the period of the Kisalian occupation of the Sanga site. As regards the geographical distribution of this type of ware, Kisalian sherds have been found at Katongo, Mwanza and the NPila cave, and several pots of a devolved Kisalian (?) are known from Mitwaba; this represents an area of about 120 by 100 miles.

The second group of pottery found at Sanga has been called 'Mulongo' ware, after the village where representative examples had previously been found. The pots have a somewhat flattened aspect with frequently cylindrical necks, decorated with deep horizontal grooves (Fig. 21a). Rather large and deep bowls are equally typical, and the trilobate bowls (Fig. 21b) already known from the Kisalian, are also present here. Copper 'croisettes' of two types were discovered (Fig. 21c and e), the larger ones clearly showing how the copper was poured into a mould; sometimes several of the smaller ones were found held together with a piece of string. Of particular interest were three copper bands found in one grave, which may possibly be fragments of a wooden head-rest (Fig. 21d). Nothing special is to be said about the iron objects except perhaps that some of the bracelets were made by spirally winding narrow strips of iron over a string core. This Mulongo ware is also known from a few sites between Kaloba and Mulongo itself, which means a distance a little under 100 miles.

The pottery forming the 'Red Slip ware' group has been

[1] J. Nenquin, 'Two radiocarbon dates for the Kisalian', *Antiquity*, XXV, No. 140 (1961), 312.

discovered at Sanga in four graves only. Large and deep bowls are relatively numerous, and several of the pots have high and slightly conical sides, with a rim sharply separated from the neck; others are more globular in shape (Fig. 21f). The most distinguishing feature, however, is the shiny red slip which covers sometimes the outer, sometimes the inner surface of the pot, sometimes both, giving an aspect not dissimilar to provincial Roman *terra sigillata*. The most numerous copper objects are the usual small 'croisettes', of which about 360 were found in the four graves. Other metal objects are the copper and iron bracelets, a small iron bell, and fragments of an iron hoe. As regards the date of the Red Slip ware, it was observed that a Red Slip burial had cut into and partially destroyed a Kisalian grave, which therefore must be earlier; another element which may indicate a relatively late date for the Red Slip ware, is the fact that certain forms call to mind modern Luba pottery.

The cultural sequence at Sanga is probably thus:

Kisalian: seventh to ninth century A.D.;

Mulongo group: no absolute date available, but with certain forms reminiscent of Kisalian;

Red Slip ware group: no date available, but in three cases cutting into earlier burials (one certainly Kisalian); many forms similar to Mulongo pottery, and at least one type very like modern Luba ware.

As might be expected in a region of lakes and rivers, fishing must have played an important part in the life of the three cultural communities which are represented by their different pottery: considerable quantities of fishbones were found during the excavations. Agricultural activity is proven by the presence of iron hoes, and a large fragment of a quartzite quern in a Kisalian burial. It is, however, the abundance of iron and copper tools and ornaments—some showing a quite astonishing degree of technical skill—which indicates the importance of this form of economic activity; it might be interesting to mention here the discovery at Sanga of the pottery body of a small bellows with twin pipes,[1] an object which probably belongs to the Kisalian.

[1] J. Nenquin, 'Excavations at Sanga, 1957', loc. cit., 231–2 and Fig. 118, 5.

14

Before finishing this short analysis of the factual material belonging to the Iron Age in Congo, Rwanda and Burundi, mention must be made of a 'culture', long known in the literature as the 'Uele neolithic'.[1] Without wishing to discuss here this interesting problem in detail, it must nevertheless be said that no evidence whatsoever exists to show that the famous haematite polished axes and adzes belong in a neolithic context, as this term is usually understood. No excavations have ever been done in Uele, and the hundreds of specimens to be seen in our museums are all the product of selective surface collecting. Recently, however, it has been noticed that a number of these beautifully polished axes show unmistakable traces of having been used as hammers, possibly in iron-working.[2] This use may be secondary, but it should be borne in mind that at least certain Uele axes—if not all—may have been used by the Iron-Age inhabitants of north-eastern Congo.

Polished axes are known from other areas of Congo as well: several were collected in Katanga, and they are not uncommon in Ubanghi (north-western Congo).[3] They have been described as forming an important element of the 'Léopoldien' Neolithic,[4] which seems to include heavy stone picks, perforated stone discs and even pottery.[5] The published evidence, however, does not permit of a definite attribution of these polished axes (or hoes?) to a Neolithic or an Iron-Age cultural stage.

A last cultural expression of possibly Iron-Age date is the rock

[1] H. Grenade, 'Instruments en Hématite Polie Recueillis dans le Bassin de l'Uele' (Liège, 1910 (?)). Fr. L. Van Noten, 'Une Typologie des Outils Polis Appartenant à l'Uelien', *Bull. Soc. roy. belge d'Anthrop. et de Préhistoire*, LXXIII (1963), 155–95; also: id. 'Slijpbanken uit het N.-O. van de Republiek Kongo', *Africa-Tervuren*, VIII (1962–3), 61–6. Fr. L. Van Noten, *The Uelian. A culture with a neolithic aspect, Uele-Basin (N.E. Congo Republic)*, (Tervuren, 1968).

[2] Francis L. Van Noten, 'Note on the "Neolithic" Stone Hammers of the Uele Basin', *Man* (February, 1963), 24, 23–4.

[3] M. Bequaert, 'Haches de l'Oubanghi', *Bull. Soc. roy. belge d'Anthropol. et de Préhistoire*, LV (1940), 110–13.

[4] J. Colette, 'Comparaison entre les Facies Uélien et Léopoldien du Néolithique Congolais', *Bull. cercle zoolog. congolais*, X, 4 (1933).

[5] G. Mortelmans, 'Vue d'Ensemble sur la Préhistoire du Congo Occidental', *Actes IVe Congrès Panafr. de Préhist. et de l'Etude du Quaternaire*, III (Tervuren, 1962), 129–64, see pp. 146–8. Also: 'Compte-rendu Sommaire des Excursions' in: id., I–II, p. 57, mentioning the discovery of a polished stone 'hoe' in a Tshitolian context.

art, but this is perhaps even more difficult to date than any other type of isolated find. Mention has already been made of the Kiantapo Cave[1] in Katanga, to which Mortelmans[2] has added a number of other sites in the same region, distinguishing two separate groups. If the arguments of this last author are to be accepted, the oldest group need not concern us here, since for it a 'Mesolithic' age is suggested. The more recent one includes incised and schematic representations of the hand (Luabo) and foot (Kanyembo), as well as series of small drilled holes in the rock, in the valley of the river Lukima. All these last, however, could be very recent indeed, as it was shown to the author that small children from the near-by village amused themselves by scratching the contour of their hands in the soft rock, by means of an iron nail or any other sharp object.

A number of rock engravings are also known from the Uele region, where they represent either hafted haematite(?) axes, or Azande iron throwing knives;[3] though these last are obviously quite recent, it is possible that the ones showing the axes belong to an earlier period and may be relevant to the present discussion, if indeed these objects are of Iron-Age date.

The last group of engravings and rock paintings is concentrated in the caves around Thysville and Kimpese, although open-air sites are not unknown.[4] Quite recently Raymaekers and Van Moorsel[5] have described in some detail the paintings and engravings found at Lovo, about 20 miles to the south of Kimpese, but no date could be proposed, although in the immediate neighbourhood a cemetery could partially be investigated, which proved to contain pottery very similar to the Group II ware from the Thysville caves (see Fig. 15b and c), as

[1] See notes 1 and 2, p. 195.

[2] G. Mortelmans, 'Les Dessins Rupestres Gravés, Ponctués et Peints du Katanga; Essai de Synthèse' (Tervuren, 1952).

[3] A. de Calonne-Beaufaict, Les Azande (Bruxelles, 1921); and R. P. B. Costermans, 'Relevé des Stations Préhistoriques dans les territoires de Watsa-Gombari et de Dungu', Zaïre, III, 2 (1949), 153–74.

[4] J. Nenquin, 'Sur Deux Gravures Rupestres du Bas-Congo', Bull. Soc. roy. belge d'Anthrop. et de Préhistoire, LXX (1959), 153–8.

[5] P. Raymaekers et H. Van Moorsel, 'Lovo; Dessins Rupestres du Bas-Congo' (Léopoldville, 1964).

described by Mortelmans.[1] We cannot, however, agree with Raymaekers and Van Moorsel where they see in a number of these signs, if not actual lettering, at least the precursors of a conventional script.[2] Equally interesting are the paintings from Mbafu Cave,[3] which are thought to represent scenes of the christianization of the Lower Congo, possibly from the first half of the sixteenth century. Some of the copper figurines and ornaments found from time to time in the same region, probably belong to this period.[4]

From the preceding pages it can easily be seen, that although some protohistoric material is known belonging to the Iron-Age cultures of Congo, Rwanda and Burundi, it is not possible yet to give a comprehensive picture of the succession, or even of the geographical distribution of these cultures. Except for Rwanda, Burundi and a very limited region of the Lower Congo and Katanga, our knowledge of the protohistoric occupation is very incomplete indeed, and large areas must remain blank on the distribution maps. This is especially true for Kasai, where a number of most interesting places are known to exist, such as Sasatshie and the Tshienda Cave, but where no systematic excavations have yet been undertaken on protohistoric sites. Practically nothing is known from the central 'Cuvette' and in northern Congo the intriguing 'Uele-Neolithic' and its possibly comparable 'Ubanghi-Neolithic' continue to pose many problems.

Probably the earliest pottery–iron association about which a certain amount of evidence is available, comes from Kivu and Rwanda, where Hiernaux-Maquet[5] have mentioned the existence of several iron-smelting sites in association with 'dimplebased' pottery. As no radio-carbon dates exist for this region, it

---

[1] See note 2, p. 190.
[2] Raymaekers et Van Moorsel, op cit., 22: '. . . . si ce n'est pas encore une écriture, c'est au moins la page avant elle . . .'.
[3] See note 4, p. 192.
[4] R. L. Wannyn, *L'Art ancien du Métal au Bas-Congo* (Champles, 1961).
[5] See note 2, p. 184.

may be useful to mention here the absolute ages relative to 'dimple-based' ware from two near-by sites:
Nsongezi: A.D. 1037 ± 150,[1] and

Kalambo Falls (site A 1): A.D. 550 ± 150
A.D. 870 ± 180
A.D. 980 ± 150
(site B 2): A.D. 1020 ± 40
A.D. 1580 ± 50

Although in the last case the pottery is known as Channelled Ware, it is described[2] as showing 'close association with the Dimple Based pottery of Kavirondo and Ruanda Urundi'; the date from Nsongezi is for the Wilton culture immediately underlying the 'dimple-base' level. This might mean a date from anything in the sixth century A.D. to the sixteenth (although this is perhaps a couple of centuries too young) for the Kivu, Rwanda and Burundi 'dimple-based' ware. De Heinzelin suggests a date between the seventh and the fifteenth century A.D. for his sites in the Semliki area,[3] which is hardly more helpful. It would be very nice indeed to have more exact information about this particular problem, since absolute dates in the seventh to ninth century A.D. are known for the very sophisticated Kisalian culture from Katanga, a culture with, as has been seen, very highly developed metallurgical and technical skill.

This is all that can be said about the Iron Age in Rwanda, Burundi and Congo. In the present state of our knowledge, it is useless to equate one particular type of ware with one well-defined population group. Study of the oral traditions[4] has done something to clarify the largely unknown history of early migrations and settlements, but it is next to impossible to

[1] S. Pearce and M. Posnansky, 'The Re-excavation of Nsongezi Rock-shelter, Ankole', *Uganda Jnl.*, 27, (1963), 85–94. For a general discussion, see also S. V. Pearce, 'The Appearance of Iron and Its Use in Protohistoric Africa' (M.A. Thesis, London, 1960).

[2] J. D. Clark, 'The Kalambo Falls Prehistoric Site; An Interim Report', *Actes IVe Congrès Panafr. de Préhist. et de l'Etude du Quaternaire*, III (Tervuren, 1962), 195–202.

[3] See note 2, p. 188.

[4] J. Vansina, 'De la Tradition Orale; Essai de Méthode Historique' (Tervuren, 1961). Id. 'Geschiedenis van de Kuba van ongeveer 1500 tot 1904' (Tervuren, 1963). A. Coupez et Th. Kamanzi, 'Récits Historiques Rwanda' (Tervuren, 1962).

correlate any part of this still very confused picture with the known distribution of certain elements of the material culture. The few attempts which have been made in this respect rest on very shaky arguments indeed, and much more analytical work is needed before the writing of a synthesis can be tried, which will stand the rigorous tests of historical criticism.[1]

[1] Manuscript submitted in 1965; bibliography completed to 1969.

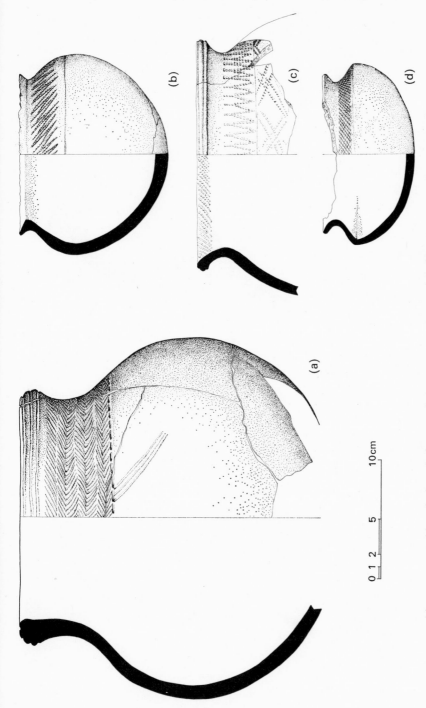

Fig. 12. (a) A-type pot (dimple-based) from Ruhimangyargya (Rwanda). (b)–(d) Pottery from the Tshienda Cave.

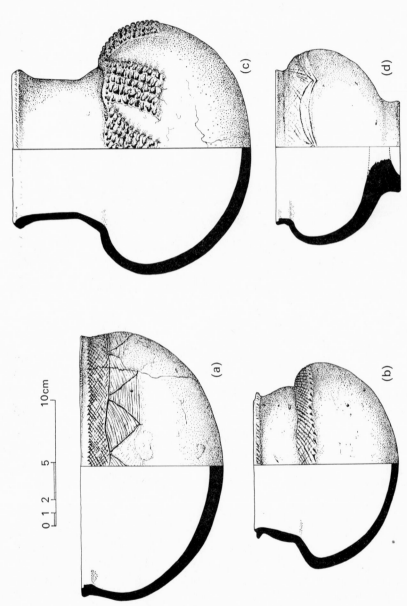

Fig. 13 Pottery from Eshilu.

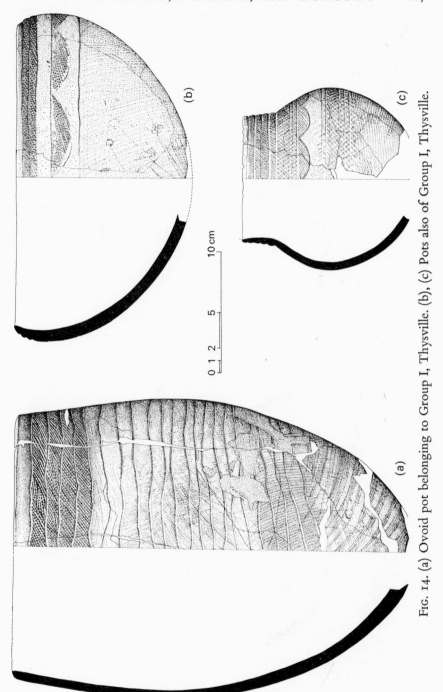

Fig. 14. (a) Ovoid pot belonging to Group I, Thysville. (b), (c) Pots also of Group I, Thysville.

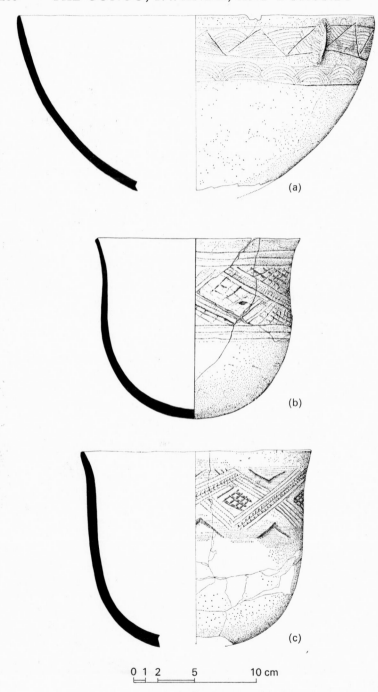

FIG. 15. (a) Group III ware, Thysville. (b), (c) Pots of Group II, Thysville.

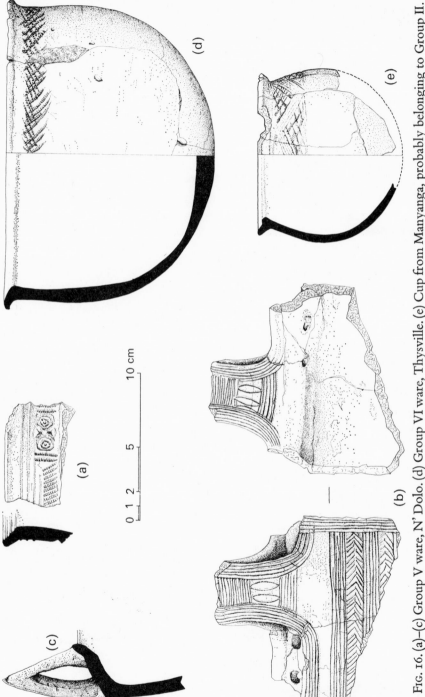

FIG. 16. (a)–(c) Group V ware, N' Dolo. (d) Group VI ware, Thysville. (e) Cup from Manyanga, probably belonging to Group II.

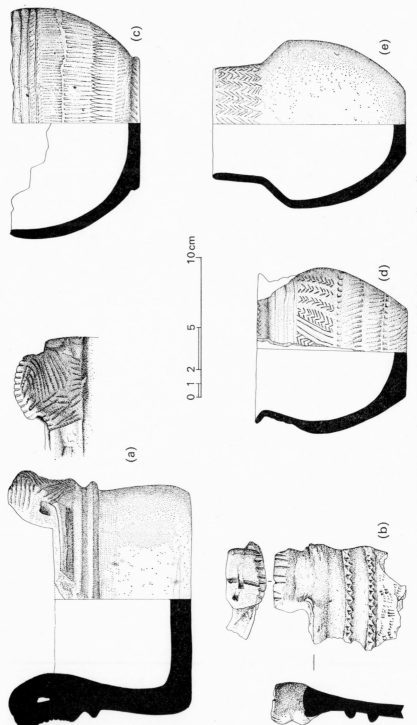

FIG. 17. (a), (b) Pottery from Kingabwa. (c), (d), (e) from Coquilhatville.

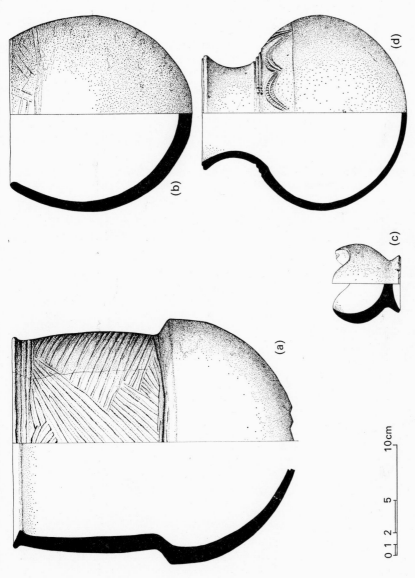

Fig. 18. (a), (b), Pots from Kapia. (c), (d), Kisalian ware from Sanga.

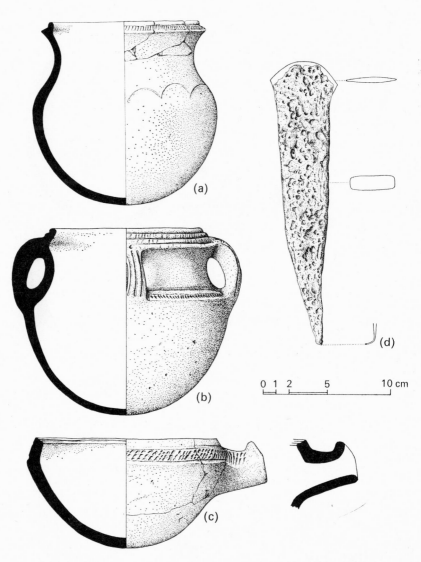

FIG. 19. (a)–(c) Kisalian ware from Sanga. (d) Iron axe, Kisalian from Sanga.

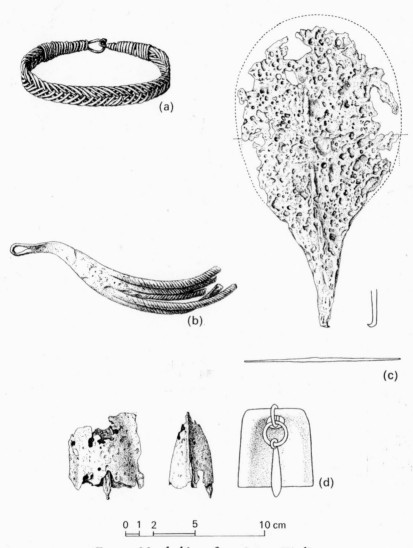

FIG. 20. Metal objects from Sanga, Kisalian.

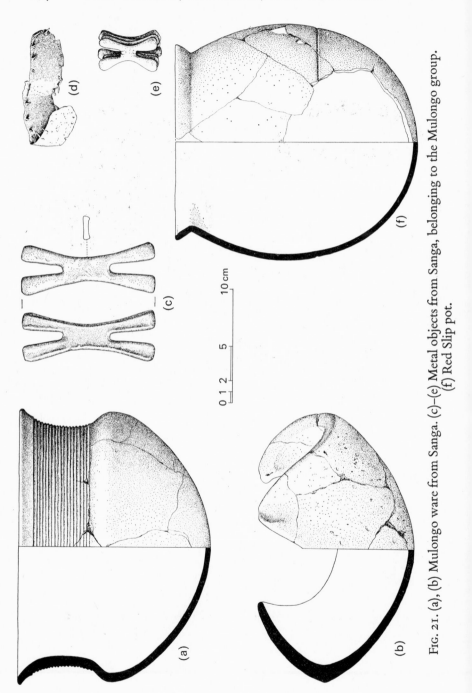

FIG. 21. (a), (b) Mulongo ware from Sanga. (c)–(e) Metal objects from Sanga, belonging to the Mulongo group. (f) Red Slip pot.

8

ZAMBIA AND RHODESIA

by

Brian M. Fagan

INTRODUCTION

RHODESIA and Zambia occupy a strategic position both geographically and historically when we come to consider the Iron-Age sequence of South Central Africa. Zambia lies astride the main migration routes from the north and north-west into southern Africa. The country is immediately to the east of the Congo Basin, whose peoples expanded eastwards across the Luapula river during the closing centuries of the Iron Age. Rhodesian Iron-Age peoples lived in a country rich in gold, copper, and other minerals which attracted the attention of foreign entrepreneurs for over 1,000 years. The Limpopo river forms the southern frontier of the region under discussion, but its geographical significance is comparatively small, since trading activities and Early-Iron-Age peoples both extended south of the river.[1]

Most of the country we are considering is high altitude plateau country lying at an average height of 4,000 to 4,500 ft. above sea level. The undulating plateau surface is broken up by deep river valleys, such as the Zambezi, Luangwa, and Kafue, which cut

[1] The original draft of this chapter was prepared in 1964; research has moved ahead so fast since then that it is impossible in a short space to do justice to all the new and exciting discoveries of recent years. Many problems posed by the new evidence are glossed over here, and the reader is referred to the reading list at the end of this chapter. This chapter was prepared before the new Terminological Code for African Prehistory was introduced.

their way down from their plateau sources to the coast. Their valley floors provided access to the interior plateaux regions, as well as low altitude environments where herds of ivory-bearing elephants abound.

The Rhodesian and Zambian plateaux are covered for the most part by *Brachystegia/Julbernardia* savanna-woodland. Monotonous tracts of evergreen trees are relieved by occasional open, grassy depressions or pans which provide good grazing grass for cattle and game. In the low-lying river valleys and in drier areas, the vegetation pattern changes, with *mopane* woodland dominant. In general the soil supporting *mopane* woodland was unsuitable for the comparatively simple agriculture practiced by Early-Iron-Age peoples. The *Brachystegia* areas were able to support a number of crops including maize, sorghum, millet, and minor crops. The woodlands of South Central Africa are abundant in natural vegetable foods as well as game, providing an important food source for farmers in years of famine. Another important ecological zone is the Kalahari sand country which covers much of the western parts of Zambia and some parts of western Rhodesia. Iron-Age peoples settled on the fringes of the *Baikiaea* woodland of the sand areas, cultivating the margins of grassy clearings and the fringes of river valleys.

The Iron-Age settlement of Rhodesia and Zambia was hindered by a number of factors. Widespread tsetse fly belts prevent the free passage of cattle and man. Trypanosomiasis is harmful to man and fatal to cattle. Such areas were naturally avoided by Iron-Age peoples; unfortunately, however, the tsetse belts are thought to have shifted their positions considerably during prehistoric times. Thus, it is impossible to draw any meaningful conclusions as to patterns of migration during the Iron Age on the basis of tsetse belts. Many diseases such as malaria and bilharzia are endemic in the area, while rindepest and other crippling diseases can decimate stock. The quality of soils is generally poor, and rainfall uncertain, rendering specialized farming techniques at the subsistence level generally impracticable.

The peoples of South Central Africa have never established large cities, practised writing, or achieved a state of urbanized

MAP 9. Zambia and Rhodesia.

civilization in the European sense. For the most part the Iron-Age peoples of the area lived in small village communities, except where there were strong economic and social incentives for a greater concentration of population. During the later Iron Age, the region was settled by peoples with complex social organizations and strongly centralized chieftainships. The immigrants introduced more sophisticated agriculture and advanced metallurgical technology, both of which led to increases in population, greater pressure on agricultural land, and to many changes in the sparse settlement pattern.

HISTORY OF RESEARCH

The development of Iron-Age research in our area is bound up with the speculations caused by the discovery of the Zimbabwe ruins in the late 1860's. The ruins were first investigated by Carl Mauch in 1870, and excavated by Theodore Bent in 1891, who ascribed a high antiquity to the site. He was followed by the Bulawayo journalist, R. N. Hall, who considered Zimbabwe to be of Sabaean origin. This view was opposed by Randall MacIver, who was commissioned by the British Association for the Advancement of Science to examine the ruins in 1905. He concluded, on the basis of careful excavations, that Zimbabwe was of Medieval age, and of African origin. The result was a furious controversy between Hall and those who considered the ruins to be of recent date, which lasted until Caton-Thompson's season of excavations at the site in 1929, also commissioned by the British Association. She was able to show that the site had been occupied several times, that it was of African manufacture, and probably dated to between the eighth and thirteenth centuries A.D. The result of her work was a reduction in controversy which led to increased field research both in the Limpopo valley at Mapungubwe, and also elsewhere south of the Zambezi. By 1950, Summers was able to summarize the Iron-Age sequence of Rhodesia, proposing two separate and parallel Iron-Age culture complexes which developed alongside each other. This concept has survived in a very modified form until the present time, the refinements resulting from further excavations at Zimbabwe in 1958, and from widespread research on Early-Iron-Age sites by Keith Robinson and others.

Iron-Age research in Zambia began with a number of minor investigations by Desmond Clark, who excavated some Early-Iron-Age pottery at Machili in the early 1950's, and later recovered important Iron-Age occupation material from the upper levels of the Kalambo Falls lake basin. Systematic research began later, with Inskeep's preliminary excavations near Kalomo in 1957, which were followed by a 3-year programme of excavations in southern Zambia by the present writer between 1960 and 1963. Excavations in this area have continued since then, with Vogel working in the Zambezi valley, while the author has worked near Batoka. At the same time, Phillipson has carried out an important survey of Early-Iron-Age sites throughout Zambia, resulting in a greater understanding of the Early-Iron-Age settlement of the territory.

In the future, the intensity of survey and large-scale excavation is likely to increase, with greater emphasis being placed on precision in definition of different cultural and stratigraphical units within the Iron-Age sequence. The outline of the Iron Age presented in this chapter can only be regarded as a preliminary account.

THE LATE STONE AGE

At the time when the first metal-workers and farmers were settling in Zambia and Rhodesia, both countries were occupied by Late-Stone-Age hunters. Bands of these food gatherers were living in rock shelters and caves, by the sides of lakes and rivers, and in floodplain areas; scatters of their artifacts are very commonly found in many places, especially in river valleys. Important concentrations of Late-Stone-Age population were centred on the Upper and Middle Zambezi valleys, in the Matopo Hills near Bulawayo, as well as in caves in northern and eastern Zambia, and in Mashonaland.

Archaeologists have distinguished several regional variants of the Late Stone Age in South Central Africa. One of them, the Nachikufan, is a woodland facies, whose distribution is confined to the north, north-west, and perhaps parts of the east of Zambia. The material culture is dominated by wood-working tools, and ground stone axes were in use. The Wilton culture, which apparently flourished in more open country, is found throughout Rhodesia and in the southern parts of Zambia. Future research will undoubtedly lead to the identification of further Late-Stone-Age variants.

Late-Stone-Age cultures were flourishing in Central Africa as long ago as 6000 B.C., but are thought to have been in their heyday in the last few millennia B.C. The hunters themselves were probably somewhat similar in appearance to the Bushmen of Botswana, but, to judge from the Wilton skeletons from the Gwisho site in southern Zambia, probably somewhat taller. They lived in small bands, hunting many different species of antelope as well as gathering seeds and fruit from the bush and fishing in lakes and rivers. Late-Stone-Age Bushmen are best known for their rock art which has been the subject of extensive study by Clark, Cooke, Goodall, and others. South of the Zambezi the hunters drew naturalistic animal and human figures in complicated palimpsests. In Zambia the artists preferred schematic designs which probably had a ritual significance to their creators.

During Late-Stone-Age times the population of South Central Africa was a small and scattered one. The hunters lived in favourable game areas from which they were ousted by Iron-Age immigrants. In some areas the Bushmen were quickly assimilated into the Iron-Age population; isolated Early-Iron-Age skeletons display signs of an intermingling of Khoisan and Negroid physical characteristics. Elsewhere, however, the Late-Stone-Age population survived untouched in isolated and comparatively infertile areas. Their presence is attested by many references in oral tradition to the *BaAkafula*, who were said to be small, vain people, who subsisted on hunting and food-gathering. Only a few small groups of Bushmen live in South Central Africa today, most of them in extreme south-west Zambia.

THE FIRST FARMERS

The exact dates when agriculture, domestic animals, and metallurgy were introduced into Rhodesia and Zambia are still unknown. The archaeological evidence is both unsatisfactory and fragmentary, most of it consisting of isolated collections of Early-Iron-Age pottery and occasional radio-carbon dates. Phillipson has recently made a detailed study of Zambian Early-Iron-Age sites which has added a considerable amount of information to that already published in the literature. The summary which follows is based to a considerable extent on the latest work. It includes an extensive radio-carbon dating programme.

The earliest dated Iron-Age site in Zambia is, at the time of writing, the Machili site on the eastern borders of Barotseland, where a few potsherds were found associated with charcoal on a buried land surface in the Kalahari Sand. A radio-carbon date of A.D. 96 ± 212 (C-829) was obtained from this horizon, the principal vessel reconstructed from the sherds being a globular vessel with a band of channelled decoration around the neck. This early date for Iron-Age pottery was for a long time thought to provide a reliable chronology for the arrival of Iron-Age peoples on the banks of the Zambezi, for a few lumps of ferri-crete, an important source of iron ore, were found with the potsherds at Machili. These pieces can only have been imported into this sandy area by man.

More recent investigations have led to a reassessment of the significance of this isolated date. David Phillipson has distinguished a number of regional variants of Early-Iron-Age culture throughout Zambia, all of which were flourishing at a slightly later date, but associated with a pottery tradition, known in general terms as 'Channel-decorated ware', a term adorning the recent literature, but now abandoned.

One of the most important of Phillipson's groups is found in the northern parts of the country, and is named the Kalambo group after the famous prehistoric site. The uppermost levels at the Kalambo Falls site have yielded an important sequence of Iron-Age occupation which has been radio-carbon dated to a period between A.D. 345 ± 40 (GrN-4646) and at least the end of the first millennium A.D. A significant amount of pottery was excavated from a series of settlements stratified the one above the other, but much jumbled by water action. The finds included an important series of channel-decorated vessels, iron slag in large quantities, and remains of pole and mud huts. A series of pits may represent graves, but no bones were found in them, nor was any economic evidence recovered.

The pottery remains basically similar throughout the long Kalambo occupation, with shouldered pots and shallow bowls dominant in the collections. Channelled or grooved decoration is common on the necks of pots, with bands of incised decoration alternating with channelling. Bevelled rims are also found, but many undecorated vessels are also represented, especially shallow bowls.

While Kalambo provides abundant evidence for a long survival of Early-Iron-Age peoples in the northernmost parts of Zambia, the evidence from elsewhere in the country is less satisfactory. Sherds belonging within the Kalambo group are widely distributed in the Northern Province, and are found in the upper levels of cave sites such as Nakapapula, near Serenje, but few stratified sites are known.

Another important series of sites is found in central Zambia, a number of settlements in the Copperbelt and Lusaka areas having been excavated in recent years. Three of these are worth mention here. Two settlements near Lusaka, Kapwirimbwe and Twickenham Road, have yielded Early-Iron-Age occupation, the former dated by radio-carbon to the fifth century, and the latter to A.D. 1055 ± 110 (GX-0662). Iron slag, traces of houses, and storage pits have been found; some fragmentary cattle bones came to light at Kapwirimbwe. The pottery from the Lusaka settlements has much grooved decoration, as well as 'false relief' chevron decoration, a motif characteristic of most Early-Iron sites in central and southern Zambia. These wares can be compared with material found at the Chondwe Farm settlement, near Ndola. A trial trench through 3½ ft. of deposit yielded Early-Iron pottery overlain by later materials. Iron slag, traces of hut wall clay, and some grindstones were present, as well as a large number of potsherds with features reminiscent of both northern and central Zambian sites. Two radio-carbon dates assign this site to the eighth to tenth centuries A.D.

In the Southern Province of Zambia, a number of Early-Iron-Age occupation levels occur at the base of Iron-Age mounds on the Batoka Plateau. These have yielded iron slag, some fragmentary cattle bones, and remains of huts. Shouldered pots with

PLATE V

The Acropolis at Zimbabwe, showing the Western Enclosure wall and the valley ruins in the right middle ground.

PLATE V

The Temple or Great Enclosure Wall at Zimbabwe. The Conical Tower is among the trees at the left hand end of the

PLATE VII

Mapungubwe Hill from the West.

PLATE VIII

Burial of a villager at Ingombe Ilede.

a band of grooved decoration and 'false relief' chevron motifs
are found in these levels, which have been dated to between the
fourth and fifth centuries at Gundu and Kalundu mounds near
Batoka and Kalomo respectively. Such vessels have similarities
with the Kapwirimbwe material, but there are some differences
in detail, which serve to distinguish the Kalundu group, as it is
provisionally named, from the Lusaka material. The exact relationship between the Kalundu and Gundu wares and the potsherds from Machili has not yet been established, largely because
the number of specimens is very small. The standard error of the
Machili date is such that it could lie within the range of those
obtained from other Iron-Age sites in southern Zambia.

Throughout Zambia, then, there is some basic continuity of
Early-Iron-Age culture, with the first appearance of iron-
working and pottery dating, in general terms, to a period no
later than the fourth or fifth centuries A.D. Many of the details
of the Early Iron Age remain to be discovered, and considerable
refinements of this picture can be expected in the future.

A link with Iron-Age cultures south of the Zambezi can be
obtained from the Dambwa site, near Livingstone, where a large
Iron-Age site has been dated by a series of radio-carbon dates
to the eighth century A.D. The pottery from this settlement is
somewhat different to that of the Kalundu group, and is characterized by the use of comb-stamping of a coarse type on the
rim band of a shouldered pot, a feature that is common on the
earliest pottery from Rhodesia.

Early-Iron-Age sites are common south of the Zambezi, but
the evidence from Rhodesia is still very incomplete. Many
settlements are known, most of them concentrated in the central
and eastern parts of the country. The most celebrated are those
included within the Gokomere culture, named after a type site
at Gokomere Mission near Fort Victoria. Gokomere occupations
are characterized by shouldered pots with bands of grooving or
channelling, associated with an obliquely comb-stamped rim
band as well as shallow bowls, many of them decorated with
comb-stamped bands. There are generalized resemblances to
Early-Iron-Age pottery north of the Zambezi, including the use,

occasionally, as at Sinoia, of false relief chevron motifs. The earliest dated settlement is Mabveni, with a reading of A.D. 180 ± 120 (SR-43), while a later settlement with similar pottery, at Malapati on the Nuanetsi river, dates to A.D. 840 ± 100 (SR-33). The Gokomere pottery tradition has a long history, and is in part contemporary with the Leopard's Kopje culture, described below, the pottery from the earlier stages of which has some affinities with Gokomere pottery.

Gokomere ware is stratified directly over a Later-Stone-Age occupation level at the type site, and represents the earliest Iron-Age occupation of central Rhodesia. Related sites are still comparatively rare from the western parts of the country, although a scatter of potsherds from the Kapula Vlei site near Wankie serve to connect provisionally Gokomere ware and the Dambwa pottery. Kapula Vlei itself has been radio-carbon dated to the ninth century, slightly later than Dambwa.

Little is known of the exact distribution of Gokomere ware, or of the economy of its makers. Gokomere people made their houses of poles and anthill clay, and the remains of a collapsed granary were recovered from Mabveni. Robinson found a jaw of a domestic sheep or goat at the same site, but no cattle bones have yet been identified, although they were almost certainly kept by the earliest farmers. Grindstones are found, indirect evidence of cereal agriculture.

A single site which has yielded Gokomere pottery is found south of the Limpopo in South Africa, at Happy Rest farm near Louis Trichardt. The pottery from this settlement recalls that from Malapati, and is evidence for the southwards extension of the earliest pottery tradition of South Central Africa into the central Transvaal.

The earliest occupation of the Acropolis at Zimbabwe took place earlier than the fourth century A.D. The end of a short period of Early-Iron-Age occupation is dated to A.D. 330 ± 150 (M-913), and Gokomere-type pottery is associated with the early horizons. Only potsherds were found in this early occupation, but finds from Gokomere itself and other sites testify to iron-working and simple iron tools, as well as to the manufacture of clay figurines of animals and humans, as well as to sporadic trading, reflected by isolated finds of imported glass beads.

A single burial of a young person was recovered from the Gokomere levels at the type site; this has not yet been studied in detail, but is considered to show Khoisan physical features. Negroid skeletons have been reported from Ziwa sites in the Inyanga District, but they have not been fully described. It is probable, however, that the skeletal evidence, when more complete, will show that the earliest Iron-Age peoples in South Central Africa were a mixture of the Khoisan and Negro physical types, perhaps with the features of the former dominant.

The extreme eastern parts of Rhodesia have yielded another variant on the Early-Iron-Age cultural tradition, named after the type site at Ziwa farm. A number of collections of Early-Iron-Age potsherds have been made from caves, burials, and settlement sites, and dated by a number of samples to between the fourth and eleventh centuries. The general features of the pottery, known as Ziwa ware, are similar to those on Gokomere vessels, but bowls are more common, and the rims on them are elaborate. Decoration tends to be more lavish on Ziwa pottery, but the differences are ones of degree rather than of cultural difference.

The picture of the earliest Iron-Age settlement of South Central Africa painted in this article is necessarily brief and incomplete as well as being subject to major modification, as the tempo of research continues to increase. We now have evidence for indicating that iron-working, agriculture and domestic animals were well established on both sides of the Zambezi by the fourth century A.D. at the latest, and that an Early-Iron-Age cultural continuum stretched from the Tanzanian border in the north to the Limpopo and further south. The radio-carbon dates for the earliest Iron Age suggest a rapid and more or less contemporary spread of iron-working into the whole of South Central Africa by the end of the first four centuries of the Christian era.

We cannot yet paint a convincing picture of the ultimate origins of Iron-Age economy in South Central Africa. Archaeologists are in general agreement that it is difficult to correlate the archaeological record with linguistic evidence. Many feel that the earliest Iron-Age settlement of South Central Africa is connected with the spread of Bantu-speaking agriculturalists outwards from a nuclear area south of the Congo forest in the southern woodlands. The only likelihood in our present state of knowledge is that iron spread rapidly throughout our area.

SUBSISTENCE FARMERS AND MINERS

We have seen how the earliest farmers in South Central Africa all belonged within the same broad cultural tradition, which in many parts of our area survived virtually unchanged until the beginning of the second millennium A.D. In the Northern Province of Zambia channel-decorated pottery makers were still living at the Kalambo Falls in the eleventh or twelfth centuries A.D. It is likely that other communities making Early-Iron-Age pottery were living in parts of Rhodesia until a few hundred years ago. In certain areas of South Central Africa, however, later immigrants arrived and absorbed the earliest farmers in the middle of the first millennium. These peoples and their predecessors made up most of the farming population of South Central Africa throughout the remainder of the Iron Age, in spite of the rule of successive generations of powerful overlords. The life of the Iron-Age subsistence farmer in Zambia and Rhodesia survived almost unchanged into the nineteenth century. The farmers benefited, of course, from trading contacts and technological advances especially in metallurgy and pottery brought in by several dominant tribal groups. The degree to which the early peasant farmers were assimilated by later immigrants is uncertain, but in Zambia the peoples who entered the country in successive waves from the Congo Basin from as early as the fifteenth century appear to have absorbed most of the earlier farming population. South of the Zambezi it would seem that many of the immigrants remained aloof leaving their unsophisticated neighbours to live in comparative isolation.

Our knowledge of the later indigenous farming population

is based for the most part on archaeological investigations in the southern parts of Zambia and in Matabeleland. The general characteristics of the early farming populations can be summarized for they were common to peasant farmers throughout Rhodesia and Zambia.

The economy of the population was based on the cultivation of cereal crops, including sorghum and millet. A number of other minor crops were also planted. The farmers kept cattle as well as goats and sheep. Dogs roamed their villages, but were not eaten, presumably being of use in the chase. They supplemented their meat supplies from domestic sources by hunting small antelope. The hunters were not afraid, however, to tackle the elephant, economically valuable because of its ivory, and other large beasts. Bows and arrows and various methods of snaring and trapping were used for hunting. Insects, rodents, and vegetable foods from the bush also played a significant part in the diet, especially in famine years. Their economy made full use of the rich abundance of the *Brachystegia* woodland in vegetable foods. Early oral tradition from Rhodesia, recorded by Abraham, suggests that these people considered cattle an important part of their economy. Evidence from archaeological sites in Zambia tends to support this view.

The material culture of the early farmers was simple. A number of regional variations of pottery have been distinguished in both countries. In general the vessels have simple shapes and bear unsophisticated decorative motifs. Their iron tools consisted for the most part of arrow-heads, razors, spear-heads and simple hoes and rings. A few copper ornaments were made. Animal and human figurines are found in the deposits of their villages. The human figures from Rhodesian sites are often of elaborate design while those north of the Zambezi are little more than cylindrical fragments of clay. At the time of writing almost nothing is known of the layout of their villages, but it seems that many communities lived in small settlements with the huts grouped round a central cattle enclosure. Such a layout has been found at the Isamu Pati mound near Kalomo in Zambia. There is an absence of evidence for either fortification or elaborate social organization, the latter always difficult to deduce from archaeological data.

Almost nothing is known of the early farming populations from traditional sources. White refers to early Bantu-speaking peoples in the Balovale district of Zambia who are said to have relied on food gathering for much of their diet, to have had a simple social organization and to have had a strong addiction for earth-spirit worship.

Such people were easy prey to the more sophisticated Iron-Age peoples who entered South Central Africa from the Congo and elsewhere during the later centuries of the Iron Age. Strong chiefs, backed by a centralized political and military organization, found no difficulty in assimilating the disorganized Early-Iron-Age peoples whom they found in the country when they arrived.

South of the Zambezi, and probably north as well, early farming communities played an important part in the development of the commercial networks between the interior and the East and West Coasts of Africa during the Iron Age. Many communities exploited the outcrops of copper and gold which lay by their villages. They had little use for the metals themselves except for ornamentation and traded them with their more powerful neighbours and with Arab traders who travelled far into the interior of Africa from the East Coast. Mining methods at the time were simple and based on open-cast working. The reader is referred to the recent article of Mennell and Summers on the subject. There is evidence to indicate that mining throughout the Iron Age was in the hands of the indigenous farming population. Later immigrants and other powerful groups merely controlled the outlets of supply, demanding tribute in metals from the miners.

A number of regional groups of subsistence farmers, distinguished by the styles of their pottery, have been recognized in the two countries. In Zambia the most important subsistence farming group yet distinguished is the Kalomo culture, centred on the southern and central parts of the Batoka plateau and extending from the Middle Zambezi valley in the east to the borders of Barotseland in the west. The Kalomo people were mound dwellers who lived on traditional village sites occupied intermittently from about the seventh to the eleventh or twelfth centuries. Such traditional settlements have yielded invaluable stratigraphical evidence, enabling us to trace the development of this culture over a period of several centuries. The earlier Kalomo people were skilled hunters, but in later times possessed large herds of cattle; food-gathering and hunting played a less important part in their lives.

Other subsistence farming cultures are known to have existed in Zambia during the first millennium, but only a little is known about them. It has, however, recently been established that the Ila/Tonga speaking peoples were living on the eastern borders of the central Kafue Basin, their present tribal homeland, as early as the eleventh or twelfth centuries. A study of the pottery from Sebanzi Hill, Lochinvar, and excavations at Gundu mound near Batoka have shown that the Tonga are one of the earliest of the present Zambian tribes. They pre-date the migrations of the powerful Congo tribes eastwards into Zambia, and probably represent one of the last surviving enclaves of Early-Iron-Age farmers in South Central Africa.

Robinson, who is the principal authority on the earlier Iron-Age peoples of Rhodesia, has distinguished an important culture in the west of the country. This is named after the type site at Leopard's Kopje near Bulawayo, and has been divided into three separate stages. Radio-carbon dates for the Leopard's Kopje culture are too few to allow a detailed discussion of its chronology. The earliest stage contains sherds which have affinities with Gokomere pottery, and the available dates for phase I and II suggest a date in the middle of the first millennium for the earliest Leopard's Kopje communities. The later stages of the culture have also yielded pottery resembling that from the Rhodesian ruins indicating some contact with Shona peoples, stage III, represented by the Woolandale site near Bulawayo, giving a reading of A.D. 1310 ± 90 (SR-44). Several early workings of gold and copper have been shown to be associated with the Leopard's Kopje people and it is likely that they provided much of the mining population in the west of the country. Various dates for the end of this culture have been proposed but there is every reason to believe that some Leopard's Kopje farmers were still living in Matabeleland during the nineteenth century.

Leopard's Kopje settlements have been found throughout Matabeleland as far south as the Middle Limpopo Valley, where the important Bambandyanalo site has been radio-carbon dated to A.D. 1050 ± 65 (Y-135-17). Other variants on the Leopard's Kopje theme are certain to be found in Mashonaland when further fieldwork has been completed.

STONE BUILDINGS AND TRADE

From the early centuries of the first millennium A.D. Asian, and later, Arab traders visited the east coast of South Central Africa. The merchants or their agents penetrated the interior via river valleys and mountain passes, established overland trade routes, trading glass beads, sea-shells, china, cloth and other luxuries for ivory, gold, copper, and slaves. The stabilizing element in this trade was the constant and regular demand for elephant ivory from Indian sources.

Isolated finds of sea-shells and glass beads have been made in Gokomere sites and in Kalomo culture villages dated to as early as the second or fourth centuries A.D. Finds of imports from the coast are never common in early sites, for the ivory and gold trade does not seem to have expanded greatly until the early centuries of the second millennium.

The Ingombe Ilede site in the Middle Zambezi valley, which flourished as a trading centre in the late fourteenth and early fifteenth centuries, has shown that trade in raw materials was well established inthe Zambezi valley by the end of the first millennium. Eleven richly decorated skeletons were found at this site (Pl. VIII). The grave goods included copper crosses, of economic importance as currency, gold beads, necklaces of sea-shells, glass beads, and traces of imported and indigenous cloth. The principal inhabitants of the Ingombe Ilede must have controlled the trade over a considerable area, for the site lies in a strategic position. Both the mineral outcrops of the plateaux and the elephant herds of the Zambezi valley itself were within easy reach of the settlement. Exotic imports obtained from Zambezi traders, as well as the salt extracted from deposits near their settlement, could be readily exchanged for the copper and ivory which was the basis of the whole trade.

Until the middle of the second millennium when the Portuguese opened up the West Coast trade routes through the Kingdom of the Kongo, commerce through Sofala with the Rhodesian interior was far more important than any commercial network north of the Zambezi. By the twelfth century coastal trading networks had penetrated far into the trade areas of Mashonaland. Those using the networks came into contact with Karanga peoples who are thought to have arrived in Rhodesia from the north by the end of the first millennium. The Karanga brushed aside the Early-Iron-Age inhabitants and achieved political dominance over them within a comparatively short period. As a result of the mining activities of their subjects, they enriched their material culture and established a commercial rapport with the Moors. By clever political manoeuvring and Moorish support the leaders of the Karanga were able to establish themselves as overlords of a confederacy of minor chiefs who paid them tribute and thus contributed to their prosperity.

The Karanga were ardent exponents of the *mwari* cult, a religion based on ancestor worship. They established a number of shrines on prominent hills which became the focal points of the nation. They increased the effectiveness of these sites by stone walling, naming them *Dzimba dzemabwe* (houses of stone). An enormous literature has accumulated over the years on the significance of these ruins, the most famous of which is Zimbabwe, south-east of Fort Victoria in Mashonaland. Gentlemen of romantic imagination have assigned Zimbabwe to King Solomon and the Phoenicians. Others have suggested, and this is the theory that is more generally accepted today, that they are of African workmanship and of comparatively recent date. Recent archaeological excavations at Zimbabwe, Khami, and other ruins have shown that there were several periods of

MAP 10. Stone ruins of Rhodesia.
Key included on map

occupation at the principal sites. Whitty has distinguished several
styles of architecture, while Robinson and Summers were able
to demonstrate that Zimbabwe was occupied at five different
periods. This sequence of occupation is used as a yardstick for
the study of all the ruin sites of Rhodesia.

The Zimbabwe ruins are dominated by the Acropolis (Pl. V),
which is a boulder-strewn hill encircled with stone walling.
The west end of the hill is mantled with deep occupation deposits

from which vital stratigraphical evidence has been obtained. In the valley below the hill lies the Great Enclosure of Temple (Pl. VI) which consists of a high, circular enclosing wall with associated features including a Conical Tower with possible ritual significance. Archaeology has shown that the Acropolis was occupied for a long period before the Great Enclosure was built. The significance of Zimbabwe itself is probably connected with the *mwari* cult and with rain making.

The earliest Iron-Age farmers to live at Zimbabwe were, as we have seen, people making Gokomere pottery, which was found in the lowest levels on the Acropolis. The closing stages of their occupation, Period I, has been dated to the fourth century A.D. After Period I there was a gap of unknown duration. Middens belonging to Period II overlie a sterile layer. The date when the new occupation began is unknown but the late stages of this phase are dated to A.D. 1075 ± 150 (M-914). From Period II there appear to be links in the pottery which extend as far as Period IV which had its heyday in the fifteenth century. The pottery of Periods II and III consists for the most part of undecorated vessels, often gourd shaped. In later centuries the quality of the pottery improves and burnishing is often used. The pottery of Period IV is typified by tall necks, whilst polychrome vessels, common in late ruin sites in Matabeleland, are almost unknown at Zimbabwe. There is good reason to believe that the occupants of the ruins from this time onwards were peoples who were at least basically related to each other.

In Periods II and III the material culture of the inhabitants of Zimbabwe was not very rich. Imported beads became more common, stylized human figurines and models of cattle were constructed and in Period III, which has been dated to as early as the eleventh century, the first stone walls were built in the valley as well as on the Acropolis. During Period III the pole and mud huts built by the inhabitants were much stronger than those of the earlier occupants, although the earlier types of houses were still constructed. The fact that there is some continuity in material culture from Periods II to IV suggests that the changes which took place were those of gradual economic development, as well as of political leadership rather than complete disruptions of the cultural sequence.

Period III led to a number of other minor innovations. Weaving and spinning began to be practised and extensive stone building took place. Karanga peoples are thought to have been the immigrants who were responsible for this phase. The term Shona was first applied to the tribes of Mashonaland by Europeans and being a linguistic term may be used as an alternative to Karanga or to the other five main dialects which it embraces. We do not know who was responsible for the Period II occupation. Little information is available on the distribution of Period II pottery on other sites in Rhodesia. It has been picked up at a number of sites in the Fort Victoria region and near Bulawayo. Some ruins and open sites have also yielded traces of Period III wares. These discoveries show that Karanga influence in Rhodesia was widespread during the twelfth and fourteenth centuries.

The southern frontier of the Karanga sphere of influence was in the Limpopo valley. The important site on Mapungubwe Hill (Pl. VII) has shown that Karanga material culture was richly endowed at this period. Mapungubwe itself has been radiocarbon dated to the late fourteenth century. It is a hill-top site probably with sacred association which was covered with elaborate huts and ritual structures. Several skeletons, buried with gold objects and copper ornaments, were found near the western end of the hill. Mapungubwe Hill was greatly revered by the local population until recent times and must have been a ritual centre of considerable importance. The site was also strategically placed to control the copper-mining activities of the farmers of the Messina region of the Transvaal.

By the fourteenth century, then, small groups of Karanga were in control of a large area of what is now Rhodesia between the Zambezi and Limpopo. They controlled the gold, ivory and copper trade and were on excellent terms with the Moors. Many of the Karanga lived in stone settlements whilst the indigenous population exploited mineral outcrops and provided grist for the commercial mills of the Kingdom of Monomotapa.

THE EMPIRE OF MONOMOTAPA

Period IV at Zimbabwe, which dates to *c.* A.D. 1450 on the latest researches, is represented by rich deposits on the Acropolis and in the valley. It reflects the full glory and importance of Zimbabwe as a commercial and religious centre. The women were making extremely fine pots and bowls which were sometimes painted with different colours. These can be directly compared to pottery made by modern Rozwi peoples. The Rozwi occupants, who were the dominant clan of the Karanga, built the Temple Enclosure Wall at Zimbabwe as well as the Conical Tower. They made use of patterned walling, modelled beautiful soapstone bowls and ceremonial bird figures and developed the gold trade to a new height. Iron gongs of Congo type and copper ornaments become more common in the deposits as well as a wide range of imports.

Many other Rozwi ruins are known from Rhodesia. One of the most important of these is the Khami ruins near Bulawayo, which consists of a series of platform ruins which were the centre of an important Rozwi chief. Polychrome decoration is a particular characteristic of Khami pottery and finds of imports, iron tools, etc. are common. Chequer pattern walling is characteristic of Khami.

The traditional history of the Karanga and Rozwi kingdoms has been studied by Abraham and others. From their work we know that by the middle of the fifteenth century a dominant clan known as the Rozwi were in control of the Karanga peoples. Their power was bolstered by Arabs who encouraged them to expand their sphere of influence and thence their prosperity. About 1440 a Rozwi chief named Mutota began a massive expansion of his domains. By 1450 he and his Arab allies were in control of a vast region bounded by the Indian Ocean in the east, the Kalahari desert in the west and by the Zambezi and Limpopo rivers. Mutota was given the praise name of *Mwene Mutapa* (master pillager) a name which has been perpetuated as Monomotapa. The empire of Monomotapa soon disintegrated into several distinct kingdoms. A vassal chief named

Changamire, a title which was later perpetuated, disengaged the eastern and south-eastern parts of the kingdom leaving the Monomotapa in effective control of only the northern parts of his domains.

The Portuguese rounded the Cape of Good Hope in the late fifteenth century and progressively extended their trading activities on the East Coast. They smashed the commercial organization of the Arabs based on Kilwa and Sofala, settling at the latter themselves. The South East Africa region came under the control of the Viceroy of Goa. The Portuguese authorities were not slow in exploring the interior. A pardoned criminal named Antonio Fernandes visited the realms of Monomotapa in 1514 and is thought to have witnessed trade in the Zambezi valley. In the following century the Portuguese made slow but consistent attempts to improve trade relations with Mono-motapa. The Arabs hampered their activities at every turn, fearing the destruction of their monopoly. During the period 1575 to 1616 the Portuguese were able to increase their influence and that of the Arabs declined. A series of trading stations was established in the northern parts of Mashonaland. European traders were unable to penetrate into Changamire's kingdom, to the south of Monomotapa's domains. In the late seventeenth century Dombo, the Changamire of the day, was persuaded by a usurper to the throne of Monomotapa, now a Portuguese puppet, to back his claim to the throne by force. He initiated a ruthless military campaign between 1693 and 1695 which expelled the Portuguese from Mashonaland and brought savage hordes to the very gates of Tete. As a result of this devastating defeat Portuguese influence declined sharply. The settlers were forced to confine most of their trading efforts to the Lower Zambezi valley, basing themselves at Sena, Tete and Feira with only occasional visits to Changamire's kingdom. It was not until the nineteenth century that the Portuguese re-established effective political control over some of the areas which hitherto had been closed to them.

The archaeology of the Rhodesian stone settlements shows that Period IV sites, associated with the dominant Rozwi clan, are by far the most common ruins. The richness and power of the Rozwi chiefs of the time is amply demonstrated by the varied and vigorous artistic and technological achievements of the day. Rozwi leaders continued to dominate the Rhodesian scene until their power was smashed by Nguni raiders from South Africa in the early nineteenth century.

INYANGA

The eastern borders of Rhodesia lie among high mountains which form part of the great chain of high ground which extends from the Cape to Ethiopia. The Iron-Age peoples who lived in these upland regions in the second millennium developed a characteristic culture, based on terrace cultivation on hillsides as well as stock-breeding, hunting and food-gathering. We know from studies of pottery at Inyanga that the peoples who lived there were of Karanga stock and contemporary with the Ruin peoples of Mashonaland. Their villages were clustered around stone-lined pits about 20 ft. in diameter and also stone-walled enclosures, in both of which they kept their stock. Forts were built on the Uplands as protection against Zimba raiders. It has proved difficult to date the Inyanga structures but Summers and his colleagues were able to assign some of the ruins to between the sixteenth and eighteenth centuries.

The material culture of the Inyanga people was poor when compared with that of their Mashonaland neighbours. They lived far away from mineral outcrops, their homeland having little attraction for traders. Only the simplest of iron objects were found including spearheads, arrowheads and razors. Pottery was coarser than in the Mashonaland ruins. The origin of the Inyanga people is unknown but there are a number of indications that they were of northern origin. Summers considers that the techniques of terrace cultivation were probably evolved at Inyanga itself quite independently of the terraces in other areas.

ZAMBIA AND THE CONGO

Much of Zambia is inhabited by tribes who have migrated eastwards from the Congo basin and Angola (Fig. 4). With the

exception of the Ila/Tonga speaking peoples and one or two
other minor groups, all the tribes of Zambia are thought to have
moved into the country within the last 600 or 700 years. The
second millennium A.D. was a period of considerable importance
for it was during this time that the copper-mining centres of
Zambia and Katanga were organized on a larger scale than ever
before. Judging from discoveries at Sanga in Katanga, the
mines were being extensively exploited by A.D. 900, but we have

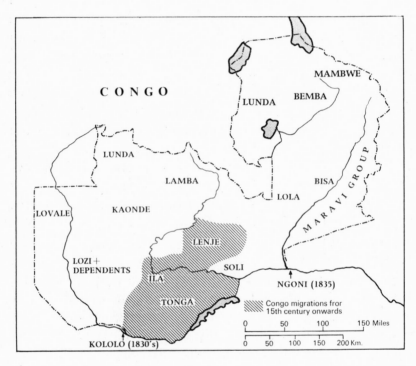

MAP 11. Zambia—distribution of tribes of Congo origin arriving since the
fifteenth century A.D.

no means of saying whether the Zambian outcrops were being
exploited at such an early date. How much copper from the
Katanga and Zambian mines went south to the East Coast trade
routes we do not know, but there is reason to believe that the
mines did not reach full production until the second half of the
second millennium.

When the Portuguese discovered the mouth of the Congo in 1482 they came into contact with the kingdom of the Kongo, an empire with trading contacts with the Luba peoples of the Congo basin. The Portuguese concentrated their missionary and commercial endeavours on this kingdom for the next 100 years and stimulated the export market in slaves, ivory and copper to new heights. In Luba a group of ivory hunters created a feudal dynasty under a hereditary chief named Mwata Yamvo. A number of peripheral states giving allegiance to Mwata Yamvo sprang up around his domains and there was a gradual dispersal of Lunda chieftains and their followers to the south and south-east across the Luapula into Zambia.

These were merely part of a long series of migrations from the Congo. The earliest immigrants whose tribal identity is known to us are the Maravi peoples of the Eastern Province who are thought to have entered their present homeland before A.D. 1500. In all probability only a few aristocratic families and their followers moved eastwards, subjugating the Early-Iron-Age farmers who were already living east of the Luangwa. In later centuries the Maravi peoples separated into several distinct groups, which today form the tribes of the Eastern Province of Zambia and parts of Malawi.

During the eighteenth century large-scale population movements took place from the west. The Bemba and Bisa, who today occupy much of the Northern Province, are thought to have crossed the Luapula river in the early eighteenth century. They were followed by the Lunda, whom traditional history suggests crossed the same river in about 1740. Both these tribes found a number of minor groups of Congo origin such as the Mambwe and Lala already living in Zambia. The Lunda were under the leadership of chief Kazambe whose direct successor still rules them today.

North-western and central Zambia is now occupied by a number of tribes of Congo origin including the Lovale, southern Lunda, Kaonde, Lamba and Soli. The exact dates of their arrival in the country are unknown, but all of them have entered Zambia within the last few centuries.

The flood-plains of western Zambia were settled by the Lozi and their dependents in the seventeenth or eighteenth centuries and a centralized kingdom was founded, it is thought, by the descendants of a female chieftainess named Mwambwa. She moved southwards from the kingdom of Mwata Yamvo and established her rule on the Barotse flood-plains.

The tribal distribution in Zambia as we see it today was established in outline by the beginning of the nineteenth century but a number of events affected this distribution during the last century of the Iron Age. The Lunda under Chief Kazembe had been in direct contact with the Portuguese on the West Coast for some time, but in 1793 some Bisa traders contacted the Portuguese at Tete on the lower Zambezi and suggested that they should open a trade route with Kazembe from the east. An expedition set out from Tete in 1798 under the leadership of Dr. F. J. de Lacerda with the specific object of trading with the Lunda. The expedition reached Kazembe, but was not allowed to proceed to the West Coast although tenuous trade relations were established. Further subsequent expeditions attempted to expand Lunda commerce. Two half-castes, Baptista and Jose, crossed from the West Coast to Tete via Kazembe's capital between 1806 and 1811, subsequently returning by the same route. A second expedition, under Monteiro and Gamitto, reached Kazembe's headquarters from the east in 1831-2, but returned to Tete without achieving anything. By this time Kazembe was aware of the dangers of allowing the Portuguese to control his strategic position in the middle of the continent and their attempts to exploit the markets of the interior never succeeded.

Where the Portuguese failed, Arab slave traders from Kilwa on the East Coast succeeded. The Portuguese never identified themselves with the political ambitions of Zambian chiefs, whereas the Arabs were careful to create an effective political umbrella under which they could operate their nefarious trade. Soon after the last Portuguese expedition left, the Arabs broke Kazembe's power by forming an alliance with the Yeke of Katanga and the land-hungry Bemba whose land was infertile. These alliances led to a period of unrest in the north and east of the country, when the Bemba expanded their territory at the expense of their neighbours, handing over their captives to the Arab slave traders in exchange for firearms.

THE NINETEENTH CENTURY

The events of the last century of the Iron Age in Rhodesia and Zambia arose almost entirely as a result of the deeds of one man. In 1818 the famous warrior Shaka became the chief of the Zulu. In the following years he extended the influence of the Nguni tribes over enormous areas of South Africa by devastating military campaigns. Several chiefs and their followers fled before the wrath of Shaka northwards into Rhodesia. One of these groups was headed by a chief named Mzilikazi who defied Shaka and fled northwards into the Transvaal. His followers played havoc with the Sotho tribes of the Transvaal, acquiring the name AmaNdebele ('those who are hiding behind their enormous Zulu war shields of stout cowhide'). By about 1840 Mzilikazi had moved northwards and finally settled near Bulawayo in Rhodesia overthrowing the Rozwi chiefs and establishing rule over what is now known as Matabeleland. Groups of Ndebele raided as far north as Tonga country and their second chief, Lobengula, who succeeded Mzilikazi in 1868, saw the establishment of European rule in Rhodesia.

In 1821 another chieftain, Zwangendaba, fled northwards from Natal. After ravaging the lower Limpopo valley his troops moved westwards to Karanga country around Zimbabwe, which they sacked. The Ngoni horde crossed the Zambezi near Zumbu in the midst of an eclipse of the sun on 28 November 1835, and fell on the tribes to the east of the Luangwa river. After Zwangendaba's death in 1845 the horde separated but the principal chief, Mpenzeni, settled in Zambia and terrorized the Bemba, Bisa, and others of their neighbours. Inevitably there were clashes between the Bemba and Ngoni, for the former were extending their territory in search of new land and slaves for their Moorish allies.

At the beginning of the nineteenth century the Lozi empire to the west of Zambia was gradually extended by conquest. The Lozi ascendancy was soon overthrown by a group of Kololo warriors under the leadership of a Chief Sebitwane. This remarkable man had moved northwards through Botswana to the Zambezi in the 1820's. In the following decade he crossed the Zambezi, defeated the Tonga and finally conquered the Lozi kingdom. The Kololo were visited by David Livingstone on his Zambezi journeys in 1851 and 1860, and he has left us descriptions of their customs. In 1864 the Kololo were destroyed by a confederacy of Lozi generals and a succession of Lozi chiefs have rules Western Zambia ever since.

When the first European missionaries and administrators arrived in our region they found the whole political situation in a state of fluidity. Slave raiding, tribal invasions and petty jealousies were changing the long established distributions of populations. The establishment of European rule led to peace and some stability but initiated another major revolution in the history of South Central Africa.

BIBLIOGRAPHY

The following references can be recommended for further reading, but the list is far from complete:

D. P. Abraham, 'The Early Political History of the Kingdom of Monomotapa (850–1589)', *Historians in Tropical Africa* (Salisbury, 1960), 61–92.

D. P. Abraham, 'Maramuca, an Exercise in the Combined Use of Portuguese Records and Oral Tradition', *Journ. of Afr. Hist.*, II (1961), 211–26.

Eric Axelson, *Portuguese in South East Africa, 1600–1700* (Johannesburg, 1960).

W. V. Brelsford, *The Tribes of Northern Rhodesia* (Lusaka, 1956).

G. Caton-Thompson, *Zimbabwe culture* (Oxford, 1931).

J. D. Clark, *The Prehistory of Southern Africa* (London, 1958).

J. D. Clark, 'The Prehistoric Origins of African Culture', *Journ. Afr. Hist.*, V (1964), 161–84.

J. D. Clark and B. M. Fagan, 'Charcoals, Sands, and Channel-decorated Pottery from Northern Rhodesia', *Amer. Anthrop.*, 67 (1965), 354–71.

Sonia Cole, *The Prehistory of East Africa* (London, 1964).

Ian Cunnison, 'Kazembe and the Portuguese, 1798–1831', *Journ. Afr. Hist.*, II (1961), 61–76.

B. M. Fagan, 'Pre-European Ironworking in Central Africa with special reference to Northern Rhodesia', *Journ. Afr. Hist.*, II (1961), 199–210.

B. M. Fagan, 'The Iron Age Sequence in the Southern Province of Northern Rhodesia', *Journ. Afr. Hist.* IV (1963), 157–77.

B. M. Fagan, 'The Greefswald Sequence: Mapungubwe and Bambandy-analo', *Journ. Afr. Hist.*, V (1964), in the press.

B. M. Fagan, *Southern Africa during the Iron Age* (London, 1966).

B. M. Fagan (ed.), *A Short History of Zambia* (Nairobi, 1966).

B. M. Fagan, 'Early Iron Age Pottery in East and Southern Africa', *Azania*, I (1966), 101–11.

B. M. Fagan, *Iron Age Cultures in Zambia*, I (London, 1967).

B. M. Fagan, 'The Iron Age Peoples of Zambia and Malawi', in W. W. Bishop and J. D. Clark (eds.), *Background to African Evolution* (Chicago, 1967), 659–86.

B. M. Fagan, 'Early Trade and Raw Materials in South Central Africa', *Journ. Afr. Hist.*, X (1969), 1–16.

B. M. Fagan and D. W. Phillipson, 'Sebanzi: The Iron Age Sequence at Lochinvar and the Tonga', *Journ. Roy. Anthrop. Inst.* 95, 2 (1965), 253–94.

B. M. Fagan, D. W. Phillipson and S. G. H. Daniels, *Iron Age Cultures in Zambia*, II (London, 1969).

L. Fouché (ed.), *Mapungubwe* (Cambridge, 1937).

G. A. Gardner, *Mapungubwe*, Vol. 2 (Pretoria, 1963).

P. L. Garlake, 'The Value of Imported Ceramics in the Dating and Interpretation of the Rhodesian Iron Age', *Journ. Afr. Hist.*, IV, 1 (1968), 13–34.

R. R. Inskeep, 'Some Iron Age Sites in Northern Rhodesia', *S. Afr. Archaeol. Bull.*, XVII, 67 (1962), 136–80.

F. P. Mennell and Roger Summers, 'The "Ancient Workings" of Southern Rhodesia', *Occ. Pap. Nat. Mus. S. Rhod.*, 2, 20 (1955), 765–77.

Roland Oliver, 'The Problem of the Bantu Expansion', *Journ. Afr. Hist.*, VII, 3 (1966), 361–76.

D. W. Phillipson, 'The Early Iron Age in Zambia: Regional Variants and some Tentative Conclusions', *Journ. Afr. Hist.*, IX (1968), 191–211.

P. A. Robins and A. Whitty, 'Excavations at Harleigh Farm near Rusape, Rhodesia', *S. Afr. Archaeol. Bull.*, XXI, 82 (1966) 61–80.

K. R. Robinson, 'Four Rhodesian Iron Age Sites, An Account of Stratigraphy and Finds', *Occ. Pap. Nat. Mus. S. Rhod.*, 2, 22A (1958).

K. R. Robinson, *Khami Ruins* (Cambridge, 1959).

K. R. Robinson, 'An Early Iron Age Site from the Chibi District, Southern Rhodesia', *S. Afr. Archaeol. Bull.*, XVI (1961), 75–102.

K. R. Robinson, 'Further Excavations in the Iron Age Deposits at the Tunnel Site, Gokomere Hill, Southern Rhodesia', *S. Afr. Archaeol. Bull.*, XVIII (1963), 160.

K. R. Robinson, 'The Leopard's Kopje Culture, Its Position in the Iron Age in Southern Rhodesia', *S. Afr. Archaeol. Bull.*, XXI, 81 (1966), 5–51.

K. R. Robinson, 'The Archaeology of the Rozwi', in E. Stokes and R. Brown, *The Zambesian Past* (Manchester, 1966), 3–27.

K. R. Robinson, 'Bambata Ware: Its Position in the Rhodesian Iron Age in the Light of Recent Evidence', *S. Afr. Archaeol. Bull.*, XXI, 82 (1966), 81–5.

Roger Summers, *Inyanga* (Cambridge, 1958).

Roger Summers, 'The Southern Rhodesian Iron Age', *Journ. Afr. Hist.*, II, (1961), 1–13.

Roger Summers, *Zimbabwe, a Rhodesian Mystery* (Johannesburg, 1963).

Roger Summers, 'Iron Age Industries of Southern Africa, with Notes on Their Chronology, Terminology, and Economic Status', in W. W. Bishop and J. D. Clark (eds.) *Background to African Evolution* (Chicago, 1967).

Roger Summers, K. R. Robinson and A. Whitty, *Zimbabwe Excavations, 1958*. Occasional Papers of the National Museums, No. 23A (Bulawayo, 1961).

A. Whitty, 'A Classification of Prehistoric Stone Buildings in Mashonaland, Southern Rhodesia', *S. Afr. Archaeol. Bull.*, XIV, 54 (1959), 57–71.

9

SOUTH AFRICA

by

R. Inskeep

WHEN I was first approached with a request to contribute to this volume my first response was one of misgiving because of the paucity and inadequacy of the documentation. After careful consideration it is still my opinion that it is far too early to attempt anything approaching an historians' synthesis of the evidence; it is so meagre as to be almost meaningless. On the other hand the volume would be incomplete without some remarks on this most southerly region. There are a few facts which can be stated, a few working hypotheses can be proposed, problems outlined, and the prospects presented as an enticement for future generations of field workers.

Before proceeding to a brief review of the evidence, a few words on the history of archaeological exploration in South Africa might help to explain our present sad state of knowledge of our Iron Age. With the establishment of the Colony, in 1652, the opportunity for an antiquarian era, comparable to that experienced by Europe in the seventeenth and eighteenth centuries was established. But South Africa, as it was known, down to the early nineteenth century lacked the intriguing field monuments which provided such attractions and such entertainment for the curious in Europe. Europe offered the comfortable prospect of digging up one's very own ancestors; Africa was hostile and impersonal, and her indigenous peoples were often regarded as an impediment to free movement rather than as a topic for investigation. Sparrman seems to have been our first field investigator in a region (the Great Fish River) which might easily have brought him into contact with the Iron Age. But apart from some delightful speculations, his efforts really produced nothing. The Stone Age received its debut at the hands of T. H. Bowker in the 1850's, and this seems to have set the seal on the pattern of South African archaeology for the next 70 or 80 years. The discovery of handaxes in the diamond rich gravels of the Vaal in the 1870's, and of the australopithecines in the second and third decades of the present century, loaded the dice in favour of the earlier periods.

By and large the period from the sixteenth century to about 1900 might be called a period of casual observation; whilst that from 1880 to 1923 could be described as a period of speculation, not always well controlled. A new era of constructive thinking and research was ushered in with the appointment of A. J. H. Goodwin as Research Assistant in Archaeology and Ethnology at the University of Cape Town in 1923. But Goodwin's work was confined mainly to the south and south-west Cape; an area which seems not to have been touched by Iron-Age occupation. It is of interest that Goodwin's excellent paper of 1935 entitled 'A commentary on the history and present position of South African prehistory with full bibliography' makes no mention at all of an Iron Age, although he comes tantalizingly near it in a section on 'Neolithic Elements'.[1] It seems curiously out of keeping that Goodwin should have missed at least a dozen papers dealing with ancient mine workings, smelting sites, burials and stone ruins in the Transvaal and Orange Free State, all published before 1935. That he considered these to lie outside the proper field of prehistory is strongly suggested by the fact that he lists no less than nineteen papers by J. P. Johnson on geological and stone age topics, but omits entirely a most interesting paper published by him in 1912 on stone-walled kraals in South Africa.[2]

---

[1] A. J. H. Goodwin, *Bantu Studies* (1935), 368–72.
[2] J. P. Johnson, *Man*, 12 (1912), 65–8.

The appointment of van Riet Lowe as Director of the newly created Bureau of Archaeology (later re-named the Archaeological Survey of South Africa—disbanded in 1962) in 1935 brought a full-time archaeologist to the centre of an area extraordinarily rich in Iron-Age remains. But van Riet Lowe remained loyal to the tradition of South African archaeology, and only seven of his 131 published papers relate to Iron-Age problems,[1] four of these arising directly from his involvement in the Mapungubwe project.

Just as Zimbabwe lies at the back of a long history of Iron-Age research in Rhodesia, so Mapungubwe has probably done more than any other site to focus attention on the Iron Age in South Africa; yet it is a sad thought that the handful of gold found by the first European visitors was undoubtedly the attraction, rather than the other evidence of occupation.

Professor Dart entered the field with a paper on 'The ancient mining industry of southern Africa' in 1924,[2] and his subsequent departure from the field of interest is undoubtedly to be associated with the discovery of *Australopithecus africanus* in that same year. It is, however, a tribute to his interest and enthusiasm that a number of early papers describing ruins in the Transvaal and Orange Free State emanate from the pens of his students. Other early contributions come mainly from a few enlightened prospectors, miners and engineers attracted to the Transvaal in the pioneering years.

The papers by van Hoepen and Hoffman,[3] van Hoepen[4] and others like them remain isolated phenomena, including the relatively recent contributions of R. J. Mason. The two major research projects in progress today[5] are much more reflections of trends, widespread in Africa today, to take note of the more recent past, than a natural outgrowth of the sporadic investigations indicated above. Both of these projects are, however, of

[1] B. D. Malan, and H. B. Cooke, *S. Afr. Arch. Bull.*, Supplement to 17 (1962), 82–4.

[2] R. A. Dart, *S. Afr. Geol. Jour.*, 7 (1924), 7–13.

[3] E. C. N. Van Hoepen, and A. C. Hoffman, *Argeol. Navors. Nas. Mus. Bloemfontein*, 2 (1935).

[4] E. C. N. Van Hoepen, *Argeol. Navors. Nas. Mus. Bloemfontein*, 2 (5) (1939).

[5] *S. Afr. Arch. Bull.*, 21 (1966), 156.

such recent origin that little has emerged in published form, and the remarks which follow are based primarily on the fragmentary, and often incomplete evidence of earlier investigations.

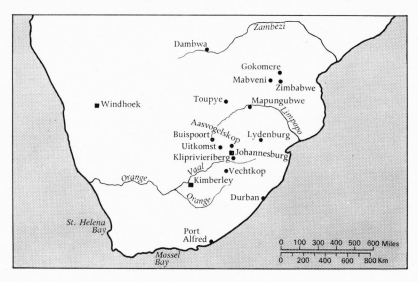

Map 12. South Africa.

Geographically the area with which we are here concerned lies south of the Limpopo, and north of a line running from Windhoek to Port Alfred, though this southerly limit is only a very approximate boundary which may well be revised, certainly clarified, in the future. South of this region, in the north-west Cape, south-west Cape and south Cape coastal region, evidence for Iron-Age occupation is entirely lacking. Da Gama makes no mention of sheep or cattle, or the use of metals when he landed at St. Helena Bay in 1497. Sheep and cattle were encountered further east, at Mossel Bay, and his description of the eastern Cape coast leaves little doubt that the area was occupied by peoples whom we would include within our compass as Iron Age. By the time of the establishment of the Dutch colony at the Cape, in 1652, sheep and cattle were present in the landscape, but still the yellow-skinned hunters and herders of the area had no knowledge of metals. Some 10 years after the establishment of the colony van Meerhof encountered Nama tribesmen, north of the Colony, wearing iron and copper ornaments. It is not entirely clear whether this was a truly indigenous Nama industry, or whether, as seems more likely, the Nama were in contact with groups belonging more properly to a major Iron-Age complex.

The idea that 'the Hottentots' migrated into South Africa—from East Africa, bringing with them sheep, cattle and ceramics, as a sort of ripple heralding the tidal wave of the Iron Age is a very old one. Unfortunately 'the Hottentot' is a rather elusive entity, recognized on different grounds by linguists, physical anthropologists, and cultural anthropologists, with little or no agreement between them. Recent blood group studies suggest that 'light skinned pastoralists speaking Nama' are African negroids with a long history of differentiation in the southern-most part of the continent.[1] The writer has argued elsewhere[2] that the yellow-skinned hunters and the yellow-skinned herders, encountered by the early explorers of South Africa, are best thought of as components of a truly indigenous later Stone-Age population which had become differentially acculturated by contact with Iron-Age societies. It was further suggested that the acquisition of sheep and cattle might have occurred at very different times in very different places; sheep from north of the Limpopo soon after the turn of the Christian era, and cattle from south-east Africa at a considerably later date. Unfortunately rock art depicting sheep and cattle is generally undatable, and pastoralists still remain to be identified within the later Stone Age. The evidence of culture contact therefore has little to offer by way of dating Iron-Age penetration in our region.

The Portuguese, Dutch and English explorers of the fifteenth, sixteenth and seventeenth centuries have little to contribute to our knowledge of the origins of the South African Iron Age, though some nineteenth-century authors have left valuable records of an ethnographic nature. Monica Wilson[3] has made a valuable contribution in this field, combining historical sources

[1] R. Singer, and J. Weiner, *Southwestern Jour. of Anthrop.*, 19 (1963), 169.

[2] R. Inskeep, in L. Thompson and M. Wilson, *The Oxford History of South Africa* (Clarendon Press, Oxford, Vol. I, 1969.)

[3] M. Wilson, *Afr. Studies*, 18 (1959), 167–79.

with tribal traditions to show that Nguni speakers were well established in the Transkei/Ciskei coastal region in the sixteenth century, and that prior to this they had inhabited the foothills of the Kahlamba mountains some 50 to 60 miles to the north. There was nothing in the recorded traditions to suggest movement from further north within the period covered by the genealogies (i.e. since A.D. 1300), so that Nguni speakers may well have been established in the region for over 600 years.

It is indeed unfortunate that so little traditional history has been recorded in the country. The excellent work of van Warmelo[1] on the copper miners of Musina stands almost alone in this respect. As yet, no serious attempt has been made to align the evidence of this splendid document with the findings of archaeology.

The evidence then, meagre as it is, lies predominantly with archaeology. What does this tell us? The evidence will lead us to the conclusions that the period with which we must deal spans a little over 1,000 years from the present, with the possible exception of the extreme north, where the period might be significantly longer, and that apart from some societies which may, through time, have lost their identity, we are dealing with the early forebears of the present Bantu-speaking peoples of South Africa. It is instructive, therefore, to ask ourselves to what extent we might be capable of distinguishing the many groupings identifiable on various grounds at the present day on the basis of the more durable components of their material culture. Since we cannot rule out the possibilities of movements to and fro across modern political boundaries we might begin by commenting on a recent list for the territories south of the Cunene, Okavango and Zambezi rivers. Lawton[2] lists ten major divisions (Nguni, Tsonga, Sotho, Venda, Lemba, Chopi, Shona, Herero, Ambo and various non-Ambo Okavango tribes). These comprise some thirty-nine sub-divisions, some of which are large groups separated from other sub-divisions

[1] N. J. Van Warmelo, *The Copper Miners of Musina and the Early History of the Zoutpansberg*, Department of Native Affairs, Ethnological Publications, VIII (Government Printer, Pretoria, 1940).

[2] A. C. Lawton, *Annals of the S.A. Mus.*, 49 (1967).

of the same major division by great distances (e.g. Nguni: Cape Nguni and Rhodesian Ndebele), and some ninety-two tribal groups. When we consider that the archaeologists' major basis for classification is pottery sherds, we shall begin to realize the complexity of the task before us. Fortunately there are other traits which might be expected to assist here and there, such as house and village plans, and other aspects of domestic architecture; ceramic products such as figurines, and clay spoons, may assist, and smelting furnaces, of which we know next to nothing. The products of metallurgy will be helpful where these survive, but at present we know little of these things for our living populations, so to a large extent the findings of archaeology must remain, for a while, unwed to the facts of ethnology.

Laidler[1] pioneered the study of pottery in southern Africa, and whilst the interest of his paper is now largely historical, it undoubtedly contributed much to the excellence of Schofield's treatment of the subject 20 years later.[2] This latter work, and the more detailed and comprehensive study of Lawton[3] indicate fairly clearly that significant differences in pottery styles do exist between major groupings (e.g. Nguni and Sotho), and further suggest that significant differences may exist at a more refined level of distinction (e.g. the *divisions* or *tribal groups* of Lawton). It must be stressed, however, that the quantity of pottery described and illustrated by Lawton does not provide sufficient data for identification of smaller units with any degree of certainty. The main lines of the ceramic traditions are sketched in, but the survey gives too little indication of the range of variation in the pottery forms and decoration for individual tribal groups. No data is available on the frequency with which the forms and decoration described, occur within the pottery of a particular group, and one suspects that the corpus is too strongly biased in favour of decorated, or otherwise 'fine' specimens, at the expense of the more humble plain pottery.

[1] P. W. Laidler, *Trans. Roy. Soc. S. Afr.*, 26 (1938), 93–172.
[2] J. F. Schofield, *Primitive Pottery*, S. Afr. Arch. Soc., Cape Town (1948).
[3] Lawton, op. cit.

It is, then, apparent that the prospects for identifying archaeological pottery, even of very recent date, at any more refined level that 'Nguni', or 'Sotho', Tsonga, etc., are not good.

The dangers of attempting to identify ethnic groupings on the basis of pottery assemblages becomes apparent when one looks at the vessels illustrated by Lawton for the Rhodesian Ndebele; the affinities are much more with Tsonga and Shona groups than with the existing Nguni, and it is doubtful whether the Nguni relationships of the Ndebele would be recognized at all from their pottery; weapons and domestic architecture may well provide better clues. This situation is understandable when one considers that the Ndebele represent a warrior incursion whose settlers presumably took wives from local tribes, and that pottery is generally the woman's business. On the other hand, it is remarkable that a very pure Nguni dialect has survived the transplantation.[1]

The interpretation of pottery attributes must proceed with great care, for not only may the features associable with a single society undergo changes through time, independent of any external influences, but such trends may be triggered off or imposed by culture contact in a variety of ways. If we consider the possibility of changes resulting from both these causes, combining with population movements and perhaps the fragmenting of societies, we can see that very complex pictures might result.

The Venda of the northern Transvaal make very fine and distinctive pottery including bowls in which the decoration is effected by the very skilful use of finely burnished red ochre and graphite, applied in bold, simple patterns without delineation by stamped, grooved, or incised lines. Precisely the same kind of bowls were recovered by the author from a cemetery in Malawi, at the south end of Lake Nyasa in 1958.[2] In addition to the painted bowls certain other ceramic features point to a relation-

---

[1] I am indebted to Professor E. O. Westphal of the University of Cape Town for this information.

[2] R. Inskeep, *Preliminary Investigations of a Proto-Historic Cemetery at Nkudzi Bay, Malawi* (National Museums of Zambia. Special Paper. 1965).

ship between the Nkudzi cemetery and Venda pottery; these
include the occurrence of 'double-tiered' pots, extensive use of
red ochre and graphite to emphasize decorative motifs formed
by grooved or incised lines, and a very low incidence of comb-
stamping. The resemblances are such that the archaeological
conclusion, based on the pottery, would be that the two sites
belonged to the same 'culture', even though differences were
conceded which might lead to one or the other being labelled 'a
variant'. In the case of the Nkudzi cemetery, however, historical
evidence is quite clear that the cemetery is Nyanja. The reasons
for the similarity are still far from known and it is not our
concern here to pursue them. The example is given in order to
underline further the difficulties of arguing from ceramics to
existing ethnic groupings in a context where some workers are
striving to identify contemporary African populations in other
places and other ages.

With these remarks concerning the inadequacy of archaeological and ethnographic research clearly in mind, and with
due regard for the difficulties of interpretation, we may review
the slender evidence available to us. In 1948 Schofield, concerning himself primarily with pottery, recognized seven classes, of
which one (his N.C.1) was considered to belong to the later
Stone Age, and can be ignored from our present standpoint.
His remaining classes may be summarized as follows:

Northern Transvaal

N.T.1. This was represented primarily by pottery from
Mapungubwe and Bambandyanalo and equated generally with
the class M.2 as described in the first Mapungubwe volume.[1] He
was unable to point to other closely related groups, but saw
some similarities with pottery from sites in Botswana. He
described small occurrences from other sites in the central and
northern Transvaal, but considered that too little was known
of this material to warrant classification.

[1] L. Fouché, *Mapungubwe, Ancient Bantu Civilization of the Limpopo* (C.U.P., Cambridge,
1937).

Southern Transvaal and northern Orange Free State

S.T.1. These were well-made wares in which contrasted colours predominated, together with the use of comb-stamped impressions. This material he also considered to have affinities with the pottery of Botswana which he linked with his N.T.1, though there is no direct affinity suggested between S.T.1 and N.T.1.

S.T.2. This class consisted primarily of pots devoid of decoration except for rim-notching. Although S.T.2 was considered to be characteristic of the corbelled stone hut settlements of the northern Orange Free State, he noted their occurrence also at ruin sites at Buispoort, Aasvogelskop and Magaliesburg in the western and southern Transvaal, none of which contained corbelled stone huts. He considered both S.T.1 and S.T.2 to have been used concurrently, and to have, perhaps, a common origin. The more elaborately decorated vessels of S.T.1 he suggested had fallen out of use in the inhospitable environment of the Orange Free State. His general remarks on the area[1] are of considerable interest: 'All of these sites are covered with the remains of stone-walled cattle-pens and dwelling-enclosures. In many instances the latter are occupied by the walls and wind-screens of huts, probably once roofed with thatch. On the completely treeless downs of the Orange Free State the thatched roofs were replaced by roughly corbelled domes of undressed stone, and thus (in this locality only) a new architectural feature was evolved that has no counterpart in the rest of South Africa. This completely treeless environment had its effects in other directions as well, for iron-smelting could no longer be carried on for lack of fuel, and we also find that all the finer types of pottery ceased to be made.'

The Natal Coastal Region

N.C.2. According to Schofield this class of pottery is found sometimes alone, and sometimes in association with N.C.3, predominantly in the vicinity of Durban, but occasionally elsewhere in Natal. The fabric is soft, and tends to be grey to

[1] Schofield, op. cit., 142.

black in colour. Burnish may be present, but colour applied to the surface has not been noted. Forms include platters, pots, and bowls, and decoration includes notching of the rim, surface pitting in a variety of ways, surface relief produced by pinching or application, grooving or incision, and comb-stamping. Schofield notes that all these features are characteristic of his S.T.2 ware as found in the stone hut settlements, and suggests that their presence in Natal results from an eastward spread from the Orange Free State with the consequent abandonment of stone architecture in a region where timber was readily available.

N.C.2D. This is regarded by Schofield as a 'phase' of N.C.2 whose affinities 'are clearly with . . . Buispoort'. Fabric and finish are said to resemble N.C.2, but stress is laid on a globular form with flared neck and bold incised decoration whose shapes are said to be very reminiscent of the western Transvaal.

N.C.3. This class presents a contrast with N.C.2 and N.C.2D. The fabric is commonly coarse, 'self-coloured', and decoration by deep grooving in the form of parallel lines, cross-hatching, and herring-bone is described as vigorous. The pottery is commonly found associated with clear evidence of iron smelting.

Whilst some new ideas may have arisen as regards the interpretation of the pottery described by Schofield, it must be conceded that his account still comprises the only general survey of Iron-Age ceramics in South Africa, and is still an indispensable source of information. Since only two other general interpretations have appeared,[1] it may be of value to summarize Schofield's own conclusions.

As between Mapungubwe and his N.C.2 class, there are clearly great differences, and one suspects that one of the weaknesses of Schofield's view is the way in which almost everything is ultimately referred back to Mapungubwe. Starting in Natal, we note that no antecedent is found for N.C.3, and an origin in the north is proposed. The bearers of N.C.2 came from the west, and Schofield accepts their association with the Hurutshe and Fokeng; this same class ultimately set the pattern for the modern

[1] R. F. Summers, *Proto-historic Cultures of Rhodesia and South Africa*, in W. W. Bishop, and J. D. Clark, *Background to Evolution in Africa* (Chicago, 1967).

Mpondo and Thembu pottery of the Cape Nguni. N.C.2 has a number of attributes, all of which[1] are distinguishing features of class S.T.2, as found among the stone hut settlements of the southern Transvaal and northern Orange Free State. In the latter area he clearly favours the view that the makers of the huts, and of the pottery, were Ellenberger's Fokeng who migrated from Ntsuanatsatsi to Natal in the sixteenth century.

We have noted that S.T.1 and S.T.2 are regarded as having a common ancestry, and being in use concurrently, the more elaborate decoration and finish of S.T.1 vanishing in the inhospitable environment of the Orange Free State. Schofield does not propose, specifically any connection between S.T.1 and N.T.1, but there seems none the less to be an implied relationship through the material described from Botswana and its alleged makers.

In the 20 years since Schofield published his *Primitive Pottery* our knowledge of Iron-Age pottery in South Africa has barely changed. Mason[2] has contributed two short papers; the earlier paper contains a rather brief, and inadequately illustrated description of four small assemblages of pottery from caves close to Johannesburg, while the later paper gives a better account of a useful assemblage of pottery from the surface of a site with a short length of ruined stone walling. The pottery of the caves was recognized by Mason as falling within Schofield's two classes S.T.1 and S.T.2, and whilst he does not refer the later collection to either of Schofield's classes it would appear from the illustrations to lie with the S.T.1 class.

1962 saw the publication of a valuable survey of the current state of knowledge of the Transvaal Iron Age.[3] In this work Mason recognizes two cultures; Buispoort, with three sites, and Uitkomst with twelve or thirteen sites. So far as three sites will permit of distributional comment, the Buispoort culture seems to lie west of the Central Transvaal, whilst the Uitkomst sites cluster well in the centre. Both are associated with stone ruins.

[1] Schofield, op. cit., 155.

[2] R. J. Mason, *S. Afr. Arch. Bull.*, 6 (1951), 71 and 7 (1952), 70–9.

[3] R. J. Mason, *The Prehistory of the Transvaal* (Witwatersrand University Press, Johannesburg, 1962).

In a recent but too brief survey, Summers[1] regards Mapungubwe as 'little more than a Zimbabwe colony'. He then goes on to say that 'It is rather more since Mapungubwe seems to have possessed certain features missing at Zimbabwe'. He does not, however, indicate what these features are. The features he mentions as providing the connection are similarities in oriental and Arab imports, and identity of goldsmiths' techniques. These may well be important, especially the latter, but the very great differences in the ceramics of the two sites would suggest that Mapungubwe might be a very different entity from Zimbabwe, linked only by gold-working techniques. The significance of this would depend very much on who the goldsmiths were, for they might, like the modern Lemba, be a small, independent class working in a number of larger communities as specialists.

Beyond Mapungubwe Summers recognizes Mason's Uitkomst and Buispoort cultures. Of the Buispoort culture Summers remarks that it is far more common in the Orange Free State than in the Transvaal. He gives it an enormous area of distribution, from Lydenburg in the north-east, to the edge of the Kalahari in the west, and from the central Transvaal, well south into the Orange Free State. He remarks that a general resemblance in the plan form between Buispoort settlements and settlements in the Limpopo is fortuitous, but holds that within the Buispoort area, as defined above, there is a close architectural resemblance between sites.

Little is said of Uitkomst other than that Toupye (Botswana) is undoubtedly an Uitkomst site, and this indicates a very considerable distribution for this culture also. The only other area mentioned in this paper is the coastal plain (i.e. Natal), and here Summers mentions N.C.2 and its affinities with Buispoort, and suggests that non-Buispoort elements in N.C.2 must hail from elsewhere, and that elsewhere may well be Mozambique. He makes no mention of N.C.3.

We have observed (p. 256) that very little field data for the South African Iron Age has been added since Schofield's day;

[1] Summers, op. cit.

any re-assessment, therefore, must be very largely in relation
to changes in our knowledge of adjacent areas, and more
particularly by the addition of a few radio-carbon dates.

In the absence of any indication, in the later Stone-Age
cultures in central southern Africa of an indigenous development
of domestication and metallurgy we must begin by regarding
our local Iron Age as introduced either by diffusion of culture
traits, or by physical immigration. Since the living descendants
of our Iron-Age societies (the Bantu speakers) represent a physical
stock which has no obvious ancestry in the later Stone Age, and
whose language homeland lies to the north, we may fairly
assume physical migration to have carried a ready-made Iron
Age south of the Limpopo. The general character of our Iron
Age is sufficiently similar to that immediately north of the
Limpopo, for us not to have to look much further for ancestral
relationships (the less well known areas of Mozambique and
Angola may well be involved) and we need not concern ourselves here with the thorny problem of the ultimate origin of the
central African Iron Age. What follows, however, may well
require modification when more is known of the pre-and
proto-history of the Portuguese territories.

The earliest Iron Age dates in Zambia are for sites in the
Zambesi valley established before the end of the first century
A.D.; seventh, eighth, and ninth century occupation is attested
at a number of sites whilst at least one date suggests that the
Kalomo culture may have been established in the southern part
of Zambia by A.D. 300. In Rhodesia where Iron-Age research is
most advanced, there is at least one date in the first century B.C.
The earliest Iron-Age occupation on the Acropolis at Zimbabwe
antedates A.D.300 and at Mabveni, some 140 miles north of the
Limpopo there is a date of A.D. 180. On this evidence it seems
most likely that our South African Iron Age will be contained
within the past 2,000 years. Furthermore, if the South African
Iron Age represents a southward extension of a movement
responsible for the Rhodesian Iron Age, we may expect to find
some evidence of this early relationship in South African
material.

No site in South Africa has received more attention in the field, nor more lavish publication than that of Mapungubwe and its twin site, Bambandyanalo.[1] Yet despite the effort, our knowledge of what these sites represent must remain vague and frustrated until further work is carried out there, and until more extensive reconnaisance and excavation give substance to the image recovered there. The earlier excavations at the site were prompted, very largely, by the discovery of gold by the first European visitors in 1932. Investigations were mainly confined to Mapungubwe hilltop, though cuttings were also made in occupied areas at the foot of the hill, and further afield at the Bambandyanalo (the K.2 of some authors) site, about half a mile distant, where upwards of thirty burials were found. The resulting report[2] described two major pottery traditions; an earlier M.2 group, mainly from the Bambandyanalo site, and a later M.1 mainly from Mapungubwe hill. These, and the numerous other remains (including pole and daga huts) were taken to represent a 'bantu' material culture, whilst the burials recovered showed no positive negro features, and were classed as dominantly 'Bush-Boskopoid'. Thus the investigators found themselves faced by the enigma of a 'Bantu culture' associated with a 'non-Bantu' physical type. The second series of excavations, carried out by Gardner at the behest of the University of Pretoria, has, as one of its objectives, the resolution of this apparent enigma. Far from achieving this aim, 5 years fieldwork, followed by a weighty and expensive tome 23 years later have served only to increase the confusion. By his own account, Gardner's system of excavation left much to be desired, whilst his recording of the disposition of finds is almost meaningless. To add to all this, he seems to have had an obsession about the role of Hottentots in the history of the site. According to Gardner there was no evidence for metal-working in the K.2 (Bambandyanalo) site, which he regarded as arising from a settlement of Hottentot pastoralists. This settlement was

[1] Fouché, op cit. and G. A. Gardner, *Mapungubwe: the second Volume* (van Schaik, Pretoria, 1963).
[2] Fouché, op. cit.

terminated by the arrival of a 'Bantu' population, suggested to be Nguni, although a blending of the two pottery traditions on the hilltop suggested to Gardner that M.2 women had survived to become absorbed (with their ceramic traditions) into the new population. The appearance of new pottery types higher in the hilltop succession was taken to represent a new 'Bantu' arrival, the Sotho, and finally the whole occupation was brought to an end by the return of a second wave of Hottentots who over-whelmed the hilltop occupants, and left a final deposit of their own remains.

Gardner's reasons for invoking Hottentots were his belief that the M.2 pottery resembled Hottentot pottery, the presence of 'beast-burials' in the K.2 site, which he compared with Fayum neolithic practices (the Hottentots deriving ultimately from north-east Africa), bone work, especially bone points which he felt must be Hottentot and the evidence of the skeletal remains. The present writer has argued elsewhere[1] against the north-east derivation of the Hottentots, and Rudner has shown conclusively that there is no resemblance between the M.2 pottery and that from later Stone-Age sites around the coast from Walvis Bay to Durban.[2] The evidence of the skeletal remains loses much of its impact when subjected to scrutiny since only seven complete adult skulls were recovered; the bulk of the burials were of infants and juveniles, neither of which can be considered good guides to the adult form. In any case, the significance of the 'non-negroness' of the remains cannot be properly assessed without a knowledge of the skeletal characteristics of a variety of southern Bantu groups, many of whom are distinctly 'non-negro' in the flesh. A close examination of Gardner's report[3] shows that at least 25 per cent of the burials contain evidence for iron- and/or copper-working, whilst no less than ten of the pits, considered to be some of the earliest features on the site, contain iron, as does the beast burial No. 6, also rated as one of the earliest features; it was this beast burial which yielded the radio-carbon date of A.D. 1055

[1] Inskeep in Thompson and Wilson, op. cit.
[2] J. Rudner, *Ann. of the S. Afr. Mus.*, 49 (2) (1968).   [3] Gardner, op. cit.

In fact there are no grounds at all for invoking Hottentots at the site, and every reason for regarding the entire complex as belonging to the Iron Age. The internal history of the site can hardly be known until a more thorough analysis is available, and it seems unlikely that this could be obtained from the published reports. It does, however, seem fairly clear that innovations occur in the ceramics of the site as between the earlier and later levels. It cannot be affirmed that these mark radical changes resulting from replacement by new, immigrant groups since the site must have been occupied for at least four centuries, and the possibility of internal developments, or development resulting from culture contact, without replacement of the population, must be allowed. Such change is evident in the Kalomo culture in Zambia. The fact that older forms, and styles of decoration persist through to the latest levels may well be an indication that this is the nature of the change, rather than successive replacement by Nguni and Sotho as Gardner suggests. Thus it becomes possible to regard the old classes of pottery, M.2 and M.1, as earlier and later expressions of a single tradition rather than as separate entities as has been the case in the past.

To what extent can Mapungubwe be taken out of isolation and related to other things? Schofield had long ago suggested that Mapungubwe sites may occur in Botswana, and more recently, and perhaps with more authority Robinson[1] has published a distribution map showing a cluster of M.1 sites north of the Limpopo, extending 50 or 60 miles into Rhodesia. It can hardly be assumed that this gives an accurate picture of the distribution of the 'Mapungubwe culture', but it does suggest that we may be dealing with a well-established entity which might well warrant 'culture' or 'industry' status, together with Zimbabwe, Leopard's Kopje, Inyanga, and Uitkomst.

What of its relationships? Robinson has, provisionally, identified three phases of the Leopard's Kopje culture in Rhodesia, and expected that these would be successive phases. Radiocarbon dating[2] suggests, however, that phases I and II may be

[1] K. R. Robinson, *Arnoldia*, 1 (1965), 3, 4.
[2] K. R. Robinson, *S. Afr. Arch. Bull.*, 21 (1966), 5–51.

contemporaneous variants, while phase III may well be a late derivative from, or expression of phase II. Largely on the basis of pottery and beads, he has suggested that Leopard's Kopje phase I may be distantly related to Bambandyanalo, but because of the stronger element of comb-stamping, and to some extent vessel forms, in L.K. I, he thinks it may be ancestral to Bambandyanalo (M.2). He further suggests that the large cylinder beads of L.K. I may be the inspiration for the 'garden roller' beads of Bambandyanalo. He sees much stronger affinities between L.K. II and Bambandyanalo in the field of ceramics, and notes that 'garden roller' beads occur in both. Whereas comb-stamped decoration is dominant in L.K. I, it is superseded in L.K. II by incised, or dragged decorations, or stylus impressions; the same general observation would be true in respect of M.2 pottery from Bambandyanalo and Mapungubwe. With regard to L.K. III, the pottery is described as hard, black or buff, frequently burnished, no comb-stamping, but carefully incised; it is compared with Zimbabwe class 3, and Mapungubwe M.I.

At this stage of the discussion dating becomes all important. We have a few isolated radio-carbon dates to serve as a basis for discussion, but we must bear in mind that they are so few that a single new, discrepant date would cause an entire argument to founder. Robinson[1] thought that L.K. I might date back to A.D. 900. This would accommodate well the evolution of L.K. I from a Gokomere type of ancestor, with the subsequent evolution of L.K. II and L.K. III moving steadily away from the comb-stamping tradition, towards one of predominantly incised decoration as in L.K. III. Bambandyanalo might, in this framework, have been regarded as an offshoot from L.K. I, not greatly different from L.K. II. The radio-carbon dates, however make L.K. II earlier than L.K. I by 200 to 300 years, and bring L.K. I (A.D. 1040) and Bambandyanalo (A.D. 1055) very much into line chronologically. L.K. III (A.D. 1310) and the M.1 levels of Mapungubwe (A.D. 1370 and 1410) also fall close together.

An alternative suggestion, summarized in the diagram, would see L.K. I and L. K. II as separate radiations from an early,

[1] Robinson, op. cit.

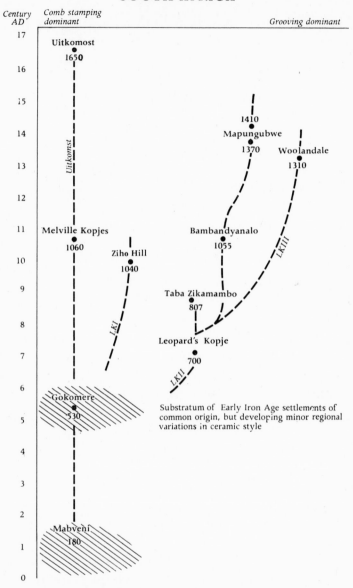

Diagram showing tentative relationship between major Iron Age entities in
Rhodesia and South Africa.

common substratum with the former retaining a stronger element of its ancestral features than the latter. L.K. II is then in a
position, both typologically and chronologically to give rise to

18

both L.K. III and Bambandyanalo (M.2) as further radiations. The position of Mapungubwe (M.1) remains even more hypothetical; it may be regarded as simply a late expression of M.2, or a re-settlement of L.K. III. In view of the apparent overlapping of M.2 and M.1 pottery types at Mapungubwe it may be better to adopt the former suggestion. That Bambandyanalo should be considered a similar but separate offshoot of L.K. II, rather than an L.K. II outpost is suggested by the distribution pattern in Robinson's map.[1]

We are left with two 'formally' named Iron-Age 'cultures', Buispoort and Uitkomst,[2] and one or two associations of pottery and/or, other kinds of remains for which formal 'culture' names have not been proposed. In every case there is an even greater deficiency of field evidence than is the case for Mapungubwe, and except in the case of Uitkomst, there are not even dates to help weld the pieces together. In the case of Uitkomst there are two radio-carbon dates; A.D. 1060 for an iron-smelting furnace in the suburbs of Johannesburg, and A.D. 1650 for the type site cave some 20 miles to the north.

The type-site of the Buispoort culture, a stone-built village, was investigated in a rather superficial manner in the early 1930's.[3] A useful plan of the settlement was recovered, and a range of pottery which has been taken to be representative of the 'Buispoort culture'.[4] The forms are said to be similar to those of the Uitkomst culture, but predominantly plain; burnishing is present, but decoration is said to be limited to nicking of the rim. The density of sites in the Buispoort area would appear to be very high, and Mason speaks of over ninety separate ruin groups in an area of 27 square miles. Further east, in the Uitkomst area, densities would seem to be less marked, though the number of sites is still impressive; a little over one per square mile for an area of almost 1,000 square miles (see Addendum p. 272). The same source shows clearly that there are large areas devoid of ruins. The full import of such density figures cannot be understood

[1] Robinson, *Arnoldia*, loc. cit.
[2] Mason, op cit.
[3] Van Hoepen and Hoffman, op. cit.
[4] Mason, op. cit.

until the survey, largely based on the study of aerial photographs, is much more complete, and until some indication is discovered of the degree of contemporaneity of occupation. Mason has remarked that there is little difference in the plan layout of ruins in the Buispoort area and those in the Uitkomst zone, but a comparison of the Buispoort plan produced by Hoffman and van Hoepen, and the air photos of Klipriviersberg does not support this. A recent survey, based on aerial photographs and supported by some ground survey, of the numerous ruins in the Orange Free State, shows that there are at least four classes of ruin distinguishable on the basis of plan layout[1] and it is expected that closer study of the Transvaal ruins will show similar variation of types.

We have already remarked (p. 257) that Buispoort pottery is quite characteristic of at least some of the Orange Free State sites, although the form of the associated ruins is quite different. Elsewhere in the Free State corbelled hut settlements have yielded pottery which is apparently indistinguishable from Schofield's N.C.2 ware from Natal. We have already seen that Schofield was well aware of the similarities, and that he proposed, by way of explanation, that Free State builders in stone moved eastwards to Natal to an area where building was more easily and appropriately effected with less durable materials. Even so, village plans should be expected to show similarities and it becomes a matter of some urgency that Natal should be explored for the living sites of these N.C.2 folk. Marked similarities between N.C.2 pottery and modern Nguni pottery have been noted with the implication that N.C.2 may be ancestral Nguni. This, however, is little more than a working hypothesis, and does not appear to receive support from a comparison of Nguni village plans with those of the corbelled stone hut settlements of the Orange Free State. There is much scope for speculation, but little hope of any real progress without considerably more field study.

To return to the Transvaal again, we find the situation here is

---

[1] I am indebted to Mr. T. M. Maggs for this unpublished information. Mr. Maggs is currently engaged in research on the Iron Age in the Orange Free State for his doctoral thesis at the University of Cape Town.

18*

equally resistant to any tidy solution. The western Transvaal
and the northern Free State present markedly different ruin
types with similar classes of pottery. But it must be noted that
rim notching occurs in at least one good Uitkomst site,[1] albeit in
combination with typical Uitkomst decoration, whilst the
Uitkomst cave yielded a single but much more characteristic
Buispoort sherd.[2] Similarly some of the Buispoort sherds would
not be at all out of place in an Uitkomst context. None the less,
whilst there may be some blurring of the distinctions between
the two, the published evidence is clearly in favour of Buispoort
and Uitkomst representing separate archaeological entities.
The lack of distinction, presumably reflecting lack of field-work,
does however, make discussion of the relationships of the Orange
Free State sites rather tenuous. Schofield read into the evidence
a south-eastward, eastward, and southward diffusion of what
was ultimately a Buispoort ceramic tradition. We should note
that in the absence of any dating of the Transvaal sites, or those
in the Free State and Natal, the only evidence for indicating the
geographic direction and chronology of the spread lies in the
similarity of the supposed end-product, certain classes of Nguni
pottery, to N.C.2. If the grounds are slender for discussing
possible derivations of Buispoort, they are virtually non-existent
for discussing its origins. The absence of any form of chronology
immediately raises an obstacle, but even so, it is not possible to
see, in any of the more or less well-known cultures to the north,
anything which immediately suggests itself as a possible ancestor.
It is not impossible that it is an offshoot of Uitkomst, but there is
barely any evidence for suggesting this even as a working
hypothesis. Buispoort must surely remain in a suspense account
until field-work has told us a little more about its character and
its chronology.

The Uitkomst culture is named from a cave of the same name
in the southern Transvaal.[3] Basically the cave contained three
Iron-Age levels, and yielded two iron-smelting furnaces,

---

[1] Mason, *S. Afr. Arch. Bull.* 7 (1952), 70–9.

[2] Mason, *The Prehistory of the Transvaal* (1962), 391.

[3] Mason, op. cit., 387.

'dozens of potsherds', and some shell, bone, wood and fibre remains. The pottery characteristics are described by Mason but the author has also had the privilege of examining the relevant collections.[1] The type collection seems to consist of approximately 150 sherds, of which about sixteen are decorated. Grooving and comb-stamping are both present, though comb-stamping is the more common method of decoration. Approximately 10 per cent of the sherds are burnished. The number of sherds and the small size of many of these make it impossible to say anything useful about vessel shapes.

Tafelkop yielded a much more useful collection of sherds. Some 216 sherds were recovered, many of them large enough to give reliable indication of vessel form. As compared with the type collection, there are some notable differences; 62 per cent of the sherds are decorated; 32 per cent of the 112 vessels recognized by Mason are burnished, and decorative motifs include coil impressions as well as comb-stamping and grooving. Mason classed forty-nine vessels as pots, and twenty-five as bowls; the author went somewhat further, recognizing sixty-five pots and thirty-eight bowls. Either of the results indicate about twice as many pots as bowls. Bowls are more frequently decorated than pots (87 per cent of bowls and 21 per cent of the pots). Several sites (five cave sites and four open sites) are attributed to the culture, presumably on the basis of shared pottery attributes. Substantial and extensive settlements built in stone are also attributed to Uitkomst culture on the grounds of association of pottery and ruins. It must, however, be admitted that the evidence could be clearer. At Uitkomst cave a wall across the front of the cave is shown to be associated; at Tafelkop the pottery was associated with a stone-built windbreak 8 ft. long and 3 ft. high; at Klipriviersberg where the ruins are substantial, only six sherds out of 'several dozen' were decorated with stamping or grooving, the remainder being plain.

The six sherds from Klipriviersberg cannot be closely matched at either Uitkomst or Tafelkop, but they are of the *genre*. The

---

[1] The writer is indebted to Dr. R. J. Mason for placing the Iron Age collections in his care at his disposal during a short visit to Johannesburg in 1962.

Uitkomst collection, whilst more limited in range, could well be accommodated within the Tafelkop collection. The Melville Koppies furnace which provides the earlier (A.D. 1060) date for the Uitkomst culture is associated on the basis of two comb-stamp decorated sherds and two plain sherds from within, or adjacent to the furnace. Three other comb-stamped sherds, and one with parallel rows of short, oblique incisions were found lower down the side of the hill, in association with ruined stone enclosures. Once again, the most that can be said of the pottery is that it is of the same broad tradition as Tafelkop and Uitkomst. There are no serious grounds for questioning the existence of the Uitkomst culture as such, but the time-range suggested by the two available dates (Melville Koppies A.D. 1060, and Uitkomst cave A.D. 1650), together with the paucity of associated remains should lead us to expect that future research will lead to a more complex picture in which changes in ceramic style, or associated settlement plans, architecture, etc., may result in the recognition of phases, perhaps successive and perhaps contemporaneous, within the culture.

There is a great deal in the character of the Uitkomst and in particular the Tafelkop pottery to suggest the probability of a close relationship with the present-day northern and north-eastern Sotho. As regards origins, there is little to go on. In so far as decoration is dominated by comb-stamping and grooving, and bowls are rather common, it seems reasonable to look to the comb-stamped pottery traditions to the north of the Limpopo, that is the complex represented by Gokomere and related sites. If, as has been suggested above, we are to consider Gokomere as possibly ancestral to the various phases of Leopard's Kopje, *and* Mapungubwe *and* Uitkomst, then it is necessary to visualize a fairly complex series of radiations. Comb-stamping seems to be more strongly present in the Uitkomst sites than in Leopard's Kopje phase I, and if this can be taken as a guide, it suggests that Uitkomst is more likely to be a related offspring of Gokomere than a derivative of L.K. I; the proposal is summarized in the diagram (p. 263). Perhaps, in suggesting these derivations, we are laying ourselves open to the mild criticism which we have

levelled at Schofield earlier in this essay (p. 255), and perhaps we
are wrong to have made the judgement. The problem is a difficult one which obliges us to raise the old cry of 'more field-
work, more dates'. The earliest Iron-Age pottery in both
Zambia and Rhodesia is characterized, perhaps more than by
anything else, by the bold and free use of comb-stamping and
grooving as decorative techniques. The basically similar character is underlined by the observation that the Dambwa pottery
(7 miles north of the Victoria Falls) is more like Gokomere than
anything yet known from Zambia;[1] the Dambwa village was in
existence a century or two after the Gokomere type site occupation. One receives, very strongly, the impression that the Early-
Iron-Age occupation immediately north and south of the
Zambezi, represented by such occurrences as Situmpa, Dambwa,
Kalundu (Kalomo culture, early phase), Mabveni, Gokomere,
Zimbabwe class I, and Ziwa, represents the arrival of a closely
related group which proceeded to settle in their new found land,
and to diversify in varying degrees of geographical isolation.
In the earlier stages, when the countryside was more sparsely
settled by village communities, there would be greater opportunity for individual development than later, when there was,
perhaps, less freedom of movement, and more contact. It seems
more reasonable to expect that much of the Bantu-speaking
population of southern Africa is directly descended from this
Early-Iron-Age substratum, than that each division, or congeries
of tribes, is here today as the result of a new migration from some
free-flowing source in the north which had not yet been identified. Whilst the roles of Angola and Mozambique are quite
unknown in all this, it is for the above reasons that the situation
given in the diagram is preferred to one in which the various
entities hang in isolation, with no permissible links.

Apart from pointing to the existence of several Iron Age
'cultures', indicating their possible relationships to each other, to
'cultures' in other areas which might be ancestral or in other ways
related, and the possible relationship of some of our 'cultures' to
extant Bantu groups, what other general observations may be

[1] B. Fagan, *J. Afr. Hist.*, 7 (1966), 495–506.

made ? No direct evidence for building in stone was forthcoming
in the earliest Mapungubwe settlement at Bambandyanalo,
though it is by no means clear that stone buildings were *not*
present with this stage. At Melville Koppies the evidence is not
unequivocal, but favours the probability that the stone-built
enclosures at the site were contemporaneous with the furnace,
and were built no later than the eleventh century; on Rhodesian
evidence it would be expected that they would not be much
earlier than this. That the art of building in stone has never been
lost, despite change and upheavals, has been shown by Kirby[1]
who, in 1931, witnessed the building of a new homestead for
Sibasa, the Paramount Chief of the Venda. Kirby's too brief
description of the site is reminiscent of the ruins at Brodie Hill,
near Pietersburg described by Malan and Brink[2] and also of the
well-known ruins at Khami, in Rhodesia. Certainly both Sibasa's
kraal and the Brodie Hill ruins are something different from the
Buispoort complex described by Hoffman and van Hoepen, and
from various Uitkomst ruins described by Mason. Buispoort
and, for example, Klipriviersberg appear to represent different
traditions of village settlement, whilst Maggs suggests four classes
of stone-built village in the Orange Free State and extending to
the adjacent Kimberley area of the Cape. One of these four
classes may be the same as, or similar to the ruins of the Buispoort
area. The indications are that in many parts of the Transvaal and
adjacent areas stone ruins are enormously abundant; it is to be
expected that this abundance will include a variety of types of
settlement plan, as well as other architectural details which may
be a valuable supplement to pottery as a means of classification.
In the Vechtkop settlement[3] the corbelled huts are fairly clearly
the sleeping quarters, though most domestic chores, and most of
the living must have been done in the open areas adjacent to the
huts. On Mapungubwe Hill elaborate daga houses were built,
reminiscent of the finer daga structures of Zimbabwe and
Khami. Elsewhere, where no obvious stone houses occur, and sur-

[1] P. R. Kirby, *S. Afr. J. Sci.*, 52 (1956), 167.
[2] B. D. Malan, and A. S. Brink, *S. Afr. J. Sci.*, 48 (1951), 133–7.
[3] C. van Riet Lowe, *J. Roy. Anthrop. Inst.* (1927).

face soil is too shallow to mask substantial daga houses, we must suppose that the main enclosing walls of the ruins surrounded huts of timber and thatch, perhaps with mud plastered walls and floors. So much may be inferred, but most awaits the attention of the excavator for confirmation. Little direct evidence exists for agriculture, though this may be inferred in many cases from the remains of hoes, and from the numerous grindstones which survive in some sites[1] as well as possible threshing places.[2] On the other hand, the very large, open, walled areas in many of the settlements can be little other than livestock enclosures, probably in most cases, for cattle.

In the absence of any obvious sources of ore in the heavily settled Orange Free State, it seems very likely that iron was traded in either from the Transvaal or from Basutoland. In the Transvaal the evidence for mining and smelting is both widespread and clear[3] and includes iron, copper, tin and gold. There is little to suggest, however, that miners south of the Limpopo took part in the flourishing gold trade channelled through Sofala.

Enough has been said to indicate that the Republic of South Africa has a wealth of evidence to contribute to the story of the Iron Age in Africa; more pertinently, to the history of the Bantu-speaking peoples of southern Africa. Enough has been said, too, to indicate that the surface of the subject has barely been scratched. There is much scope for interdisciplinary collaboration, and, in the archaeological sphere, for the application of special techniques in the search for a deeper understanding. Might not phosphate analysis provide solutions to the problem of where cattle were penned, whether fields were manured, or whether burials ever occurred beneath the numerous stone mounds which commonly occur in settlements where no cemetery is found? Could not pollen analysis assist in the study of cultivation associated with farming settlements, or the analysis of metals and ores perhaps point to the sources of iron in the

[1] Mason, op. cit.
[2] Johnson, op. cit. and T. R. Jones, *S. Afr. J. Sci.*, 32 (1935), 528–36.
[3] Mason, op. cit., 415–23.

Free State, or trade patterns in various metals in other areas? Interpretations will always be fettered as long as dating is absent, and yet the frequency with which dates must be asked for makes radio-carbon a prohibitive method. It is encouraging to note that a research programme in thermoluminescence is well under way in the University of Cape Town.

Finally, a word on recording and publication. Even a casual perusal of excavation reports emanating from field-work in southern Africa (and other parts of the continent) is enough to reveal serious shortcomings when compared with European and Near-Eastern examples. The tradition of detailed investigation, accompanied by scrupulously thorough recording, and complete publication of the procedures followed, the facts observed, and the range of objects recovered, has barely established itself in Africa; nothing less should be acceptable, at least from the professional investigator. If pottery is a primary tool for classification and chronology, then pottery must be illustrated expertly and freely as exemplified in reports on the archaeology of Roman Britain. Settlement archaeology is new in most parts of Africa; it presents problems and opportunities unmatched in the investigation of hunter-gatherer camps, and the new generation of field-workers in Africa have a unique opportunity to benefit by the study of all that is best in the literature of other countries, where decades of experience have pointed the way to success.

ADDENDUM

The high figures given by Mason for sites in the Transvaal result, in part at least, from his method of designating 'sites'. It would appear that any stone structure which is not contiguous with another, and does not lie within an enclosing wall, is listed as a separate site; this approach is used to obviate the difficulty apparent in many areas of determining where one settlement 'unit' ends and another begins.

A site discovered a few years ago at Lydenburg, Transvaal, has yielded a group of terracotta heads so far unique in Southern Africa.[1]

[1] K. L. von Bezing, and R. R. Inskeep *Man* 1 (1), March 1966.

The site has not yet been investigated, but the associated pottery bears a strong resemblance to Schofield's N.C.3. The contrast between this pottery and traditions further inland, such as Buispoort, Uitkomst, Leopard's Kopje and Gokomere suggests the possibility that a separate and distinct culture tradition may be found to occupy a more easterly zone along the coast, from Tanzania, through Mocambique, to Natal, barely impinging on the highveld zone.

INDEX

Date Due